Paul Sheehan's work has appeared in the *New Yorker*, the *New York Times*, and the *Atlantic Monthly*, but most of his writing has been for *The Sydney Morning Herald*, where he is a senior writer. He has served as the *Herald*'s chief of staff, day editor, and New York correspondent. He was a Nieman Fellow at Harvard University, and was educated at the Australian National University and Columbia University in New York. A piece he wrote for the *New Yorker* was selected for the *Best American Essays 1997*.

*To Mike
best wishes
Carmel*

AMONG THE BARBARIANS

PAUL SHEEHAN

RANDOM HOUSE
AUSTRALIA

Published by
Random House Australia Pty Ltd
20 Alfred Street, Milsons Point, NSW 2061
http://www.randomhouse.com.au

Sydney New York Toronto
London Auckland Johannesburg
and agencies throughout the world

First published in 1998
Copyright © Paul Sheehan

All rights reserved. No part of this publication may be reproduced, stored in a retrieval system, or transmitted in any form or by any means, electronic, mechanical, photocopying, recording or otherwise, without the prior written permission of the publisher.

National Library of Australia
Cataloguing-in-Publication Data

Sheehan, Paul, 1951– .
  Among the Barbarians

New ed.
Bibliography
Includes index.

ISBN 0 091 83999 8.

 1. Multiculturalism—Australia. 2. Twenty-first century—
Forecasts. 3. Natural resources—Australia. 4. Australia
—Politics and government—1990–. 5. Australia—
Forecasting. I. Title.

305.8

Design by Yolande Gray
Typeset by Asset Typesetting Pty Ltd
Printed by Griffin Press Pty Ltd

10 9 8 7 6 5 4 3 2 1

For the colourblind

Take the women out of publishing
and you don't have a publishing industry.
The women who made this book possible
were Deborah Callaghan, Jennifer Byrne,
Jane Palfreyman and Jody Lee.

CONTENTS

	THE TROGLODYTE	ix
PART ONE		
1	THIS DOG BITES	1
2	IT WASN'T LUCK	17
3	BLACK RAIN	41
4	AMONG THE BARBARIANS	57
5	AN EMPIRE OF THE SOUL	77
PART TWO		
6	THE MAN WHO WASN'T THERE	91
7	THE BILLION DOLLAR BLUFF	109
8	A KICK IN THE TEETH	139
9	IN THE FOOTSTEPS OF ALEXANDER	155
10	THE VOTE EATERS	165
PART THREE		
11	STRIP MINING	181
12	THE BIG NOWHERE	201
13	LOVE AT FIRST SIGHT	221
14	THE BIG PINEAPPLE	241
15	THE REVENGE OF THE DESPISED	257
PART FOUR		
16	WHITE DREAMING	279
17	A GRAND AND POWERFUL COUNTRY	295
18	GREEN THUNDER	307
19	NOMADS	315
Afterword: A DANCE WITH THE THOUGHT POLICE		341
SOURCES		351
INDEX		363

SECOND EDITION

Among the Barbarians was published in May 1998, and immediately became the biggest-selling book in Australia. It stayed on best-seller lists for five months. Tens of thousands of Australians have bought the book for the same reason I wrote it—to lift the veil of intimidation that hangs over discussion of the most important subjects in Australian life.

So much happened in those five months—including a federal election—that we have produced an updated edition.

The 1998 federal election said plenty about the Australian people, most of it good. This second edition also visits the impact and behaviour of the news media, where the story is not so good.

Some cuts have been made from the original edition to make way for new facts and two new chapters, 'The Revenge of the Despised' and 'The Big Pineapple'.

Three other chapters, 'The Billion Dollar Bluff', 'The Vote Eaters' and 'Nomads' have been extensively rewritten to accommodate a wealth of new material. New material has also been added throughout the book.

None of the defining arguments or facts of the original edition have been removed.

Some material has come from the several hundred letters and phone calls I received in the wake of the first edition, contacts which ranged from the bizarre to the sublime.

THE TROGLODYTE

THE ABUSE STARTED FLOWING immediately. It came by letter, by fax, by phone, by e-mail, by radio interview.

> Geraldine Willesee, SBS Radio:
> *Paul Sheehan hit a grubby rock-bottom ... his story got truly scary ... From which dung-heap did he dredge this offensive, patently stupid and dangerous garbage ... badly researched bile ... the worst of gutter journalism.*
>
> Sonja Marsic:
> *Mr Sheehan's article was a betrayal of all that is truly Australian.*
>
> Camilla Nelson:
> *It's a pity that Paul Sheehan's psychosexual problems have turned out to be so unutterably boring ...*

This outrage was prompted by a story published in the *Sydney Morning Herald* on 25 May 1996. It was the first step in describing one of the greatest political myths in Australian history.

Published under the front-page headline THE MULTI-CULTURAL MYTH, the story described an industry of tax-fed lawyers, political operatives and racial axe-grinders that has grown like an enormous parasite out of Australia's heroic commitment to cultural diversity.

Despite the flow of outrage most of these responses were positive.

> *Eureka!* wrote Nick Jones. *Finally an attack on reverse racism.*

> D. Eastman:
> *Thank you for debunking the newest form of cultural cringe and self-loathing.*

> A.K. Singh:
> *I sit nightly gnashing my teeth at the passing parade of 'ethnic leaders' on television speaking on behalf of me and the 'ethnic community' ... Where do they get their mandate from?*

The bulk of the letters were from people who felt themselves to be members of a silenced majority. They believed their tolerance had been abused and their voices patronised and dismissed. But the most powerful responses and the most interesting letters were hostile. Some of the insults were marvellous, and all of them were useful.

> Noel McGuire:
> *The problem with the troglodytes opposed to multi-culturalism ... is they find it distasteful working alongside Buddhists and Moslems, as if they're less than human.*

THE TROGLODYTE

Paul seems to be well on the way to gaga land ...

Al Grassby, former Minister for Immigration in the Whitlam government:

[It] seemed to have been written in the twilight of 1939.

Penny O'Donnell, communications department, University of Technology, Sydney:

Australia cannot afford another generation of journalists like Paul Sheehan ... What kind of example of tolerance does this offer to media students in National Reconciliation Week?

Jane Gibian, writing in a student publication at Sydney University:

Cultural imperialism and insensitivity ... demonstrates a thinly disguised anxiety regarding his own identity ...

John Minns, office of the Department of History and Politics at Wollongong University:

Racist—in the worst traditions of yellow journalism.

Stepan Kerkyasharian, Chairman of the Ethnic Affairs Commission of New South Wales:

I now await the sequel—The Myth of Quality Journalism.

E. Vasilopoulos:
Biased, irresponsible and disturbing.

AMONG THE BARBARIANS

Graham Barry:
Good rabble-rousing jingoistic stuff—nonsense.

Caroline Alcorso, Director of the Working Women's Centre in Sydney:

An incoherent concoction of misleading assertions and half-truths.

Gary Crokett:
... sloganistic nonsense ... a flawed, directionless and myopic grab-bag of assertions ... vulgar and insulting ...

Malcolm Long, then Managing Director of SBS, speaking on ABC radio:

It's a bitter little document.

Yet nowhere in 'The multicultural myth' was there any criticism of Australia's ethnic diversity. Just the opposite. What was rejected was the notion that Australia does not have a distinct dominant national culture that binds and forms society. The story also emphatically rejected the large tax-fuelled industry whose members used, with great effectiveness, the accusation of racism to snuff out criticism or even debate.

The person who went to the most trouble in attacking the article and its author was Geraldine Willesee of SBS, who wrote a heated, hyperbolic, six-page response intended for publication. Ms Willesee, the daughter of a former Labor senator, was the reader who asked, 'From which dung-heap did he dredge this offensive, patently stupid and dangerous

THE TROGLODYTE

garbage?' Strangely, the memo which opened 'The multicultural myth'—a complaint about racism against 'Anglos' at SBS radio—came from Ms Willesee herself. She wrote it, a fact she admitted in her response. That was the dung heap from which the story first sprang.

Her reaction to the story, and all the other hostile responses, shared several characteristics:

They were personal. They concentrated on the writer rather than the arguments.

Nearly all who identified their place of work were on the public payroll. Most were part of the multicultural industry.

There was no middle ground, no possibility of concession. Opponents were extremists and racists and xenophobes. Pauline Hanson had not yet given her maiden speech in Parliament, so the Frankenstein's Hanson had not yet been created in the news media's laboratory, otherwise they would have all used the convenient new label of Hansonism.

The 1996 book *The Good Life and Its Discontents,* by the American economist Robert Samuelson, captured the neurosis mirrored in Australia today.

Our attitudes are shaped more by unattained ambitions than actual achievement. We seem to have lapsed into a selective view of the national condition and into tortuous self-criticism.

Three years earlier, that great Australian export Robert Hughes summed up the same neurosis in just three words, the title of his best-selling book, *Culture of Complaint.*

AMONG THE BARBARIANS

Attacking this culture of complaint triggered the standard response against all those who have ever threatened the industry's power and, more importantly, its funding.

To summarise the hate mail:

> *The author of* The Multicultural Myth *is a desperate, ranting, racist, xenophobic, jingoistic, unintelligent yellow journalist from gaga land who writes biased, flawed, directionless, myopic, vulgar, insulting, strange, wildly inaccurate, truly scary, malicious, misleading, glib, bitter, offensive, patently stupid, dangerous, irresponsible, disturbing beat-ups, incoherent concoctions, inflammatory rubbish, badly researched bile, sloganistic nonsense and garbage, a betrayer of all that is truly Australian, an insensitive cultural imperialist that Australia cannot afford, a hegemonist whose thinly disguised cultural anxiety has led to a grubby rock-bottom dung-heap, the worst of gutter journalism. In short, a troglodyte with boring psychosexual problems.*

And this is the voice of tolerance.

PART ONE

Eucalypts are thirsty beasts, and they love firestorms, which farmers don't ... They are the tree of Siva. They are the tree of the future. They are the enemy of the farmer, the friend of the hunter–gatherer. 'Your days are numbered,' they say to us.

David Foster, *The Glade Within the Grove*

1
THIS DOG BITES

THE EUCALYPTUS IS THE pyromaniac's tree. It loves fire. It is aggressive, adaptable, pragmatic. With fire as its great ally, it has colonised the Australian continent to the snowline, to the edge of saltwater mangroves, to the limits of sandy deserts and the last remaining rainforests. A dominant army, its discreet colours flying—the red gum, the blue, the grey, the black, the stringy-bark, the ghost, the scribbly, the ribbon, the coolibah, ironbark, bloodwood, jarrah, mugga, yellow box, red box, white mallee, yellow mallee, red mallee, rose, salmon, tallow wood, sugar, blackbutt, river red and river peppermint. An American scholar, Stephen Pyne, left this homage in his brilliant but largely forgotten book, *Burning Bush: A Fire History of Australia*, published in 1991:

> *Eucalyptus has given the bush its indelible character. It is not only the Universal Australian, it is the ideal Australian—versatile, tough, sardonic, contrary, self-mocking, with a deceptive complexity amid the appearance of massive homogeneity; an occupier of disturbed environments; a fire creature.*

The eucalypt asks for trouble. As drought withers the bush, turning it into fire fuel, the eucalypt, especially the stringy-bark, drapes incendiary streamers of tinder. The oil in its leaves is flammable. When fire inevitably comes, the eucalypt sheds its tough bark like protective plates. Eucalypts infiltrate places disturbed by fire. Fire opens areas to sunlight, allowing eucalypt seedlings a chance to outgrow more shade-tolerant rivals. During fires, seeds rain down from the charred canopy. The fluffy ash buries them in an environment of mineralised biochemicals. Fire purges the ground of antagonistic micro-organisms. Fire sweeps competition away.

Fire and drought. The crown of the eucalyptus is continually reshaped for maximum efficiency. (The name eucalyptus comes from the Greek *eu*, meaning 'well', and *kalyptos*, meaning 'covered'.) The canopy drapes downward to reduce leaf temperatures. The leaves are hard, to reduce moisture loss. They are shed infrequently, to preserve energy. As dry periods extend, the root system can grow vast as it compensates for the poverty of the soil. It obsessively retains and recycles nutrients. Seedlings can remain dormant for decades.

It is only in recent years, with the rapid advance of science and the development of environmental history, that the full power of Australian history is being described and understood. Stephen Pyne, a professor at the University of Arizona, provides a compelling history of the natural drama that has shaped Australia; in *Burning Bush,* he retells the history of Australia as a history of fire. He describes the eucalypt as a tree that burns 'readily, greedily, gratefully'.

THIS DOG BITES

The calendar of modern Australian history is marked with great conflagrations. Red Tuesday, 1 February, 1898; Black Friday, 13 January 1939; another, even worse, Black Tuesday on 7 February 1967 causing the largest loss of life and property on any single day in the history of the Australian continent. Pyne described it as, 'an apparition, like some Pleistocene beast, exhumed from the ice, that had come to life in an uncontrollable rampage'. On 2 December 1997, yet another Black Tuesday, two veteran firemen died on Scotsman's Hill overlooking the main street of Lithgow. That night the hills above Lithgow looked like lava flows.

By the time the Europeans arrived in 1788, the structure of the forest reflected multi-millennia of fire farming. Firestick farming had created a fragile system that coevolved with the Aboriginal people. The arrival of a new people from a different environment quickly dissipated ancient patterns of conservation.

The early European settlers could not know that they were entering the alien realm of a fire-loving species. The ensuing struggle with the eucalypt would define the nation and the national character even more than the struggle with the people displaced by the onrush of a European tide. The bush and its lore have always been the central metaphor of Australian mythology, but the early Australians raped the environment they found. Anyone who has read one of the new generation of environmental histories of Australia—William Lines's 1991 book, *Taming the Great South Land*, is a pioneer of the genre—will have no doubt that rape is the only word for what took place. Only the eucalypt was able to stand up to the onslaught. Lines describes the fate that awaited the continent's only long-lived deciduous tree, the red cedar, which used to grow right along Australia's east coast, until early settlers discovered that it cut easily, warped little, was durable, versatile and grew in a straight bolt up to 45 metres high. Today, not even a stump remains. The pillage extended as far as the new settlers could reach, land and sea. Lines describes the natural cornucopia that was soon swept away.

> *Mariners in the southern seas in those days sailed through an abundance of marine life unimaginable to Australians today. Indeed, the southern oceans served as a vast undisturbed sanctuary for the sperm whale and the right whale ... every beach of the Tasman Sea, each rocky promontory of Bass Strait teemed with rookeries of elephant seals and fur seals.*

At the time of Federation, the pillage was ongoing. Two thousand lyrebird tails were exported in three years. In 1924 two million koala skins were exported. In 1959, the year before native bird exports were banned, 400 000 birds were trapped with only 100 000 surviving for export.

Yet Australians have always paid homage to the bush. The national colours are wattle and green. Gradually we have begun truly to see what we have around us. This maturing clarity shows up in a multitude of ways: from the recognition of native title as a national priority, to the new love of native flowers, to the didgeridoo becoming the unofficial national instrument, to the revival of the classic homestead architecture, to the burgeoning of superb Australian cuisine, to the explosion of popular interest in Aboriginal art and design, to a taste for wattleseed ice cream. The list goes on and on, a mosaic of large and small details. It is a collective, effortless embrace of nativism while also absorbing what the world has to offer, as Australians have always done. It is a recognition that Australia is not Europe, it is not Asia, and it is not California. It is another way in the world.

It helps to leave Australia for a while to fully appreciate the country. During visits home from New York where I lived for a decade, I was struck by how much Australia was *not* America. The scale of Australian culture is less grandiose, more human, more sensual. The new generations are growing colourblind. You see it on the streets, young mixed couples, Asian and European, black and white.

The Australia I returned to is better than the Australia I left and the prodigal eye rejoices in the undulating procession of the seasons, the streets carpeted in mauve as the jacarandas explode and shed, the crimson bottlebrushes and their feeding flocks of rainbow lorikeets, the red December flashes of the flowering gum. The mornings have the visceral thrill of kookaburras' calls. Cockatoos, currawongs, magpies. At night, fruit bats hang upside down in palm trees holding fruit in their claws. They shake the branches of the big Moreton Bay fig trees, and by morning they have left scattered fruit debris on the street below. Beauty is commonplace.

Yet another bit of bush mythology—sheepdog trials—is enjoying a quiet boom. The Australian National Trial Dog Championships are held each March at the Hall

AMONG THE BARBARIANS

Showgrounds outside Canberra, a bumpy oval surrounded by stands of red gum, yellow box and Cootamundra wattle. The old skill of herding with sheepdogs is enjoying a comeback, and the number of dogs competing is rising. The trials have their own laconic drama. In the last run of the 1996 championships, I watched the defending champion, Clyde, with the national title at stake, make a stand, like Horatius, on the bridge.

One of the tests in a sheepdog trial is the bridge, where a dog must direct three sheep up a ramp and over a small bridge before it can move on to the next obstacle. In the last run of the championships all three of Clyde's sheep charged him on the bridge, normally a disaster. Clyde did not flinch. He went chest to chest with the big lead ewe, then bit her on the nose. If this trial had been held in Britain, where sheepdogs have been trialling for more than 120 years, Clyde would have been disqualified immediately. European judges will not tolerate a biting dog. But the Australian merino is much bigger and more aggressive than European sheep. It is almost a free-range beast, used to wide spaces, and some of them can grow powerfully attached to wide spaces unless brought up sharply.

Clyde was not disqualified. He was not even penalised. He received a perfect score on the bridge for showing courage and doing good work. After the confrontation he quickly penned his chastened sheep and won the national championship. Clyde's owner, Greg Prince, the most successful sheepdog trainer of the modern era, explained his victory to me afterwards:

THIS DOG BITES

'An Australian dog is allowed to stand up for itself.'

Australia is described as a young country, yet in many ways it is old. It is one of the world's oldest continuous democracies, with political and social structures that have a direct lineage to a thousand years of historical and legal evolution. Australian democracy is so sinewy and instinctive that it is taken for granted, like a gift of nature. (In the United States, supposedly a paragon of democratic virtue, the quadrennial national election campaigns last more than a year and cost several billion dollars. Democracy for sale. In Australia, a national election campaign lasts barely longer than a month and costs less than a single Senate race in California.) Australia's modern culture has evolved over more than two centuries, since before the Industrial Revolution which transformed the world. Australia's physical environment is the most ancient, and the core of its human ecology—the diverse Aboriginal clans—comprises the world's oldest continuous civilisation. Thousands of kilometres of Australian cliffs and rock-faces are daubed and scraped with indigenous rock art older than the millennia of Christianity.

In global ecological terms, the most important people in Australia are the surviving traditional indigenous clans. Some of them are preserving systems of values and laws older than any of the legal systems of Europe and Asia. These islands of vestigial ancient culture also present moral dilemmas for an enlightened, law-based nation like Australia. These dilemmas are all personified in Stephen Barnes Jungarrayi.

Stephen Barnes Jungarrayi did not mean to kill his twenty-three-year-old nephew in March 1996. (The name of the dead nephew has been withheld by the Northern Territory police in accordance with Aboriginal custom not to publicly name the dead.) Both men were drunk at the time. The fight started in the backyard of the home they shared in Darwin, where they were preparing the evening meal. When the argument became heated, Jungarrayi picked up a kitchen knife. His nephew picked up an Aboriginal fighting stick. Jungarrayi later told a court he went for his nephew's leg, but the knife rode up the fighting stick and into the nephew's chest. It sliced the coronary artery. The nephew bled to death within minutes.

Jungarrayi was arrested, charged, and placed in custody. He remained in jail for twenty months, until 29 November 1997, when Justice Dean Mildren of the Northern Territory Supreme Court sentenced Jungarrayi, who by then was twenty-eight and had been an alcoholic since his early twenties, to a four-year prison term for manslaughter. Then the judge let him go. Justice Mildren said Jungarrayi had already served twenty months and was also facing 'payback' punishment in his own community. 'A spearing and a beating is envisaged. I take it into account, as I am obliged to, not because the court approves of payback as a form of punishment but because it is not right that a person should be punished twice, both in his own community and by the courts.'

As soon as he was released, Jungarrayi, a fully initiated member of the Warlpiri clan, travelled the 700 kilometres to his community in Lajamanu to face *yawarra*, a Warlpiri word for blood. Lajamanu, a community of some 1000 people, is about 200 kilometres from Tennant Creek. It is often isolated during the wet season. Warlpiri is a distinct language and its geographical reach ends at the edge of the Great Sandy Desert, the Gibson Desert, and the Barkly Tableland. It is surrounded by the languages and dialects of the Arrernte, Papunya, Kukatja, Warumungu, Mutpurra, and Gurindji.

Like many other traditional communities, Lajamanu imposes an alcohol ban, enforced by the elders, the same elders who decided that Jungarrayi must face *yawarra*. He was to be speared by close relatives of the dead man, and beaten by members of his own immediate family. *Yawarra* required that he be seriously wounded. Even this punishment was a compromise, a recognition that the traditional clans must live in a nation defined by white law. 'In the old days that Jungarrayi would have been killed, but times have changed and we have to move with the times,' the Lajamanu council president, Martin Johnson Japanangka, told reporter Maria Ceresa. 'We have moved our *yapa* law [Warlpiri clan law] to fit in with *kartiya* [white] law but *yapa* must come first. We are living under *kurruwarri kujarra*—two laws.'

The payback took place within days of Jungarrayi's return. It was done in the traditional way, in a place of ritual. The entire Lajamanu community, including children, was allowed to witness it. Close kinsmen supported Jungarrayi by both arms. Before the first spearing they told him to look away. A relative of the dead nephew plunged a wooden spear into Jungarrayi's leg. The spear tore muscle, glanced off the thigh bone, but avoided the femoral artery. Cutting that artery would cause death. The ritual was repeated five times, each blow tearing deep into Jungarrayi's muscle. His blood poured onto the ground. He was then speared eight more times by other members of the nephew's family. He could no longer stand and was being held up by his kinsmen. But his punishment had not ended. He had to be beaten by members of his own family. His sisters and a woman he called 'mother' used traditional clubs, nulla-nullas. They clubbed him about the head, drawing more blood. He blacked out. When he regained his senses the women hit him again. They hit him four times before it was decided he had suffered enough. Jungarrayi was carried to a waiting air ambulance and flown to Katherine Hospital, 350 kilometres away, to recover from his wounds. He checked himself out after five days, earlier than the doctors advised, and returned to Lajamanu with his legs swathed in bandages. He could barely walk.

The punishment drew divergent reactions. The Katherine Region Aboriginal Legal Aid Service said Jungarrayi's imprisonment had postponed the proper resolution of the matter. 'Under Aboriginal law, which is community based, the punishment would be meted out as soon as possible,' said Glen Dooley, a spokesman for the service. 'The issue would then be resolved, and the sooner this happens the better. When an offender against tribal law is in prison, this merely postpones the community's resolution. Let the tribal punishment occur first, and then the European court. We would like to see an amendment to the Bail Act allowing release for tribal punishment.' A bail application on those grounds was made, but the judge who heard the application said

Jungarrayi was facing the infliction of grievous bodily harm and the law clearly prevented him from allowing the court to be a party to such a crime.

The then Attorney-General of the Northern Territory and later Chief Minister, Shane Stone, scoffed at suggestions that the release of Jungarrayi could be a case study in favour of using tribal punishment. 'This custom, under Aboriginal law, is barbaric and will not be condoned by this government. Bashing, beating and stabbing are not condoned by the government. Tribal law is not a substitute for penalties set out in the criminal code. The court can't release people to go through tribal punishment.'

Amnesty International agreed. It described as 'cruel and inhuman' the punishment given to Jungarrayi and drew attention to the International Covenant on Civil and Political Rights. 'To allow such cruel punishment to occur without government response would mean to allow human rights violations to be perpetrated with impunity,' said Amnesty's Dr Heinz Schurmann-Zeggel. 'We cannot accept that the difficult legal and human rights questions involved remain forever in the too-hard basket.'

Indigenous clans practising traditional law not only practise ritual violence but also genital mutilation. In some clans men must undergo the ghastly ritual of subincision, where the penis is split open from the tip to the urethra.

It is brutal and primitive and unacceptable in the wider society, but if traditional indigenous clans are to have any cultural sovereignty, the elders must have the right to enforce tribal law. This can extend from initiation mutilations to banning the sale of grog, a problem imported from the white world.

An entire book, *Grog War* by Alexis Wright, has been written about the campaign to ban the sale of alcohol to the Aboriginal community at Tennant Creek, not far from Lajamanu. Wright, an Aborigine, provides plenty of grit from the front-line of this little cultural war, quoting the women who bear the brunt of the problem.

> 'Wife get bashed all the time.'
>
> 'Parents saying, "if we smash your drink", they saying they will go up the road and commit suicide.'
>
> 'That five-litre cask killed a lot of people. Some not even old.'
>
> 'Go around stabbing people when drunk and sniffing petrol.'
>
> 'That's why they buy that long neck wine, port wine, for a weapon. They can buy it and smash it. And hurt each other proper hard.'
>
> 'They cut themselves all over. He got habit of taking pocket knife in his pocket. When someone else steal grog that person take a knife or a glass and start cutting themselves. They got scars everywhere.'

Paternalism has its limits. Indigenous problems need indigenous solutions. You have to be there, under the skin, to really understand. Yet even the issue of cultural sovereignty shrinks compared with the larger question of indigenous identity. Who is an Aborigine? About forty percent of the indigenous population is now made up of uninitiated, nontraditional people of mixed race living in cities, and their number is exploding. In the 1996 census, 352 970 people described themselves as indigenous Australians, an increase of thirty-three percent in just five years. This explosion in numbers, surely a positive sign, has its own problems. A cultural ocean exists between communities such as the Warlpiri at Lajamanu and nontraditional urban blacks. Yet a myth has grown up among white Australians that the indigenous populations are somehow a homogeneous group. This is ridiculous. Later on this book will be looking at this and other myths as we travel among the barbarians. But right now we are looking at just one Australian, Stephen Barnes Jungarrayi, and he is difficult enough.

Jungarrayi is a drunk who has killed someone. He has never held a steady job. The system of justice that freed him has also sometimes been abused in the past by being used merely to avoid incarceration. Violence against women in the indigenous communities is endemic, appalling by the standards of the wider society. The people on both sides of the Jungarrayi case have powerful moral arguments, which is why these issues are so difficult.

Despite all the problems, I'm going with Jungarrayi and the Warlpiri elders. Justice Mildren was right to free him for traditional punishment. The law is already winking in this direction. Those who administered the bloody ritual punishment to Jungarrayi are liable to punishment of up to life imprisonment if a court were to find they had inflicted premeditated grievous bodily harm, which certainly was the case. But no-one, before or after the payback, has ever suggested that any legal action be taken against those Warlpiri people who exacted ritual retribution. What happened to Jungarrayi was not unusual. There is still plenty of tribal punishment and payback meted out in the traditional clans, below the sight and reach of *kartiya*, white law. No matter what the Chief Minister and the judge say, there is *kurruwarri kujarra*, two laws, in the Northern Territory.

The jargon about 'human rights violations' from Heinz Schurmann-Zeggel of Amnesty International is sanctimonious. His comments about crimes 'perpetrated with impunity' is typical of the imperial thinking that still afflicts Europeans in their dealings with other parts of the world. Stephen Barnes Jungarrayi went to his own brutal punishment willingly. The enactment of the punishment was difficult for everyone and was carried out according to custom. The punishment itself was modified by the wider context of white law. Moral and emotional issues were resolved by the people most directly involved. Until Dr Schurmann-Zeggel has sat down and talked to Martin Johnson Japanangka and the other elders who are trying to save an ancient culture, he can hold his punctilious advice.

I know a white man, exactly my own age, also from Sydney, who while the rest of us went to university, or began careers, or travelled the hippie trail looking for enlightenment, went up to the centre, out of curiosity, and stayed twenty-two years. He learned Warlpiri and developed skin relationships and learned the complex skin systems. After he had been abused enough times by drunken Warlpiri men who called him less than a man because he wasn't initiated, he became fully initiated. The Warlpiri are subincision people, so they opened him up all the way. He married a Warlpiri woman with the right skin relationship and they had three children. He has always worked hard, but when I saw him in February 1998, he had moved to Alice Springs. He was worn out. Twenty-two years as a human bridge across the chasm between two worlds had finally washed his family out of the bush. How many of us really understand the distance he had travelled? Very few.

We'll leave the last word to Stephen Barnes Jungarrayi.

The courts should realise we are still living traditional around here. I was really glad I was able to face my family in the traditional way. My family has accepted me back, started talking to me again, and things are starting to get back to normal ... After what I have been through, bad times, bad experiences, I will try to teach the young people in this community both ways, traditional and reading and writing.

Asked if, prior to the attacks, he had thought of returning to jail and Australian law, Jungarrayi said:

No ... Sometimes [in prison] *I considered doing something to myself or hanging myself. I knew what was coming to me. It's always been the way ... I had to face it.*

2
IT WASN'T LUCK

CHARLES DARWIN DESCRIBED NEW South Wales as 'a very paradise to the worshippers of Mammon' after he visited the colony in January 1836 during his now legendary journey aboard HMS *Beagle*. He was struck by the wealth and energy of the young colony. In a letter sent back home, he wrote of Sydney:

> *Ancient Rome in her imperial grandeur, would not be ashamed of such an offspring ... Can better proof of the extraordinary prosperity of this country be conceived than the fact that 7/8th of an acre of land in the town sold by auction for 12 000 pounds sterling? There are now men living, who came out as convicts (and one of whom has since been flogged at the Cart's tail round the town) who are said to possess without doubt an income from 12 to 15 000 pounds per annum ...*
>
> *It is an admirable country to grow rich in; turn sheep herd and I believe with common care, you must grow wealthy.*

This was just two generations after the arrival of the First Fleet. The colony's almost instantaneous distinctiveness and progressiveness is described in Alan Atkinson's groundbreaking and award-winning 1997 history, *The Europeans in Australia, Volume One*.

> *From the very beginning, Australian political culture ... was remarkably original, especially when we take into account the remoteness and smallness of early European settlement ...*
>
> *White settlement began here during the 1780s, a decade of extraordinary creativity, the climax of the European Enlightenment ... A century whose climax was marked by great political revolutions in North America and France, and by vast and unprecedented demographic and industrial change, especially in Britain, was not 'a static time ...*
>
> *The First Fleet sailed from England two years before the outbreak of revolution in Europe, and for many years in this remote corner of the globe the eighteenth century stood still. For an entire generation, European order was worked out in Australia as if all the exquisite promises of the Enlightenment might still come true.*

Throughout the crucial first fifty years of modern settlement when the enduring core of Australia's character was set in place, Britain was at the height of its military strength, administrative reach, and cultural certainty. It had developed a vigorous bureaucracy to run an empire, with the services of superbly trained officers from the Royal Navy and the British army. Australia was administered with relative efficiency,

IT WASN'T LUCK

probity and equity, especially when measured against the standards of the time and the brutish behaviour of the other Imperial powers of Europe. Above all, Australia was meant to be an egalitarian society. This point is central to Atkinson's history. He describes 'the chemistry which created social order' in which leading ex-convicts were central to the management of the economy from an early stage. 'The original British plan [was] for a "community of peasant proprietors" in the Antipodes,' Atkinson explains. He challenges the argument, put most famously by Robert Hughes in *The Fatal Shore*, that formative colonial Australia was designed as the world's first concentration camp:

> *Botany Bay, it has been argued, was meant as a Gulag before Gulag ... Nothing could be further from the truth. In autumn 1786, if not later, New South Wales was envisaged as a land of Englishmen where the rights inherent in living conversation, the rights admired by the more old-fashioned advocates of liberty, would prevail ... At Botany Bay, so it was thought, the convicts would be peasants in a country of their own ... It was not, so* [Lord] *Sydney hoped, to be a place where the Crown might tighten its hold on humble, helpless Englishmen. So Sydney hoped.*

Atkinson's work builds on the myth-demolishing work of Professor Alan Frost, who has challenged and largely dispelled some of the mythologies in popular history surrounding the First Fleet.

That Aborigines were devastated by smallpox contracted

from the settlers of the First Fleet. This is one of the grim cornerstones of the thesis of Australian genocide against the indigenous people, so the facts are crucial. Frost argues that the documentary evidence does not support the speculative contention of smallpox transmitted to the Aborigines by the settlers. He has written that none of the Europeans on the First Fleet contracted smallpox, and that any contaminated materials, such as blankets, which may have left England between 1786–87 would have lost potency during such a long sea voyage. He has also found that the pattern of smallpox in the Pacific region at that time points to the disease travelling south through Australia, from Asia, rather than from the new settlers.

Frost's work is supported in the *Medical History Australia 1997*, which states: 'The gruesome spectre of the smallpox epidemic of 1789, that extraordinary calamity which struck the aborigines about Port Jackson, has haunted the medical history of the early settlement of New South Wales. Its origin is a conundrum that historians have tended to solve by intuition and bias. The most judicious survey of this phenomenon and the most reasonable and carefully reasoned explanation of the disease's origin is to be found in chapter 10, "The Curse of Cain?", of Alan Frost's book, *Botany Bay Mirages: Illusions of Australia's Convict Beginnings.*'

That New South Wales was conceived solely as a colony of exile. Wrong. The Pitt government also wanted to expand British commercial trading, pre-empt French expansionism, and find a new source of naval materials.

That the First Fleet was so incompetently assembled that

it lacked such basics as ploughs, seed potatoes and adequate clothing for the convicts. Wrong. All these items were included. Among many examples of good planning cited by Frost, scurvy did not afflict the fleet, and the fertility of the women suggested they were in good health.

Thus, the enterprise of penal servitude was not the only element that forged Australia. Early Australia was not built by convicts, but largely by *ex*-convicts. Nearly all convicts had only seven-year sentences and all had served at least a year by the time they landed in New South Wales, and some three or four years. They could not be kept in bondage once their time was up. Hope and optimism were also strong. Watkin Tench and David Collins saw bright hope on the faces of those setting out in the first journeys to New South Wales. Collins wrote that 'joy sparkled in every countenance' as the fleet sailed.

These first arrivals could not know how hard the eucalyptus domain would be. By the time of Federation a century later, ecological and economic crisis was the backdrop of Australian history. The long depression of the 1890s overlapped exactly with the Long Drought. A bank collapse in 1891 fed into the global depression of 1893 and forty percent of Australia's export income went to service British debts. Cropfields and pastures were left to return to bush. Overstocked herds were culled. Tracts of farmed land blew away in clouds of dust. The rabbit plague reached catastrophic proportions. The Red Centre expanded. Society was retreating from the hinterland. The years following Federation saw Australia lose population. The eucalyptus forests burned.

AMONG THE BARBARIANS

This environment demanded egalitarianism. A European population spread thinly through the fire forests of the continent could not sustain the social hierarchies of Europe. Even by independence on 1 January 1901, Australia's population was barely three million. The full extent of colonial Australia's defining battle with the environment is only now being truly understood. It has been fashionable in recent decades for historians to trivialise the process of nation-forming for ideological purposes. That fashion is now under assault from the weight of later histories not deformed by the requirements of ideology. Among the new histories, Robert Birrell's *A Nation Of Our Own* (1995) confronts the distortions of ideology head-on:

> *Two decades of revisionist writing have diminished the reputation of the early nationalist leaders and the institutions they created. This soiling of the early years of our national experience has helped to undermine Australians' faith that there is anything in their heritage worthy of inspiration ...*
>
> *There is a widely held view that the achievement of Australian nationhood in 1901 was little more than a shabby administrative deal between colonial leaders, motivated in large part by a desire to remove impediments to intercolonial trade. According to this perspective, nationalism was not a crucial factor ... Thus Manning Clark's devastating comment that federation was 'one of those constitutional devices recommended by apologists for bourgeois democracy for containing political equality'.*

What was the historical basis of Manning Clark's claim? Helen Irving's 1997 history of the Australian Constitution, *To Constitute a Nation*, looked for evidence and couldn't find any. The claim that there was a conscious conservative strategy, even conspiracy, has been subjected to scrutiny by several historians and has been found to be without corroboration, Irving writes. 'The fact [is] that almost no direct evidence exists of conservative opinion or advice along such lines, and that many of the most conservative also opposed Federation …'

The nonchalant and cynical dismissal of the struggle to create Federation is now being challenged by scholars undeformed by outdated Marxist analysis. 'Australian nationhood cannot be explained in these terms,' writes Birrell. There were too many obstacles to be overcome in the form of intercolonial jealousies and too little in the way of shared grievances against British control. Each Australian colony had pursued its own development independent of the others. Their main external links were with Britain, not the other colonies. Each colony had developed its own railway system in order to prevent neighbouring colonies from attracting cross-border traffic. Each colony had its own well-developed sense of identity. In Victoria at the time of Federation, seventy-nine percent of residents were Australian-born, but only six percent were natives of other states. In New South Wales, eighty percent were native-born, but only eight percent were from other States. To win Federation required incumbent politicians to give up powers and privileges to an unknown federal authority. The anchor of political inertia was heavy.

But the sheer scale of the problems facing Australia in the 1890s overmatched the ability of the colonies to deal with them individually. The sense of siege helped create a collectivist response. The experience of the United States, far from serving as a beacon, served as a warning of a racially divided society. Helen Irving points out what many people have missed: that the Civil War, so historically distant from us now, was a matter of living memory for even the youngest of the delegates to the federation conferences in the 1890s. Even as late as 1898, debate was continuing in Australian newspapers over the causes of the Civil War and its lesson for Australia.

Out of all this came a mood from which to create a new nation, a new Constitution and a new government, despite the fears of the small States that any national parliament would be dominated by New South Wales and Victoria. The success depended on the ability to mobilise support across the class spectrum, and from both city and country. Alfred Deakin and his federation supporters expressed their ideas around the theme that Australia was to become a 'new world' free of 'old world' social divisions. This ideal was the rallying point for the diverse electoral coalition the federationists constructed. 'An emotional commitment to the establishment of an Australian nation, primarily among native-born colonists, was a crucial factor in overcoming obstacles,' writes Birrell.

Helen Irving, too, debunks the cynical view. She points out that the framers of the Constitution were working with the conceptual tools they had at hand. After scouring the history of the Australian Constitution, she does not dismiss the collective idealism of the people. Australians were capable of both pragmatism and romanticism, writes Irving, and this practical blend made Federation possible. It was certainly not the work of British imperialism, which by the 1890s had been reduced to a mainly ceremonial role in the governance of the colonies.

When Federation passed overwhelmingly in 1899 (though only narrowly in New South Wales) with sixty percent of adult males voting, independence unleashed a sequence of egalitarian social legislation that was unprecedented anywhere in the world. State funding for free state education was extended to secondary school. Women won the vote. Maternity benefits, creches, kindergartens and playgrounds, nursing services, pure food and milk supplies were all funded by the state. By 1910 the infant mortality rate in Australia had fallen to 71.7 per thousand while in Britain the rate was 105 and in France 111. In 1908 an Old Age and Invalid Pension Bill was enacted, paying double the value of the pension paid in Britain.

Australian nativism was active across the full range of culture. Artists such as Streeton, McCubbin and Roberts fed off the bush to create a distinctive Australian art. Australian Rules Football was a response to the popularity of soccer among British immigrants. Australian labour was protected by a tariff wall, and government imposed itself in the setting of wages, hours, conditions, demarcations and collective bargaining. A protective wall also went up around Australian industry. Neither protective wall would come down for seventy-five years. The sense of self-reliance extended to military spending. By 1911–12, writes Birrell, Australia was approaching the per capita defence expenditure of Britain and substantially exceeding that of Canada, the United States and even Germany. Through the period between 1901 and 1909, when legislation was passed to establish a civilian militia based on compulsory training, the British military authorities advised it would be more appropriate to develop a field force which could be integrated with the Imperial defence forces. This advice was rejected.

Australia's military commitment would be tested soon enough. By the end of 1914, just months after the outbreak of World War I, 52 561 men had enlisted, from about 820 000 eligible for service. Patriotism and adventure were the greatest factors, but drought and hardship were also important. In 1914 the wheat crop had been reduced by two-thirds, and unemployment in the bush was high. The collective character of the young Australians who went to war is captured in their letters, used by Bill Gammage in his brilliant 1974 book, *The Broken Years*. Ellis Silas, of the 16th Battalion, wrote these words in 1915 just before the first Australian wave landed at Gallipoli:

> *We have been told of the impossible task before us, of probably annihilation; yet we are eager to get to it; we joke with each other about getting cold feet, but deep down in our hearts we know when we get to it we will not be found wanting ... for the last time in this world many of us stand shoulder to shoulder. As I look down*

IT WASN'T LUCK

the ranks of my comrades I wonder which of us is marked for the land beyond.

The disaster of Gallipoli did not prevent the Australian army from prodigious achievement over the course of the war. During the final nine months of the war in 1918, the Australian army opposed thirty-nine divisions and defeated them all. They took 29 144 prisoners (twenty-three percent of the British total), 338 guns (23.5 percent), and forty miles of ground (21.5 percent), and made possible the gaining of much more. Yet they made up less than ten percent of the British army.

These achievements were also made in inimitable style. In 1917 three Australian divisions recorded twelve times the number of absence without leave convictions than the twenty-two other divisions of the Third Army. In March 1918, 9000 Australians were in field prisons, compared with fewer than 2000 in every other British or colonial force. Bill Gammage wrote that Australian forces received some visits by the King in stolid silence. He also described, 'the fierce individualism with which he fought Turks, Arabs and English staff officers'. Gammage describes the Australian light-horseman as laconic, practical, with the equanimity and resourcefulness of the bushman. 'Probably his kind will not be seen again for the conditions of war and romance that produced him have almost entirely disappeared.' The words of an Australian soldier, writing in his diary in 1917, would reverberate through the nation:

Adieu, the years are a broken song,
And the right grows weak in the strife with wrong,
The lilies of love have a crimson stain,
And the old days never will come again.

Australians' character would soon be tested again on an even greater scale in a war of national survival. Gavan Daws in *Prisoners of the Japanese*, a history of the Allied prisoners in the Pacific theatre of World War II, describes cultures stripped down to their most elemental basics.

> *I started coming across national differences in behaviour from the very first days of my research, and the evidence kept piling up. When I tried to think of simple expressions to describe what I was finding, the words that came to mind were* tribes *and* tribalism ... *Tribalism has always had enormous power: it still does. And certainly it did in the prisoner of war camps.*
>
> *I would go so far as to say that it was nationality above all that determined, for good or ill, the way POWs lived and died, often* whether *they lived or died.*

In the camps Australians discarded their differences (the biggest was the suspicion between Catholics and Masons which even showed up in the camps until crushed by the conditions) and became a tribe, a tribe which was always the most successful group. The core of this success was an ethos of mateship and egalitarianism which not only survived the ultimate dehumanising duress of the death camps, but shone through as the dominant Australian characteristic.

IT WASN'T LUCK

The juices crushed out of the POWs were of course human in the most fundamental sense. But at the same time, all the way down to starvation rations, to a hundred pounds of body weight and less, to the extremities of degradation—all the way to death—the prisoners of the Japanese remained inextinguishably American, Australian, British, Dutch ...

The Americans were the great individualists of the camps, the capitalists, the cowboys, the gangsters. The British hung on to their class structure like bulldogs, for grim death. The Australians kept trying to construct little male-bonded welfare states ...

[Unlike Americans] Australians could not imagine doing men to death by charging interest on something as basic to life as rice. That was bloodsucking; it was murder. Within little tribes of Australian enlisted men, rice went back and forth all the time, but this was not trading in commodities futures, it was sharing, it was Australian tribalism.

One of the most memorable passages in *Prisoners of the Japanese* is a survivor's description of what happened after the sinking of a Japanese freighter, the *Rakuyo Maru*, filled with prisoners of war:

When the Rakuyo Maru *went down with seven hundred Australians and six hundred British aboard, it was the Australians who tried to preserve the biggest prisoner tribe. On the third day in the water, some Englishmen who were almost finished sighted a mass of black shapes. As we drew nearer we saw there were about two to three hundred men gathered on a huge pontoon of rafts. They had erected a couple of lofty distress signals, coloured shorts and other bits of clothing fixed to spars of wood. As we paddled up we saw there was a large outer ring of rafts linked to each other with pieces of rope. Inside the circle were other rafts, unattached but safely harboured. They seemed organized compared with the disintegrated rabble we had become during those last two days. They may have been drifting aimlessly as we had; but at least they all drifted together. A lot of them still wore those familiar slouch hats—we had caught up with the Aussie contingent. One of them looped us in with a dangling end of rope. 'Cheers, mate,' came the friendly voice. 'This is no place to be on your lonesome'.*

It is important to remember the privations of these wars, and the pervasive sense of dread for the millions of Australians who lived through them. The world wars are rapidly receding into historical abstractions, and as they fade from the collective experience it is becoming discreditable in universities to invoke the memory of these struggles. It is almost as if the past is now mainly invoked for what was lost, not won. But the red stain across Australian history was not left only by the receding Aboriginal tribes. Stoicism in the face of pain was ingrained in the evolving Australian character from the earliest days, a characteristic duly noted by Robert Hughes in *The Fatal Shore*:

IT WASN'T LUCK

The scarred back became an emblem of rank. So did silence. Convicts called a man who blubbered and screamed at the triangles a crawler *or a* sandstone. *(Sandstone is a common rock around Sydney; it is soft and crumbles easily.) By contrast, the convict who stood up to it in silence was admired as a* pebble *or an* iron man.

Something happened to Australian stoicism and nativism during the comfort and success of the boom after World War II. A key record of this change was Donald Horne's *The Lucky Country*, first published in 1964. It was a huge bestseller, reprinted for many years thereafter, and became a formative document. *The Lucky Country* is a lucid book but also an extremely patronising book. More than any other postwar work, it created and legitimised the practice of sneering at Australian culture. Again and again, Horne's tone is one of unambiguous embarrassment, the embarrassment of a provincial intellectual:

The possibility that the world should become like Australia would profoundly alarm most cultivated people in the world …

Australia is a lucky country run mainly by second-rate people who share its luck. It lives on other people's ideas and, although its ordinary people are adaptable, most of its leaders (in all fields) so lack curiosity about the events that surround them that they are often taken by surprise. A nation more concerned with styles of life than with achievement has managed to achieve what may be the most evenly prosperous society in the world ...

It is usually not possible to conduct in Australia the kind of conversation that would be immediately acceptable among intellectuals in Europe, or New York ...

Intellectual life exists but it is still fugitive. Emergent and uncomfortable, it has no established relation to practical life. The upper levels of society give an impression of mindlessness triumphant ... at the top the tone is so banal that to a sophisticated observer the flavour of democratic life in Australia might seem depraved, a victory of the anti-mind ...

In Australia people get away with things that would be exposed in a more sophisticated nation ...

But the tiredness and cliche-thinking of opinion-makers is unable to capture the skepticism of the people. It is almost a conspiracy of tiredness of the spirit ...

Australia did not 'earn' nationhood by struggle against the oppressor or civil war. It could have become a nation earlier than it did, if it had wanted to. At the end of the 19th century there was a desultory debate for twenty years as the six separate Colonies began to talk about federating. Finally there was a referendum. Sixty per cent of Australians voted in it; altogether forty-three per cent of all electors voted 'yes'.

IT WASN'T LUCK

The Lucky Country must be judged in the context of its time, and in this context Horne's comments were intelligent and forward-looking. His book was a resounding success in the marketplace of ideas. The social context of his arguments was the provincialism of the 1950s and 1960s (though similar provincialism existed in most places around the world if one cared to look). Taste-makers like Horne, in helping to shed the narrowness of postwar Australia, also laid the foundation for a much more destructive and methodical assault on Australian history in the 1970s and 1980s—fuelled partly by the idealistic folly of the Vietnam War—an assault led first by academic Marxism and then by the multicultural industry.

'Advocates of multiculturalism tend to resist arguments that a unique Australian society and identity emerged with Federation, and especially the expectation that this identity should be the basis of immigrant assimilation,' says Bob Birrell, the Monash University demographer and historian. 'One way to discredit such expectations is to argue that the early Australian nationalists did not in fact create a society or culture which can be regarded as distinctly "Australian" ... In response to those who insist that Australia is distinctive, people like Stephen Castles argue that much of this is mythical, or worse, a cover-up of a rather seamy historical reality.'

> *Australia grew up as part of the British Empire. Unlike the USA, India or Britain's other far-flung possessions, Australia never managed a decent independence movement, let alone a liberation struggle. Australia was made a nation by an Act of the British Parliament in 1901. The*

> *creation of a nation in a struggle for independence is usually the pre-eminent moment for the definition of national character, language, culture and myths. Australia has missed out on this.*

The authors of this summation, an echo of Donald Horne, were Stephen Castles, Mary Kalantzis, Bill Cope and M. Morrissey, writing in *Mistaken Identity, Multiculturalism and the Demise of Nationalism in Australia* (1990), a work typical of the genre. During the years of Labor's ascendancy in Canberra, Castles, Kalantzis and Cope were key players for the ideology of multiculturalism. Their ideology was, and remains, hostile to the mythology of Australia's egalitarian tradition:

> *It has been racist, justifying genocide and exclusionism, and denying the role of non-British migrants. It has been sexist, ignoring the role of women in national development, and justifying their subordinate position. It has idealised the role of the 'common man' in a situation of growing inequality and increasingly rigid class divisions.*

This view of Australia's past manages to turn success into failure. Since World War II no other nation in the world has remade itself so comprehensively and so seamlessly as Australia, absorbing and adapting a wide range of cultural influences and immigrants. In 1964, the year *The Lucky Country* was published, Australia's population was 11.25 million. In the year 2000, the population will be nineteen million, an increase of two-thirds in little more than a generation. This transformative thrust was not the vision of a self-satisfied, narrow nation.

David Malouf, in his foreword to the third edition of the *Macquarie Dictionary* (1997), the superb and now ubiquitous cultural reference point which did not exist when Donald Horne produced *The Lucky Country*, wrote of his changing country and its changing language:

> *For a long time we tended to see our local world, for all its vastness and the variety of its landscape, as uniform, not because it was, but because we had not yet found a use for variety and for that reason had no eye for it.*

'It's miraculous!' another acute Australian writer, Clive James, said in 1997. 'It is so striking after you come home after a long time away because back in the 1950s I can remember how short of culture we felt we were. And now there's no question of shortage. For a long, long time, people were spending a lot of time talking about what Australian culture should be, and not realising that culture grows like a coral reef, through accumulations, through accretions, often through the deaths of a lot of little anonymous creatures.'

Success and solidity has been built over the long haul. The wealth which so amazed Charles Darwin in 1836 has not, as in so many other naturally wealthy countries, been dissipated. Australians are, on average, almost five times richer than they were at the start of the twentieth century, according to a 1997 study by the CSIRO. The average life has increased between the 1890s and the 1990s from forty-nine to seventy-eight. The adult life of the average Australian has almost doubled in a century.

The World Bank, which now uses a complex formula to measure the relative wealth of nations, including 'natural capital' and environmental stewardship, rates Australia the sixth wealthiest nation in the world after the United States, Switzerland, Canada, Japan and Norway. 'Australia's quality of life looks even better than the purely economic index,' Professor Fred Gruen told me in 1996.

Australia is still called the lucky country, and the description is still not a kind one. It implies a nation that lives off an inheritance. But Australia, distant from its markets, sparse in its population, living off a largely threadbare continent, has taken what was available and used its advantages, despite mistakes, logically and efficiently. It wasn't luck.

In *The Lucky Country* Donald Horne looked back and quoted Vance Palmer who, beneath the shadow of social annihilation in 1942, with everything at stake, wrote:

> *The next few months may decide not only whether we are to survive as a nation, but whether we deserve to survive ... If Australia had no more character than could be seen on its surface, it would be annihilated as surely and swiftly as those colonial outposts white men built for their commercial profit in the East— pretentious facades of stucco that looked imposing as long as the wind kept from blowing. But there is an Australia of the spirit, submerged and not very*

IT WASN'T LUCK

articulate, that is quite different from these bubbles of old-world imperialism ... sardonic, idealist, tongue-tied perhaps, it is the Australia of all who truly belong here ... And it has something to contribute to the world. Not emphatically in the arts as yet, but in arenas of action, and in ideas for the creation of that egalitarian democracy that will have to be the basis for all civilized societies in the future. That is the Australia we are called upon to save.

That is exactly what has happened. The half century 1947–97 saw a social revolution in Australia that was bloodless, gradualist, democratic and open-minded. In 1947, the Australian population was just 7.5 million; it was ninety percent Anglo-Celtic; it was ninety-nine percent European; the Aboriginal and Asian populations combined were less than one percent of the overall population; public policy still enshrined White Australia, which had helped define the nation since independence; links with Asia were minimal; the British Privy Council was still the ultimate court of appeal; Aborigines did not have citizenship, and had barely any role in society. There were no computers. There was not even television. There was no gaping hole in the ozone layer, or global warming. The nation had just fought a monumental struggle for survival against a powerful and ruthless Asian invader.

Fifty years later, no other nation in the world, not even the United States, had remade itself so comprehensively, so equitably, and with such unselfconscious ambition, as

Australia in the era after World War II. The overt culture of the nation—its language, cuisine, music, writings, film, dance, architecture, design, sport—all, at their highest expression, have become sophisticated, exuberant, worldly and distinct.

This backward glance at Australia's history—and it is no more than a glance—suggests that in demolishing the myth of Australia the triumphant innocent we are in danger of creating a new myth of Australia the genocidal despoiler.

Cultural pride does mean cultural complacency. Stephen FitzGerald, in his 1997 book, *Is Australia An Asian Nation?* put the challenge eloquently:

> *We have to start to be* [more] *intelligent, intellectual, forward-thinking and long-term, and not lazy, about ourselves, our values, our institutions, or our region ... not clutch at protectors or a white man's world now gone or a past which cannot be retrieved ... We have to be Australian and not European, we have to be quiet not strident, we have to learn humility and listen to silence. We have to care intensely about the future and the survival of this democracy, one of the oldest in the world, and the preservation of the innate democratic instinct of the people.*

The myth of the lucky country is dispelled by dozens of countries with abundant natural wealth that have failed in the past fifty years. It is dispelled by the many countries, the great majority of nations, that have not matched the dexterous, adaptable, democratic joy of Australian culture, and by the many countries where ethnic divisions have led to violence. The myth is dispelled by all the blood in the pages of Australian history. The myth of the lucky country needs to die. The truly lucky ones have been the perpetrators of this myth. It's time their luck ran out.

3
BLACK RAIN

AN ENTIRE ECONOMY DISAPPEARED in 1997. Seven hundred billion dollars. Gone. The twelfth-largest economy in the world, much bigger than the gross national product of Australia.

Evaporated.

The crisis took physical shape in August when thick smoke rolled over the green hills and grey cities of South-East Asia and the sky disappeared. Fires burned, thousands of people became sick, millions hid indoors, and in Papua New Guinea hundreds died and half a million people went starving. The dense haze drifted from Papua New Guinea to Malaysia, a distance wider than Australia. Something was badly wrong in Asia.

Even the once impregnable rainforest of Borneo, a forest canopy so large it appeared from the air like an enormous rolling lawn, has been so gashed by decades of logging that when the monsoon failed and the land dried, tens of thousands of hectares of rainforest peat caught fire and burned through July, August, September, October and into November. Twenty million Indonesians were exposed to chronic pollution, and millions more around the region. Airports were closed, flights cancelled, travel and trade disrupted. In the evergreen forests, poorly adapted to fire, trees were dying. By the time the monsoon finally came in November, the crisis had taken a different form. An electronic, computerised deluge—a black rain—had engulfed the entire region, reaching Japan, South Korea and Hong Kong as well.

On 30 June 1997 the combined value of the dynamic stock markets of Asia—Japan, South Korea, Taiwan, Hong Kong, Malaysia, Indonesia, Singapore, Thailand and the Philippines—had been almost exactly 3000 billion dollars, according to the American bank Morgan Stanley. Six months later, after fires, bank failures, property market collapses, currency shocks and stock market meltdowns, the combined value of those same nine stock markets had dropped to around 2300 billion dollars. Seven hundred billion dollars carried away in an electronic typhoon.

Add to the market crash the Asian property crash, the Russian crash, the tens of billions in unrecoverable loans to Japanese banks, and the debased value of some currencies, and the total losses created in 1997–98 were much more than twice the size of the Australian economy—the disappearance from the global balance sheets of one of the world's ten largest economies.

Flimsy banking structures exposed flimsy political structures. Factories were burned down in Thailand amid rioting. There were more riots in Indonesia, where unemployment rose, prices soared, panic buying stripped supermarkets of food, and people began hoarding. The plutocracy looked frail. In strict accounting terms, Indonesia was insolvent. The value of the stock market was much less than its debts and its capacity to pay those debts, many of them in now extremely expensive foreign currencies. South Korea was also technically insolvent, amid mass demonstrations, bankruptcies, a currency free-fall, a market collapse and a blow-out of foreign debt. The IMF had to provide more than 100 billion dollars in loans to prop up South Korea, Indonesia and Thailand, the largest bail-out in the IMF's history.

Malaysia refused to go to the IMF, but its problems were among the worst. Cracks began to appear in the economy as early as July, and they were made worse when the Prime Minister, Dr Mahathir Mohamad singled out the world's leading individual financial trader, New York-based George Soros, describing him as a 'self-serving rogue'. The government-controlled media suggested Soros had been a Nazi sympathiser—even though he is Jewish—and also had links to 'the international Zionist conspiracy'. Mahathir then made another attack on Soros, describing him as a 'moron' and a 'criminal'. Months earlier, Mahathir had already banned the movie *Schindler's List*, with its portrayal of the Jewish Holocaust.

On 4 September 1997 the Malaysian government attempted to stare down the international currency market by backing the ringgit. The government lost thirty billion dollars in a single day. This sent the Malaysian stock market plunging. Mahathir harangued the 'rich and powerful' nations who continued to give orders to the rest of the world. He accused George Soros of conspiring against the ringgit, pointing out that he was Jewish. 'Incidentally, we are Muslims, and the Jews are not happy to see the Muslims progress ... The Jews robbed the Palestinians of everything, but in Malaysia they could not do so, hence they do this, depress the ringgit.'

Asia's speculative excesses were the cause of the Tiger crisis, and the overheated economies were engulfed by an existential deluge. It came out of the future, not the past. It was an electronic black rain of volatile trading that dwarfed all the economic structures of the world. Money and value were being reinvented, redefined, repackaged and resold in multiplying combinations. Markets were being made not just in common stocks, but in preferred, participating preferred, second-preferred, prior-preferred, cumulative preferred, bond convertible, treasury, DARTS, ARPS, warrants (put, instalment, endowment, capital plus, subscription), subscription rights, debenture stocks, SCOREs, PRIMEs, stock options (naked and covered), ADRs, PIKs, index funds, bond index baskets, futures (stock, commodity, currency, index) and futures options. Bonds: junk, savings, dollar, euro, eurodollar, Yankee, yen, Aussie, gold, CTBs, CBBs, baby, put, convertibles, convertible preferred, coupons (zero, liquid yield, current, short, long, full and registered), MIGs-1, -2, -3 and -4; pass-throughs, pickups, citizens, cushions, flowers, obligations, adjustments, resets, perpetuals, super sinkers, IDBs, MITs, ARMs, ARM fixers, LYONS, REDs, HITs, BAN's, RTCs, CMOs, RANs, RAMs, TABs, TANs, REITs, REMICs, GAINS, FIGS, FEARS, STRIPS, TIGERs, CATs and LIONs.

These multiplying products didn't exist except on computer screens, traders' receipts and owners' accounts, but they had real meanings and real consequences. In nominal value the derivatives trade towered over the global equity and bond and commodity markets. The value of interest-rate swaps alone was more than 25 *trillion* dollars a year. More than ninety percent of the stupendous multi-trillion global electronic money flow was speculative. Less than ten percent was for trade or investment or travel.

The losses in Asia in this global financial casino were staggering. Imagine the Australian stock market falling from 2600 to 1600, or your retirement nest egg from $100 000 to $40 000, and you get a sense of what it was like to be a Tiger in 1997. Imagine your bank is technically insolvent.

One of Australia's finest economic writers, the late T.M. Fitzgerald, warned in the 1990 Boyer Lectures about the increasing velocity of global currency flows:

> *The economic situation that we have to address now is more difficult than anything that I have ever seen because so many things are now beyond our control. Australia is now on sufferance to foreign lenders of huge amounts of volatile short-term funds. In the past ten years the transformation has been total: an overwhelming preponderance of a vastly bloated capital inflow on very short term ... Naturally, that locust plague has tended to drive away most of the traditional bedding-down kind of capital, apart from money to effect takeovers of existing Australian enterprise by foreigners.*

Dr Doom had also warned us. In a major speech in New York on Anzac Day 1994, Dr Henry Kaufman, known on Wall Street as Dr Doom, had warned about what he called 'the

Americanisation of finance' for the roiling mountains of financial turbulence:

> *The technology is in place for a cascade of selling by investors ... The market is driven by an expanding group of high-octane portfolio managers using new trading techniques, especially derivatives, who are free to roam throughout the financial sphere, in and out of currencies, equities, bonds, commodities, derivative instruments, with primarily a near-term focus, and no particular loyalty to any national marketplace.*

Dr Doom correctly predicted the emergence of traders commanding portfolios worth around 500 billion dollars roaming the world. The most famous of these was George Soros, the ultimate black rainmaker, the man so reviled by Dr Mahathir Mohamad. George Soros was worried. He saw great potential danger in the markets he had ridden to such wealth and influence. Prior to the 1997 currency shock, he wrote:

> *Although I have made a fortune in the financial markets, I now fear that the untrammelled intensification of laissez-faire capitalism and the spread of market values into all areas of life is endangering our open and democratic society ... The present situation is comparable to that at the turn of the past century. It was a golden age of capitalism, characterized by the principle of laissez faire: so is the present. The earlier period was in some ways more stable ... The earlier period had the gold standard; today the main currencies float and crush*

against each other like continental plates. Yet the free market regime that prevailed 100 years ago was destroyed by World War I. Totalitarian ideologies came to the fore and, by the end of World War II, there was practically no movement of capital between countries. How much more likely the present regime is to break down unless we learn from experience!

After the crash of 1997, Soros's urgency became pronounced.

I cannot believe that the present global boom will not be followed by a bust ... The recent turmoil in Asian markets raises difficult questions about currency pegs, asset bubbles, inadequate banking supervision, and the lack of financial information ... There is no international regulatory authority for financial markets, and there is not enough international cooperation for the taxation of capital ... What started out as a minor imbalance has become a much bigger one that threatens to engulf not only international credit but international trade.

Soros was alarmed because he knew just how reckless cowboy capitalism was becoming. He was proved right in September 1998, when a major New York hedge fund, Long-Term Capital Management, was caught with an exposure to the derivatives market of US 1.25 *trillion* dollars. LTCM was run by John Merriwether, who had first appeared in Michael Lewis's best-seller, *Liar's Poker*, as the trader willing to bet US ten million dollars on a single hand of liar's poker. Now his firm needed $US3.6 billion in emergency funds to avoid creating a cascading ripple of defaults through the global system.

When the financial ministers of the world's seven largest economies, the G7, met as this LTCM debacle was being revealed, Britain's Chancellor of the Exchequer, Gordon Brown, expressed the growing fears of all governments:

> *The world's financial system is over-exposed, over-extended, under-supervised, under-performing and in need of far-reaching reform.*

George Soros, meanwhile, was starting to worry about China. With its huge foreign reserves, big trade surplus, strong currency, and robust domestic growth, China had been the bulwark of Asia during the economic crisis. Soros, however, saw potential for crisis in China. Again, he was quickly vindicated, when a Chinese economist, He Qinglian, revealed an economy riddled with insolvency, inefficiency and corruption on a scale far greater than generally thought in the West.

From now on, whatever China does will have large-scale repercussions for all of Asia, including Australia. The economic emergence of China is one of the reasons why the Tiger economies suffered a meltdown in 1997. Ten years earlier, Indonesia, South Korea, Malaysia, Thailand and the Philippines had all enjoyed large trade surpluses. By 1997 they all had trade deficits. Professor Lester Thurow explains why: 'Their swing from surplus to deficit is directly traceable to China's decision to concentrate on increasing exports as its engine of growth. Since China could offer better educated but cheaper workers than Southeast Asia, and since it has a much bigger internal market for its own products, it quickly gained a US forty billion dollar trade surplus, taking export trade away from other Asian countries.'

But because of the huge pool of underemployed workers built up during the decades of Communism, China, unlike Australia, must maintain high levels of economic growth just to maintain the status quo. Even the official *Chinese Daily* estimates that the cost of China's environmental degradation caused by unrestrained development is equal to about seven percent of the gross domestic product each year.

'In China,' wrote the international environmental law experts, Andre Dua and Daniel Esty, 'provincial governments and local entrepreneurs often conspire to build stripped-down, low-cost, and thus highly polluting, power plants which generate the maximum amount of electricity per dollar of capital invested. American companies that have included pollution control technologies in their proposals for electricity-generating facilities have been told to eliminate these features, and cut the cost of their bids accordingly, or lose the chance to be chosen for the project.'

China plans to build more than a hundred new power stations during the first decade of the new century.

The American reporter Mark Hertsgaard travelled through China in 1996 to study China's ecology. He would go for days in a country where, 'the land had been scalped, the water poisoned, the air made toxic and dark'. He found places like the Chongqing Paper Factory, perched near the intersection of the Jialin River and the mighty Yangtze, the artery of central China, which Hertsgaard described in the *Atlantic Monthly* in November 1997.

> *The astringent odor of chlorine attacked our nostrils, and once we reached the stream's edge, the smell was so powerful that we immediately backed away. Below us, where the discharge emptied into the Jialin, a frothy white plume was spreading across the slow-moving river ... a vast, roaring torrent of white, easily thirty [metres] wide, splashing down the hillside like a waterfall of boiling milk.*

There are at least 100 000 raw polluters like the Chongqing Paper Factory. Acid rain is endemic in China. Five Chinese cities, including Beijing, are ranked in the world's top ten cities with the worst air pollution. The levels of total suspended particulates in the air—soot, dust and faecal matter—are more than ten times greater than in major Australian cities.

Fertile cropland lost in China since 1950 is greater than all the arable land in Australia and equivalent to all the farmland in the United Kingdom, Germany and France. China's population is growing each year by sixteen million, almost the population of Australia. China is bursting with excess workers. Rural underemployment is estimated at about thirty-five percent, or 175 million people. Underemployment in the bloated state sector, which employs 110 million workers, is also chronic. The huge steel and textile industries will shed at least twenty percent of their workforce as they modernise to compete on the world market.

'China's estimated economic growth will turn the country into an environmental nightmare,' the Regional Institute of Environmental Technology, based in Singapore, warned in 1997. Its report said about eighty percent of China's urban river systems are polluted, commonly with ammonium, nitrate, volatile phenol and oxygen-consuming organic materials. The Institute estimated that fifty billion dollars would need to be spent to protect the nation from acid rain, smog and polluted drinking water. Mark Hertsgaard, after his trip through the country, wrote:

> *China is a greenhouse giant. It has already surpassed the former Soviet Union to become the world's second largest producer of greenhouse gases, trailing only the United States. With its immense coal reserves, huge population, and booming economic growth, China is very likely to triple its greenhouse emissions by 2020.*

China also carries a mountain of bad loans piled up by the four big state-owned banks, estimated at about twenty percent of the loans outstanding in the Chinese financial system. The state banks will not be able to survive without massive injections of China's foreign reserves. Thousands of state enterprises are zombie companies kept alive by government subsidy. China's political system is also one of the world's most corrupt. The killing floods along the Yangtze in 1998, which displaced millions of people—the worst floods in two generations—were partly caused by excessive timber-cutting and government mismanagement.

When all the elements are factored into the reality of

modern China—despoliation, vandalism, poor health, increasing fertility, high debt and high corruption—the Chinese miracle becomes, in part, the Chinese mirage.

An even darker conclusion is reached in the first major analysis of the Deng Xiaoping era to emerge from within China—*China's Pitfall*, by the economist He Qinglian, which has sold several hundred thousand copies in China since it was first published in 1997. In a cover story for the *New York Review of Books* in October, 1998, Liu Binyan and Perry Link conclude:

> China's Pitfall, *the first systematic study of the social consequences of China's economic boom, vindicates the skeptics so resoundingly as to reconceive what 'reform' has meant ...*
>
> *He Qinglian writes that from the outset the urban 'reform' amounted to, 'a process in which power-holders and their hangers-on plundered public wealth. The primary target of their plunder was state property that had been accumulated from forty years of the people's sweat, and their primary means of plunder was political power ...'*
>
> *Future Chinese generations will have to reckon with another, even larger, debt that the economic boom has both incurred and postponed, and that is the debt to the environment ...*
>
> *Few people in the outside world appreciate how pervasive the attitude and practice of zai (rip-offs) have become in China. Probably in no other society*

today has economic good faith been compromised to the extent it has in China. Contracts are not kept; debts are ignored, whether between individuals or between state enterprises; individuals, families and sometimes whole towns have gotten rich on deceitful schemes.

He Qinglian sees the overall situation as unprecedented. 'The championing of money as a value has never before reached the point of holding all moral rules in such contempt.' She finds the collapse of ethics—not growth of the economy—to be the most dramatic change in China during the Deng Xiaoping era.

Where does all this leave Australia? Amid all the problems of Asia, Australia proved something during the 1997 Asian meltdown. It proved to have a political, financial and social system that could weather a storm. It proved that economic wealth and rapid growth are not enough. A nation needs rigorous institutions and financial transparency. While the East Asian stock market (except China and Taiwan) saw forty per cent of its market value wiped out, the Australian stock market rode out the crash. The Australian dollar was like an innocent bystander, knocked down by a car out of control, yet it staged an orderly retreat against the US dollar as commodity prices declined, several major Australian export markets went into free-fall and tourism from the wounded economies fell off a cliff. The Australian property market grew while Asian property bubbles burst. Jobs increased. Unemployment held steady. Interest rates stayed near historic lows. The federal budget was close to balance. The Australian dollar rose against most Asian currencies. Politically, the country was as steady as a rock.

'Australia was remarkably resilient, and it has been resilient and adaptable over a long time,' said the economist and columnist Max Walsh. 'And unlike most of Asia, it has built a clean financial system.'

Australia firmly weathered the region's crisis, but the Tiger meltdown of 1997 was the harbinger of further volatility.

As the Asian contagion spread to Russia in 1998 and the Russian economy collapsed, Australia was buffeted even more by external forces over which it had no control.

SEOUL FIGHTS OFF COLLAPSE, THAIS BEG FOR MERCY

CHINA: MIGHTY YUAN STARTS TO CRACK ON BLACK MARKET

CHAOS FEARED AS MIGRANT MILLIONS FACE EXPULSION

INDONESIAN ECONOMY CRASHES

RIOTERS KILLED IN INDONESIAN RACE-HATE RAMPAGE

$A PLUNGES AS GLOBAL CRISIS GROWS

BLACK RAIN

Then came the big daddy of all headlines, in *The Sydney Morning Herald* of 29 August 1998: WORLD MELTDOWN

We are in for a rough ride. Collapsing markets in Asia, disappearing flight-loads of tourists, factory closings and a relentless swell of electronic currency trading—on which the Aussie dollar bobbed like a sloop on the open sea—all fed a sense of insecurity in Australia. If George Soros was feeling uneasy about the stability of the global financial trading system, he had plenty of company Down Under.

The vision of Asian splendour which so intoxicated many Australian public intellectuals will be a more arduous road than expected. Australia's stability in the 1998 crisis was the third time in four years the nation had been challenged by the formidable new realities of Asia. In 1995 China had competed directly and aggressively against Australia when it sought the glittering prize of hosting the first Olympics of the new millennium. China built Olympic facilities. It held huge rallies for the International Olympic Committee. It called in diplomatic debts. It mobilised political power. China was the giant in this contest. Beijing the great Imperial capital. Its only serious rival was Sydney. Almost one in every five persons in the world lived in China, while Australia had just 0.25 percent of the world's population. China represented the next frontier of international markets, while Australia was an important yet mature and secondary market.

It seemed an unequal contest. It was not. While Australia had only 1.5 percent of China's population, its gross national product was one-third the size of China's. Australia, not China, had a long and distinguished Olympic tradition.

Australia, not China, had long-term political stability and commitment to democracy, the rule of law, and individual freedom. Australia, not China, had superb communications infrastructure and a professional, worldly and untainted public sector. Australia, not China, was untroubled by endemic corruption. Australia, not China, had a globally traded currency, open equity markets and a transparent and efficient financial system. Australia, not China, was integrated into the greatest economic and cultural force in history—the alliance of English-speaking nations led by the United States.

China's Olympic city, Beijing, was coated in the squalor of its own lungs, a permanent brown haze so foul it made the normal metropolitan pollution problems of rival Sydney appear inconsequential. When the International Olympic Committee made the long trip to Sydney, they found a team that was ready and a city built around one of the great visions of the world, a place where, as a former Sydney boy Clive James once wrote: 'In Sydney Harbour the yachts will be racing on the crushed diamond water under a sky the texture of powdered sapphires.'

China lost.

4
AMONG THE BARBARIANS

IN HIS ESSAY 'TO SCREW Foreigners is Patriotic', China scholar Geremie Barmé points out that Beijing's pride was deeply offended when Australia defeated China in the international contest for the 2000 Olympics:

The internal propaganda campaign for a Beijing Olympics emphasised the primacy of a unique Chinese national spirit and the ability of the people to 'move mountains and drain the oceans' ... The eventual failure of the Chinese bid was deemed to have been orchestrated by Western bullies, and the Olympic Committee's decision to give the 2000 Olympics to Sydney was seen as an affront to Chinese national sentiment ...

The Chinese government's attitude to the Games has not exactly been in the spirit envisaged by the Olympic organisers.

On 8 January 1998, after years of controversy and accusations and improbable performances by Chinese athletes, Australian customs officers seized a drug growth hormone from the bag of a member of the Chinese swimming team as the squad arrived to take part in the World Swimming Championships in Perth. Officers found thirteen vials of a substance labelled Somatropin, a synthetic human growth hormone which can be used as a substitute for anabolic steroids and is undetectable. They also seized thirteen vials of saline solution, used to dilute the Somatropin before injection.

The following week, four Chinese swimmers failed drug tests. All tested positive for a banned diuretic called Triamterene, used to dilute the urine and thus mask the effects of steroids or illegal hormone treatments.

All four Chinese swimmers were from the Shanghai club, coached by Zhou Ming, who had been previously suspended for drug involvement when seven of his swimmers were caught using steroids in 1994. Chinese athletes had already been involved in twenty-three positive steroid tests since 1990, and innumerable accusations. In the previous world championships in Rome in 1994, China, having never been a swimming force in previous decades, won twelve of the sixteen titles. Seven of the swimmers, including two of the new world champions, tested positive for steroids at the Asian Games a month later.

In 1995 the journalist and oral historian Sang Ye, an Australian citizen who had immigrated from China, interviewed a member of the Chinese national athletics team. The interview, published in the literary journal *Heat* in 1997, suggested the problem was even worse than it appeared.

I've taken part in three major competitions: two world championships and one Olympics. I wasn't in very good form, so I didn't win any medals. But it's not a matter of pitting athletes against each other in competition. What you're really doing is comparing drugs. If the drugs we're using aren't any good, you don't have a hope. We Orientals are biologically different from foreigners; we've got the skills and quick enough reflexes, but we just don't have the stamina. Relatively speaking we need to use drugs, and they're pretty effective ...

The improbable performances of Chinese swimmers and athletes appeared to be as systematic and blatant as the illegal drug regime of East Germany, a national sports system which, after the collapse of the East German communist regime, was exposed as rotten from top to bottom. A German historian who has specialised in the East German drug sport era, Dr Gisether Spitzer, has unearthed evidence that more than 10 000 athletes across a range of sports had been given performance-enhancing drugs.

Sang Ye's Olympian also added rampant nationalism to the mix:

When [we] take part in an international competition ... We've got our backs to the wall. 'The Motherland and the People are waiting for you to fight a victorious war. You must achieve glory for the nation!' And it's just like going to war, too. The pressure is intense ... I bummed out in the Olympics and didn't get a place, and so people back home started abusing my mum and dad for having produced a birth defect like me, one that had lost face for the nation. Someone slashed my dad's bike tyres too, and my younger brother was beaten up ...

Nationalism was not merely the province of mainland Chinese. The Olympian found some overseas Chinese even worse:

> *They* [the overseas Chinese] *have it pretty good but they always have this inferiority complex thing going. They hate foreigners and see us as representing China in their own war with whitey.*

The year that Beijing lost the Olympics to Sydney, the most popular tele-series in China was *A Beijing Man in New York*. It told the story of a Chinese hero making his way through an avaricious, amoral America. In an especially popular scene, the Beijing man hires a busty blonde prostitute and, while showering her with dollars, orders her to cry out repeatedly, 'I love you, I love you'.

> *'A Beijing Man in New York',* writes Barmé, *was broadcast at a time when both the Chinese authorities and segments of the population were becoming increasingly irate about their (perceived) position in the New World Order and the attitude of the United States towards China. It also represented, perhaps, the coming of age of Chinese narcissism, and bespoke a desire for revenge for all the real and perceived slights of the past century.*

Plenty of Chinese resentments can be found about Australians, too. This is not surprising given the dynamic chauvinism at the core of Chinese culture. Yet Australia's national debate is dominated by the view that the only racism which matters is white racism. This extraordinary attitude is not only myopic, self-absorbed and neocolonial, it is also dangerously naive. In *The Year the Dragon Came*, a 1996 book by Sang Ye about Chinese immigrants to Australia, especially the so-called Bob Hawke Tiananmen Square immigrants, it does not take long before the insults against Australians start flying.

> *You can only speak like this to Chinese, you know. The Australians are dogs. Can't expect them to understand.*

That's on page 2.

So many insults flow through the book that Sang Ye, who interviewed more than 100 Chinese immigrants, warned readers in the introduction:

> *China is a country with a strong xenophobic, isolationist tradition; a place where deeply racist sentiments are not uncommon ... Nearly all of the interviewees here referred to Australians as 'devils' (guizi) or foreign devils (yang guizi) or the slightly more polite 'foreigners' (laowai or waiguoren), apparently oblivious to the fact that in Australia, it's they who are foreigners.*

Sang Ye, a delightfully friendly man and best-selling author in China, says he didn't choose the most provocative interviews for his book, merely the most interesting. He believes they represent an accurate reflection of what he heard. It isn't good. After being called 'dogs' in the first chapter, things don't improve much for Australians thereafter. China scholar Jamie Mackie, in a review of *The Year the Dragon Came*, wrote: 'Read this book to rid yourself of stereotypes and illusions about Chinese immigrants. And ponder whether (and how) Australian society or culture has been either enriched by the presence of these immigrants or put under strain.' Neil James, writing in the *Australian's Review of Books*, said of *Dragon*: 'The portraits do not make for comfortable reading. Above all else, the voice of self-interest sets the tone.'

Chinese self-interest and cynicism in Australia is not exactly hard to find. It can be found in official pronouncements from Beijing, in the Chinese-language news media, and in books such as *I Married a Foreign Woman*, *My Fortune in Australia*, and *Australia—Beautiful Lies*, the last two published in Australia under the title, *Bitter Peaches and Plums: Two Chinese Novellas on the Recent Chinese Student Experience in Australia*. Professor Bruce Jacobs and Dr Ouyang Yu, in their introduction to *Bitter Peaches and Plums*, write:

> *The image of Australia presented in these novellas is quite limited ... [They] concentrate on the Chinese student communities, communities which are basically inward-looking and which have very little interaction with Australian society as a whole ... They lived extremely frugally and, as shown in* Beautiful Lies, *developed numerous illegal tactics to save money. Most had borrowed money in China and had heavy debts to repay.*

'It is common knowledge that there are all kinds of immigration schemes among Chinese immigrants,' says the head of the anthropology department at the University of Sydney, Dr Richard Basham. 'A lot of so-called students from the PRC arrive with big debts to pay back.' Also common knowledge is the booming racket in phoney marriages. A remarkably high percentage of Australian marriages—thirty percent—currently involve offshore spouses, says Bob Birrell of Monash University, and ethnic Chinese immigrants provide the largest flow. The final passage of *Australia— Beautiful Lies*, contains sentiments that are common in Chinese writing about Australia, and are not exactly grist for romantics.

> *It can be said that Chinese students who went to Australia have varying degrees of hatred towards this kangaroo kingdom. But did the Australian government or people commit any crimes? How can the present situation of Chinese students in Australia compare with China's modern history, replete with servility and humiliation?*

The beauty of immigration is that most of the children of the Chinese wayfarers who stay in Australia will not share such alienation. Although there is widespread grumbling among Australian-born students and parents that Chinese students prefer to mix with each other, the historical experience of immigration shows that the intense peer pressures of adolescence is more powerful than cultural insularity and by the second generation the children of all immigrant groups walk, talk and think like Australians. School is the fulcrum of social formation. The Chinese students now in Australia, already distinguished academically, will add to that long, tough, durable, creative seam of Chinese history in Australia, which began on the goldfields of the nineteenth century.

The imponderable ingredient in this new mix, and the big difference between the new generations of Chinese-Australians and the previous waves of post war immigrant Australians, is that the bristling chauvinistic bulk of China will dominate the politics of Australia's hemisphere in the future. China has shown itself a superpower with a chip on its shoulder and the Chinese have an enormously long cultural history of regarding non-Chinese as lesser beings. This feeling was mutual among the generations of settlers who formed Australia. White Australians feared the Chinese and excluded them (just as some still fear them and wish to exclude them). Helen Irving, in her history of the Australian Constitution, *To Constitute a Nation*, wrote that the small Australian population at the time of Federation was shaped by the alien magnitude of China:

> *While every other question raised during the Federation campaigns and debated in the Conventions produced several lines of major disagreement, no significant group of opinion favourable to Chinese immigration existed in Australia by the 1890s ...*
>
> *With racial divisions came the risk of civil war. To Australians the Chinese appearance, language, script, way of working, dressing, worshipping, relaxing and eating were all utterly unlike anything they understood.*

A century later, in a world run by an international middle class, most Australians can see that Chinese drive and intelligence can be a national asset and a trading bridge. In *The Tyranny of Fortune*, two Australian Asia experts, Reg Little and Warren Reed, urge Australians to show a greater respect for the emerging forces in Asia.

> *Australia is in the process of becoming the plaything of forces, possibly tyrannical, outside the control of its people ...'*
>
> *East Asian organisational skill, which is today arguably the world's most effective and competitive, is the product of a rich and powerful civilisation which is understood by few Australians. The people of that tradition of civilisation often look on Australian individuality, for example, as a form of simple-mindedness, bordering on barbarism.*

Ouch! Geremie Barmé, a senior Fellow at the Australian National University, is one of the scholars watching the resurgent nationalism of China. What strikes him, and other China watchers, is how this new nationalism transcends political divisions. The racial nationalism of emerging China extends to overseas Chinese. The young Chinese Olympian interviewed by Sang Ye was positively scathing about the chauvinism of many of the ethnic Chinese who live outside China.

> *When people back home insult you after you've lost a competition overseas it's not that big a deal ... But the*

overseas Chinese! If we win we're national heroes; if we lose we're nothing more than traitors and scum ...

If you can't get the five-star flag of the People's Republic up there fluttering, if you don't make them feel like bigshots in front of all the foreigners, then you're nothing more than a big traitor.

In an essay called 'Computer Insect', Sang Ye describes a brilliant young computer hacker in Beijing who personifies what he calls the 'in-your-face China' that will be much more common in the future:

The way I see it, pirating software is no big deal. The four Little Dragons [Hong Kong, Taiwan, Korea and Singapore] *created the wealth and prosperity they enjoy today by pirating. You tell me what those little shits in Hong Kong have ever discovered? Zilch. They're a pack of pseudo foreign devils who started out as tailors and cobblers ... Foreign devils* [Americans] *are just plain unreasonable. To be honest, they've been getting away with ripping off the Chinese for ages. What's all this stuff about intellectual property? Whose ancestors got it all going in the first place?*

For more than a hundred years China has been abused, exploited and lectured to by Western powers. Australia has done its share of misreading China. Australians still tend to regard Chinese as one-dimensional abstractions, oblivious to the deep ocean of Chinese culture. Australia has never had a revolution. China endured three cultural revolutions in three successive generations and yet continued to grow as a great nation. In Australia even minor structural change provokes fits of outrage from vested interests. Australia's softness compared with China, its naivety, its sometimes second-rate diplomatic and trade performances, its failure to understand the central place of China and the overseas Chinese in the culture and business practices of the hemisphere, have been pointed out by a number of Australian experts on Asia.

Australia has, however, embraced large-scale immigration by ethnic Chinese. The Department of Sociology at Monash University studied the 14 750 citizens of the People's Republic of China present in Australia in 1989, the year of the Tiananmen massacre, and found that by 1993 they had brought an additional 13 900 spouses and dependents to Australia, none of whom were subject to skill, asset or English proficiency tests. The 14 750 had thus grown to 28 650, and the study projected, accurately, that the Bob Hawke immigrant stream would increase to 40 000 by the mid-1990s, pushing the number of ethnic Chinese in Australia to more than 300 000.

The reactions to the new nationalism in China among those 300 000 ethnic Chinese in Australia ranges across the spectrum from those who despise anything that comes out of official Beijing to those who mimic the Beijing line. After the pastor of the Ashfield Uniting Church, which has a partly Chinese congregation, flew the Tibetan flag on Tibetan National Day in 1996, Councillor Spencer Wu, a member of Ashfield Council, wrote an angry letter to the press.

> *The Tibetan flag raised at the Uniting Church did not escape the notice of the Chinese population of Ashfield. They were outraged enough to [be] ready to storm the church ... Without my timely intervention dozens of eggs would have landed on the ground. The Chinese population now believes [the] Uniting Church is an anti-Chinese political organisation ...*

There is a strong resemblance between the logic of this micro-rhetoric and the big rhetoric coming out of Beijing. When Prime Minister Howard met the spiritual leader of Tibet, the Dalai Lama, during Howard's first year in office, the official organ of Beijing, the *People's Daily*, frothed:

> *What is really inconceivable is the absurd philosophy of this Australian politician. If it is not out of his ignorance about Chinese and Tibetan history, it is because he deliberately wants to rudely interfere in China's internal affairs.*

Anyone who studies the history of China's mendacity in Tibet (and books such as *Fire Under the Snow*, published in 1998, are finally revealing the full extent of that mendacity) can only be appalled by the brutal and methodical suppression of Tibet's 2000-year-old culture and language since China's invasion in 1950. It follows that one can only be shocked by the open support or the blind eye turned by some Chinese in Australia toward China's continuing ethnocide in Tibet.

The New China News Agency has been splenetic when the

United States government issued reports about China's success in suppressing domestic dissent. This is a typical outburst: 'Enough is enough. What qualifications do you have to talk about these issues in front of the Chinese people who have a 5000-year-old civilisation?'

Despite these outbursts, recent Australian governments have managed to handle the relationship with China quite well. They have not fallen into line with the United States. They have not lectured the Chinese on human rights, thus throwing away the relationship for no gain. They have sought to build trade ties with painstaking patience. Above all, they have opened Australia to immigration by ethnic Chinese. And China/Hong Kong has become Australia's second-biggest trade partner.

China, in turn, has treated Australia as a nation it can do business with, and has made Australia an official tourist destination, a freedom the government has not extended to most countries. The 1998 agreement between Australia and China to allow the adoption of Chinese babies by Australian parents represented, through the basic human need to love, a potentially significant cultural link between the two countries. Hopefully the relationship will flower.

Australia's prudence is wise. Modern China is increasingly in a position to back its rhetoric with action. After the show of American military power in the Gulf War, defence spending in China began rising even faster than its double-digit economic growth. China has also become the biggest buyer and holder of US debt, overtaking Japan. Chinese investments have become important to the stability of the US bond market. During the 1997 Asian currency and market meltdowns, China's stock market and currency held steady, with the Chinese market even rising amid the surrounding turmoil. China also absorbed Hong Kong with smooth efficiency.

Chinese irritation with lectures from Western governments is reflected in Beijing's failure to censor ultranationalist books such as *China Through the Third Eye*, and *Winds in the Wilderness*, and the best-selling, *China, Just Say No!*, which mimics the anti-American Japanese best-seller, *Japan Can Say No*, with chapters such as 'Burn Down Hollywood' and 'Don't Fear Declaring, Prepare For War'.

In Australia, when the Howard government began making changes to the immigration system, the Independent Council for Refugee Advocacy, a lobby group for Chinese immigrants, informed the Minister for Immigration that the plan to impose English-language tests on immigrants was 'racist' and 'based on a false premise that English speakers are superior'.

When the Haymarket Property Owners Association, made up of ethnic Chinese property owners in Sydney's Chinatown, was denied a development permit by the Sydney City Council, the president of the association, Tony Ma, accused the City Council of race discrimination and threatened action under the Racial Discrimination Act. The Lord Mayor of Sydney, Frank Sartor, dismissed the accusation as 'nonsense'.

When Councillor Ted Seng, Deputy Mayor of Randwick in Sydney, an ethnic Chinese who immigrated from Malaysia, called for a three-year moratorium on immigration from Asia because of the social stresses it was causing, he was attacked in the local Chinese-language media. 'My view is that Asian migrants should adopt what I describe as core Australian values, whilst at the same time retaining their cultural heritage,' Seng told me. 'Some of those core Australian values include a fair go for all, free speech, real environmental consciousness, and maintaining the fight against corruption.' This is not quite how his views appeared in some local Chinese-language reports. One headline proclaimed: THE EMERGENCE OF THE FIRST CHINESE WHO IS IN AGREEMENT WITH HANSON'S VIEWS. An insulting photo caption depicted Ted Seng as 'The Deputy Mayor Who Can't Write His Own Name in Chinese'.

The issue of cultural insularity among overseas Chinese has been raised by a number of Australian scholars, most elegantly by Nicholas José in a 1996 essay for the *Australian Book Review*.

> *China has the numbers. Further, Chinese culture has proved adept at absorbing useful elements of other cultures while remaining relatively impervious to being absorbed in return—particularly in the encounter with the West, which has been regarded as a source of specific modernising ideas rather than posing a wholesale cultural alternative. Then, since Chinese culture exists most strongly in intangible things, customs, thoughts and attitudes can be transferred even when the outward and visible signs are excluded or rejected. Chinese culture is disposed to survive, even in a hostile environment.*

When I asked one China scholar why complaining about Australia was so prevalent in the local Chinese community, he replied: 'It's a technique.' If so, the technique has worked. Criticism of ethnic Chinese is treated as racist. Thus, the prevailing myopia of an obsession with any hint of white racism, while excusing or ignoring Chinese cultural chauvinism. This myopia is the result of several factors: the arrogance that the only morality that matters is white morality, the lingering presence of Australia's outdated cultural cringe, the residue of guilt over the old White Australia Policy, and the willingness of some Chinese lobby groups to portray Chinese in Australia as victims.

History is written by the powerful, and China is beginning to shape the history of Australia's region.

Stephen FitzGerald, Australia's former Ambassador to Beijing, wrote in 1997, as China was absorbing Hong Kong:

> [Australia's] *future will not be one in which the United States, or any other power with which we have shared cultural heritage or political philosophies or processes or institutions, is the determining force in the part of the world in which we live. The dominant political force and cultural influence will be* [a] *coalition of East Asian states ... under the pervasive and dominant influence of China.*
>
> *This will be an utterly new experience for Australia ...*

The rise to power and influence of the Chinese people in the twentieth century is embodied by Lee Kuan Yew who, more than any other individual, helped show the world the enormity of Chinese potential. In 1993 I interviewed Lee in his office in the Istana complex, a white colonial palace with Gurkha guards, set in lush quiet grounds near the heart of Singapore. Only two people had offices in the palace—Lee on the second floor and the Prime Minister of Singapore on the third. Lee, who gained one of the most brilliant passes in the history of Cambridge University, became Singapore's founding father at the age of thirty-five and ruled the country for another thirty-five years. Although he stepped down as Prime Minister in 1990 at the age of sixty-eight, he remained for a time the de facto head of state and in retirement he continued to personify the Confucian ideal of hard work and civic service, working six days a week, ten hours a day. If four decades of power had left their mark on him, it was only lightly.

It did not take long for the bemused attitude felt by many educated Chinese towards Australians to reveal itself in Lee Kuan Yew. 'I've had innumerable anecdotal accounts of Asians [in Australia] who just give up and begin to work at the pace of Australians ... That's OK if you're selling your services only to Australia, but not when you're selling your services to the world ...

'I think you will have to take your unionists and your educationists on a tour of East Asia and see how other societies start from kindergarten: the intensity and the dedication, not only of the child, but of the parents and the siblings and of the school, the teachers, the class monitors, in getting every student to put in his best.'

His words echoed the brilliant record of success by Chinese students in Australia.

Lee Kuan Yew is the world's most famous employer of Confucian values, which he used to justify political and social repression as he built the dazzling economic success, stability and efficiency of his Singapore city-state. But Chiam Yau-ming of La Trobe University has critiqued Lee's selective Confucianism. 'Lee's party, the People's Action Party ... does not tolerate criticism or even mini electoral losses. PAP leaders have openly threatened that constituencies that vote for non-PAP candidates risk losing public infrastructure development. It is doubtful whether Confucius would have applauded.'

During my interview with him, Lee broke taboos observed by Western politicians. He is one of the few leaders secure enough to venture into discussions of racial characteristics and the differences in national character, although this habit finally caught up with him in 1997 when he managed to sour Singapore's tender relations with Malays with comments about the level of crime committed by Malaysians. He was just as blunt with me, citing his experiences with the British military officers who built Singapore to describe the toughness of the Chinese:

> *When doing a project they would put the Chinese in the middle and put the Indians at the side, and the Indians were expected to keep the pace of the Chinese. And there was a hell of a problem, because one Chinese would carry one pole with two wicker baskets of earth, whereas two Indians would carry one pole with one wicker basket between them. So it's one quarter. Now* that's *culture.*

Maybe it has to do also with genetic characteristics, I'm not sure. But any doctor will tell you in our hospitals, that even if you just touch an Indian with an injection he is howling. The Chinaman isn't. He has got a very high level of tolerance for pain.

Listening to this tough little parable it is easy to see the guiding hand behind the housing laws in Singapore which effectively prevent the formation of ethnic enclaves of Indians and Malays. Most housing clusters must have ethnic occupancy in the same ratio as the general population, which guarantees a dominant ethnic Chinese majority and the dispersal of the non-Chinese population. And although Singapore wants to boost its population, it is not turning to immigration to do the job. Lee did not speak of Singapore as a new culture. He spoke of '4000 years of folk memory'. So I asked him if 4000 years of tradition of centralised, monolithic, autocratic power meant it was naive for the West to believe that China would ever change.

'Four thousand or 5000 years of centralised government and hierarchy also have to adjust to the conditions of the world today. A modern industrial society requires large numbers of educated people, managers, engineers, technicians, accountants, entrepreneurs, who are in constant touch with their counterparts throughout the world via fax, via satellite, and who will travel freely. Therefore, there is bound to be some osmosis and the forms cannot remain unchanged ... I think it will evolve, but it will still be, in my view, a hierarchical society.'

Given Australia's commitments to democracy, individualism, egalitarianism, environmentalism and the blending of sport and play into the texture of life, I suggested Australians could not compete in the world on Chinese terms nor were even interested in doing so.

Lee smiled, paused, then replied: 'I'm not sure you will lose every time. There are certain areas where you have natural advantages. Look, I don't believe, however hard they try, Singaporeans will make world-class tennis players.'

5
AN EMPIRE OF THE SOUL

THE GIGANTIC BREATHING SPREAD of Australia's desert, mountain, forest, farmland, scrub, cities, towns, coasts, reefs, continental shelf, islands, rivers, deepwater ocean, seamounts and Antarctic icecap is as large and as real as any empire built by conquest. In sheer size, it is the third-largest legal entity in the world.

It is also no longer the same country built by the time-travellers of the eighteenth century who colonised Australia.

> *Until the late eighteenth century no European had ever seen a eucalypt, and very strange they must have looked, with their strings of hanging, half-shed bark, their smooth wrinkling joints (like armpits, elbows and crotches), their fluent gesticulations and haze of perennial foliage. Not evergreens, but evergreys: the soft, spatially deceitful background colour of the Australian bush, monotonous-looking at first sight but rippling with nuance to the acclimatised eye.*

Robert Hughes, writing in *The Fatal Shore*, understood the magnitude of the alienation that these Europeans faced, even if they did not fully understand it themselves at the time. Another superb historian, Simon Schama, saw how much

Australians were formed by their environment rather than the other way round. 'Australia has never had a sense of omnipotence in the way the Calvinists had when they first arrived in America, or the generation who opened up the American West, who thought the whole continent was a Christmas present given to them by God,' Schama told me. 'For Australia, it was bloody hard to just survive on the fringe of the continent.'

Australia's ingrained cultural modesty was imposed by fire, drought, ironbark, distance and isolation. Still, the nation has been growing and thriving in an age that has been hard on the old Imperial vanities, when the maps we grew up with have been redrawn along the true dividing lines of history—geography and blood. On 16 November 1994 a whole new set of lines came quietly into force around the world when the United Nations Convention on the Law of the Sea redrew the world's sovereign boundaries. No nation gained more under this law than Australia, which now has legal stewardship and exclusive economic rights over a prodigious expanse of land, coastal sea and continental shelf. It is one of the three largest claims, though the final legal boundaries are still years from being resolved. When Australia's historic though dormant territorial claim and legal responsibilities under the Antarctic Treaty are included, the total amount of Australian Territory is 28.4 million square kilometres, including 16.1 million square kilometres of ocean territory. It is as big as North America and twice the size of Europe. Though a sparsely inhabited and fragile expanse, it is, by definition, the legal claim of an eco-superpower.

On 15 November 1994, the day before the Law of the Sea convention came into force, the then Minister for Industry, Science and Technology, Senator Peter Cook, told the Senate:

This imposes on us a huge responsibility ... It is like European civilisation landing on the shores of Australia, but with twenty-first century knowledge about the environment. We have a chance to get it right from the beginning ... The Convention has given Australia vast new territory to manage and exploit, but it also demands that we manage this exclusive economic zone in a sustainable way to ensure that the living resources in it are not destroyed, depleted or irreparably harmed.

Four nations emerged under the Law of the Sea with greatly expanded sovereign borders: Australia, the United States, Canada and Russia. Much of the enormous claims by Australia is sea. The magnitude of Australia's claim, both in size and moral obligation, is captured by the author Tim Winton, writing in 1997.

In coming to terms with the sea Australians will have to turn their heads and look hard into the glare and see the reality of our relationship with it. And half of that reality involves our relative ignorance of it. Less than one tenth of one per cent of the deep sea has been explored. Some say we know more about the surface of the moon. If most of life on Earth is indeed aquatic, then humans could do with a little modesty, a sense of perspective. We are a part of life; we are not life itself. We depend upon the sea, more so because we are islanders. Our coasts and waterways are among our most significant treasures. Half our marine species are found nowhere else.

Gone is the casual sense of infinity and the unblemished openness that shaped the nation. Australia has gathered unto itself greater power, knowledge and, like all mature entities, responsibilities.

Perhaps the greatest single challenge to Australia is preserving the thin and fragile layer of soil that has been wasting since long before the European settlers arrived in 1788. It is the most immediate threat to Australia, more urgent than the depletion of the ozone layer or global warming. 'The loss of rivers, lakes, soils and forest will have far more damaging impact on people than climate change or ozone depletion,' says Dr Graham Harris, head of the CSIRO Land and Water division. 'Many ecologists have lost the plot. A very worrying picture is emerging and we can't go on ignoring it. Yet you could read professional ecological journals for years and never realise there's a global crisis in landscape sustainability.'

A major 1996 survey by the Australian Bureau of Statistics warned:

In the two-hundred years since Europeans first settled in Australia, vast changes have been made to the natural vegetation ... The transformed landscape is more susceptible than natural ecosystems to land degradation including: erosion by water and wind, soil salinisation, soil acidification, and soil structure decline.

A nation cannot be an eco-superpower if it is destroying its environment, and two of the world's largest powers, China and Russia, have shown rapacious indifference to the long-term costs of environmental degradation. The green world will continue to go brown for decades to come. The United Nations estimates that by 2025 two-thirds of the world's eight billion people will be suffering 'water stress' caused by a shortage of unpolluted water.

Into this shrinking world goes Australia, with one enormous advantage: the environment defines the nation and its national character. On Australia Day 1997, when a national poll asked people what defined an Australian, the category that topped the list, by a wide margin, was 'Concern for the Environment'.

When historian Lyn Spillman compared national identity building in the United States and Australia, she found Americans spoke most about their freedom, while Australians spoke most about their land. The environment is Australia's great engine of national and international purpose. Even the national anthem is packed with geography:

> *We've golden soil and wealth for toil*
> *Our home is girt by sea*
> *Our land abounds in nature's gifts*
> *Of beauty, rich and rare*

Size is not the only determinant of a nation's ability to project power and ideas. If Australia is to act like, and be treated like, a superpower in any form, it has to learn to pick its battles, concentrate on its strengths and not waste precious resources on matters over which it has little control. Contrast the Sydney 2000 Olympics triumph, a contest where Australia was playing to its strengths, with Australia's crushing defeat at the United Nations during the same period, when it sought to win a seat on the United Nations Security Council.

France was one nation quietly delighted by Australia's defeat at the UN. The previous year, France became the first nation to test Australia's role as an emerging ecological power and had been bruised by the encounter. Australia fought a diplomatic war where it was strong. France's program of nuclear testing in the South Pacific, the last significant vestige of European imperialism in the region, became the catalyst which moved Australia toward assuming a more global environmental role. The clash between the two countries was an almost pristine representation of old vanities confronting new realities. The foreign affairs columnist for the *New York Times*, Thomas Friedman, reacting to the story 'Australia superpower' in *The Sydney Morning Herald*, saw the broad sweep of change that lay behind this diplomatic struggle:

> *Beneath the surface, this is a war. It is a war between two very different concepts of sovereignty, and one we are going to witness more of in years ahead. It is a clash between a traditional, inward-looking nationalistic form of sovereignty ... and a very broad, expansive, outward-looking new notion of sovereignty embodied in environmentalism ...*

This clash between France and Australia, observed the Australian writer Paul Sheehan, will be the first real confrontation between a traditional superpower and an ecological superpower.

France's decision to test nuclear weapons in the South Pacific was entirely about the past, the obsession with its collaborative humiliation during World War II. Australia's zeal in this dispute was all about the future. In a world of ocean dumping, oil spills and drift-net fishing, the emergence of several eco-superpowers with broad maritime jurisdictions and strong conservation agendas would be an essential barrier to the despoliation of the oceans.

The Exclusive Economic Zones (EEZ) under the Law of the Sea are not mere diplomatic window-dressing. It did not take long for disputes to break out after these zones became part of international law. Even polite Canada was roused to the point of military violence over fishing rights on the edge of its EEZ, seizing a Spanish fishing trawler and cutting the lines of another during a confrontation with Spain, which then sent its own naval vessels to protect Spanish fishing boats off Newfoundland. When Japan declared a 200-nautical-mile EEZ around its coast in 1996, it provoked public bitterness and diplomatic protests from China and South Korea.

Australia and the United States have quietly sniped at each other over Law of the Sea, as befitting the two nations with the most far-reaching maritime claims. 'The Australians claim they're not claiming Antarctica under the new rules,' the State Department's chief ocean policy geographer, Robert

Smith, told me with scepticism in 1995. The Americans do not even recognise the Australian Antarctic Territory or parts of its huge continental shelf claims under the Law of the Sea convention. The Australian government rejects US policy.

Once again, the debate over Antarctica is not merely symbolic. Australia's Antarctic claim and Antarctic EEZ (as large as the Australian continent) is aimed at protecting the last pristine continent, a place which Australia has played an integral role in exploring and conserving. It is also aimed at Antarctica's potentially enormous farming future. The CSIRO predicts that the farming and harvesting of Australia's EEZ waters could overtake beef as an export industry early next century, especially given the voracious Asian appetite for seafood. 'By every global measure the sea has twice as much biological richness as the land,' said Dr Peter Bridgewater, Director of the Australian Nature Conservation Authority. 'Our attitude to the sea has to change. Provided we develop our marine science, the opportunities are almost limitless.' Australia's rights under Law of the Sea extend to harvesting the sea, the seabed and the subsoil beneath. The CSIRO calls the coming era of aquaculture 'the blue revolution'.

Australia's ocean territory is like its soil: lots of it but mostly poor. Despite having one of the world's most extensive fishing zones, Australia ranks only fiftieth in fisheries production because most of the waters around the Australian continent do not have the major upwellings of nutrient-rich deep water from the ocean floor. Like arid land, these seas are fragile. Serious overfishing of southern bluefin tuna, gemfish and rock lobsters has already shrunk the sustainable levels of these valued species in Australian waters. Australia's only three major commercial fishing grounds have all been reduced by overfishing.

As a child, Tim Winton used to snorkel in abundantly rich waters on the reefs near Trigg Point, off Perth. He saw 'tumbling masses of tailor, lines of crayfish marching out to sea in single file. Plankton passed like dizzy spots before my eyes.' When he left and then returned years later, he found the everyday abuse of a crowded coast had changed everything:

> *I returned to my old haunt, the reef I had snorkeled over obsessively since age eight. But the abalone seemed small and scarce. There were hardly any fish. No tarwhine, no sweep. Every scalyfin and red-lipped morwong had a spearhole high on its back.*

Australia now has obligations to protect not only its coasts and coastal waters but also to preserve the marine environment stretching out into the Exclusive Economic Zone. The challenge is to heal the damage on sea and on land, to concentrate on managing the huge area of the earth's surface where Australia actually has territorial rights.

Governments come and go, and in time the intrinsic nature of Australia's ecological strengths and obligations should prevail over political short-sightedness. If Australia takes full responsibility for the 28.4 million square kilometres under its Law of the Sea and Antarctic Treaty claims, a huge and varied system of the earth's surface will be in relatively safe hands. New laws, new communal standards and new ways of thinking can have an enormous impact on the land and sea we have inherited. On Tim Winton's plundered reef off Perth, the local authorities banned spear guns and embargoed the taking of abalone. This is what Winton found when he finally went back:

> *Nowadays, I see as many abalone on the reef as I used to and many more fish than I saw even as a boy. In the midst of a sprawling city, children can swim and snorkel and experience a living reef.*

Asia may still be degrading at an alarming rate, but Australia is renewing. At a time when many advanced cultures are growing in wealth though not in peace of mind, the great step Australians can take is to recognise the extent of their strengths and see the enormous, fragile expanse of their territory as an empire of the soul.

BIG
World's largest
countries (land only)

1 Russia
2 Canada
3 USA
4 China
5 Brazil
6 Australia
7 India
8 Argentina

BIGGER
World's largest
countries (land and sea)

1 Russia
2 Canada
3 USA
4 Australia
5 China
6 Brazil
7 India
8 Argentina

HUGE
World's largest claims
under Law of the Sea and Antarctica

1 Russia
2 USA
3 Australia
4 Canada
5 China
6 Brazil
7 France
8 Indonesia

PART TWO

Over time there has been a disturbing historical pattern—the crack and fall of civilisations owing to a morbid intensification of their own first principles.

George Soros

6
THE MAN WHO WASN'T THERE

> WILSON TUCKEY: *All you have done is finance growth with debt.*
>
> PAUL KEATING: *You boxhead, you would not know. You are flat out counting past ten.*
>
> TUCKEY: *You are an idiot. You are just a hopeless nong ...*
>
> KEATING: *Shut up! Sit down and shut up, you pig.*
>
> TUCKEY: *You could not even deliver Christmas presents to Warren Anderson.*
>
> KEATING: *Why do you not shut up, you clown? ... This man has a criminal intellect ... this clown continues to interject in perpetuity.*

On Friday 26 April 1996, ten days before the new Parliament was about to be convened, a Parliament in which Paul Keating would be reduced from Prime Minister to backbencher, Keating tendered his resignation. He thus became the first federal Labor leader in history to decline to take his seat after his government had lost power. All previous Labor prime ministers defeated in battle—Watson, Fisher, Scullin, Chifley and Whitlam—returned to sit in the Opposition benches. Not Keating. For thirteen years he had used the government frontbench to taunt and harangue and patronise his opponents, John Howard in particular.

> 'From this day onward Mr Howard will wear his leadership like a crown of thorns and in the Parliament I will do everything I can to crucify him.'

> 'He is the classic non-deliverer of Australian politics. He is the one person who cannot cut the mustard. The game is too hard for him. Lurking in this chest is not a heart for the political fight, but a split pea.'

> 'I am not like the Leader of the Opposition [John Howard]. I did not slither out of the Cabinet room like a mangy maggot.'

When John Howard, Prime Minister, led his new ministers into the House of Representatives, Keating, the hard man, was nowhere to be found. The people of Blaxland had voted overwhelmingly to give him the honour of representing them, but he declined to turn up. Ten days before the new Parliament was to begin, he submitted his resignation to the Governor-General when, by convention and as a courtesy to the House he had served so long, it should have been submitted to the Speaker of the House.

'I leave the House of Representatives with my faith not just intact but very much stronger,' his resignation letter said.

THE MAN WHO WASN'T THERE

'I leave very proud of what the Labor government did, of what the labour movement did, and of what Australians did in the past decade to build a competitive Australian economy and marry it to a good Australian society.'

Keating was right to be proud. He had a glorious career in politics. He was, and always will be, a character who stood out in the mostly stunted ranks of Australian party politics. His structural legacies on superannuation, financial deregulation, native title, the republic debate, plus many other reforms over more than a decade, mark him as a man of vision. As for the manner of his leaving the parliamentary stage, he spent the day of the opening of Parliament at his Canberra home in Red Hill. The contrast was extreme between his absence and the full power and pungency of his parliamentary leadership, where he had refined the art of extemporaneous head-kicking:

> *... all through Question Time those two pansies over there want retractions of the things we have said about them. They are a bunch of nobodies going nowhere.*

Hansard records only the sanitised Keating. The private Keating built his career on backroom tantrums, corridor eyeballings, and the long, crude telephone soliloquies when he told opponents, especially journalists, what he thought of them.

'In and out of the cat's arse.'

'Like a dog returning to its own vomit.'

Keating's departure from politics was no more tainted than his arrival. Twenty-six years earlier, on St Patrick's Day, 1970, Paul Keating, aged twenty-five, rose before the House of Representatives at 10.26 a.m. and uttered his first words in Parliament. It is a bizarre speech when read a generation later in the context of a very different Paul Keating and a very different Australia. It shows how much a man, and a country, can change in twenty-six years.

> *As this is my first speech in the House of Representatives and the beginning of my first term in this place I desire sincerely to thank the 55 000 electors of the Blaxland electorate for the honour of allowing me to represent them here. I wish also to thank the members of the Australian Labor Party for the assistance and unselfish help that they gave me throughout the course of the election campaign.*

Unselfish help? Keating got his red-ribbon seat in 1969 through the time-honoured tactic of branch stacking. Keating lost the 1969 preselection vote on the first and second ballots and won only after the right-wing New South Wales executive intervened and allowed his stacking to stand, thus defeating a left-wing candidate. (The frantic events leading up to this outcome included a late-night motorcycle dash by Laurie Brereton, who would parley his role as a Keating gofer into a long parliamentary career.)

Keating couldn't wait to put Blaxland behind him. During his maiden speech in 1970, after he had thanked the electors of Blaxland 'for the honour of allowing me to represent them here'. He continued, 'I would like to be able to describe my electorate as a scenic district, as something of beauty, but unfortunately I can't.'

Blaxland never became scenic for Keating. His electoral office was on the second floor of a neat courtyard lined with palm trees. There was a tiny waiting room with four chairs, and copies of a pamphlet called 'Sole Parent' on a table. The office sat between a McDonald's and the Bankstown Adult Migrant Centre. The migrant centre is important. Bankstown, the heart of Keating's electorate, now has one of Australia's largest concentrations of non-English speaking background (NESB) immigrants. Bankstown Plaza is filled with East Asians, Muslims and Pacific Islanders. The chadore, head-cover for Muslim women, is common at Bankstown Square.

This is what the young Keating had to say about immigration in his maiden speech:

> *The government hopes to be able to offset the present* [small] *population situation by immigration. It is time we considered the enormous cost of bringing migrants to this country. We must bear in mind this cost when we consider the cost of subsidising Australian families ... These figures may sound high but they are not when we compare them with the cost of bringing migrants to this country. After all, the best migrant is the infant Australian.*

Paul Keating left Blaxland as fast as he could. He moved to Canberra full-time. Long before he left politics to pursue a career in business, he had moved as far as spiritually possible from his constituents in Bankstown. After the Lodge, he moved back to Sydney and paid 2.5 million dollars for a mansion on Queen Street, Woollahra, the antiques capital of Australia. Good luck to him.

A man must be judged by his own rhetoric, and this is where Keating has a few problems. Keating spoke often about reconciliation and left some courageous legislative legacies which sought to tackle the intractable problems of indigenous Australians. But the years of Labor government also coincided with an increase in neo-paternalism, welfare dependency, double standards, mismanagement and financial rorting within the Aboriginal aid apparatus. At high social and economic cost, the Labor governments subsidised a multicultural industry with a vested interest in ethnic divides. For twenty-five years, since the days of Gough Whitlam's immigration minister, Al Grassby, Labor and its surrogates pursued an ethnic strategy.

The strategy worked up to a point. The only electorates that withstood the anti-Labor landslide in 1996 were the heavily NESB electorates in Sydney and Melbourne that Labor has so assiduously, and expensively, cultivated. Labor spent more than a billion dollars building a system of patronage, dependence and influence among ethnic groups. After the Keating government lost office, the new government imposed stricter reviews to uncover fraud and abuse and immediately saw results, as the following exchange in the Senate on 29 October 1997 shows:

SENATOR NEWMAN [Minister for Social Security]: *I*

THE MAN WHO WASN'T THERE

am now tabling the Department of Social Security fourth quarter report on compliance activity ... The Labor Party said the system was as tight as a drum when they were in government—as tight as a drum. Former Minister Peter Baldwin claimed that it was of world leading standard. It is also interesting that the Labor Party's own review, after they lost the election last year, found that almost everyone in Australia thought they knew a welfare cheat.

SENATOR BOLKUS: *Play to the prejudices. Go on, keep playing to the prejudices.*

SENATOR NEWMAN: *You just listen ... The taxpayers want this, and so do those who are genuine social security recipients.*

—Opposition senators interjecting—

SENATOR NEWMAN: *During 1996–97 there were over 55 000 tip-offs from the public; that measure alone led to over 12 000 cancellations and reductions. Over three million reviews were conducted during 1996–97; that is up almost twenty-eight percent over the previous year. Also, 333 120 payment cancellations or reductions were put in place; that is an increase of over forty percent over your time in government. Debts recovered were $369 million, which is up forty-seven percent over the previous year. And just remember this: almost $28 million every week—$28 million every week—was saved as a result of compliance activity during 1996–97.*

The numbers quoted by Senator Newman amounted to only about one percent of total security payments, and the bulk of the cancellations would presumably have involved Australian-born recipients. These are important qualifications, but anyone who believes the social security system is ninety-nine percent honest and ninety-nine percent efficient is conveniently naive.

The figures have their own eloquence. The 28 million dollars saved every week, if extrapolated annually, represented payments of more than 1.4 billion dollars a year. The forty-seven percent increase in debt recoveries was a stratospheric increase in just one year. So, too, was the forty percent increase in cancellations of pensions.

A porous social security system was not even the biggest problem. The Labor government also used millions of 'soft' dollars under the grant-in-aid system which funnelled money, jobs and influence into Labor electorates. The grants-in-aid system brought down the Minister for Sport, Ros Kelly, who resigned in the wake of the 'whiteboard scandal'. Other ministers were spending more. Labor spent more than one billion dollars in grants-in-aid to ethnic organisations during its thirteen years in office. A survey of the grants made in New South Wales during its last full year in office shows that ninety-seven percent of the money went to organisations in Labor electorates. The second-largest recipient was the Prime Minister's seat, Blaxland, with its heavy and growing NESB population. In 1994–95 Blaxland received grants totalling $484 304.

The justification for this generosity in Keating's seat and

THE MAN WHO WASN'T THERE

in other Labor seats was that the majority of NESB immigrants moved into Labor electorates. This same cycle of political convenience (which would be repeated, on a much lesser scale, by the Howard government's schemes for assisting 'regional' electorates, that is, mainly Coalition seats) enabled the Labor government to spend billions in Labor electorates on welfare and job training schemes among immigrant communities which had comparable rates of unemployment to those registered during the Depression.

'By the time it left office Labor was blatantly targeting opinions and votes in a wide range of interest groups through an array of taxpayer-funded grants,' Dr Des Moore, a former Deputy Secretary of the Treasury, wrote in 'How Labor Targeted Votes and Opinion,' a study published soon after the 1996 election. Moore estimated that at least 143 million dollars in identifiable community grants were spent in Labor's last full year in office and the true value was probably greater than 200 million dollars. Moore's study revealed that among the places where this money went were the following:

Twenty-three million dollars to ethnic community organisations, almost all based in Labor electorates, and ranging through the alphabet from the Afghan Community Support Association ($93 200), to the Amal Charitable Association ($89 617), the Assyrian Australian Association ($126 047), to the Immigrant Women's Speakout Association of New South Wales ($99 684) which, by the way, never returned my phone calls (so much for speaking out).

The biggest recipient among ethnic groups was the Vietnamese community of New South Wales, which received twenty-one grants totalling $844 209, plus another $510 064 for the Migrant Resources Centre. At the same time, Labor was building a political alliance with elements in the Vietnamese community through the Communication Electrical Plumbing Union (CEPU), which had a heavy Vietnamese workforce in the mail centres. The CEPU itself received grants totalling $621 303 that year.

Advocacy groups which appeared to be financially independent in fact received subsidies under the community grants system. The Ethnic Community Councils of the various States were completely dependent on government funding. In New South Wales, the Council appears to have received $510 000 in various grants from the federal government in Labor's last full year in office.

The use of federal funds became so pervasive under Labor that charities were receiving more than half their funds from the federal government. The cost and breadth of State support for the multicultural industry has become enormous, and the annual reports of the various federal and state agencies committed to diversity reveal a neurotic compulsion towards diversity for the sake of diversity:

- Somali Community of NSW Inc. $2500. To teach the youth the traditional dances of Somalia like zeila, berey and other.
- Serbian National Defence Council in Australia. $2000. To promote the development of folkloric drama from the numerous provinces and states from the former Yugoslavia.
- Pukapuka Women's Culture Group. $1000. To maintain and promote Pukapuka culture and traditions in Illawarra.

- Fleanh Na Locha. $2000. Traditional Celtic Folk Festival. To maintain and promote exchanges of cultures, [sic] involvement youth.
- Echoes of the Cook Island. $3000. Costumes and traditional instruments.
- Woolgoolga Organising Committee. $5000. Purpose: 8th annual national Sikh Games.
- Hamazkaine Armenian Cultural Association. $1500. Assist in the purchase of costumes and venue hire for a folkloric dance performance.
- Austral Slovenian Society 'Tivoli' Newcastle. $1000. Maintain a cultural and social life for the well-aged people in the Slovenian community.

These lists, which go on for hundreds of pages, eventually add up to a very big number. Most of it goes on salaries. The link that all these programs have is that the government sector now regards ethnic groups as mendicants that must be helped. The great mystery is how Australia managed to sustain a prodigious and successful postwar immigration program for thirty years without all this new-found bureaucratic and political sensitivity.

An even more blatant political use of the federal grant-in-aid system under Labor was the payments to unions, which received grants totalling 16.5 million dollars. The money went to hundreds of specific projects such as 'developing modules for delivery of language and literacy support for the building industry'.

The close links between Labor's ethnic strategy and its

trade union power base was exemplified by endemic branch stacking using ethnic groups reaching historic proportions. Bitter factional fights in western Sydney saw infusions of thousands of Lebanese, Macedonian, Greek and Vietnamese in branch-stacking campaigns. The former Labor minister, Rod Cavalier, described these campaigns as unprecedented in their scope, even including the historic ALP–DLP split in the 1950s.

The Liberals, too, have played ethnic politics. One report by the New South Wales Auditor-General found that during the early 1990s, the Liberal government had increased discretionary payments to ethnic community groups from one million dollars a year to four million a year. The Auditor-General noted: 'Anecdotal evidence suggests that grants could have been made where there was no application and perhaps no immediate need for taxpayer support for the beneficiary.' Peter Collins tried to use the race card, making an attack on New South Wales Labor Premier, Bob Carr, a committed environmentalist.

> *Scrape away this thin veneer of contrived environmental concern and you have Bob Carr blaming immigrants for urban sprawl and environmental degradation. At a time when the community cries out for healing, Bob Carr opens the wound.*

It was a disgraceful remark, especially as Carr has an Asian-Australian wife who has been a gracious First Lady.

The following exchange, which took place in the New

THE MAN WHO WASN'T THERE

South Wales Parliament on 3 June 1998, was as revealing as it was unedifying.

> BOB COLLINS [Liberal leader and leader of the Opposition]: *In order to restore some order let me draw the attention of the House to the honourable member for Cabramatta, whose Canley Vale branch includes Phuong Ngo and two others who face serious criminal charges, which I will not go into in this place. The Cabramatta branch, the largest ALP branch in New South Wales, is comprehensively stacked. The honourable member for Cabramatta lives in fear of that branch, and rightly so.*
>
> REBA MEAGHER [Labor member for Cabramatta]: *Are you saying that all Asians are criminals? You're a racist.*
>
> COLLINS: *The honourable member for Cabramatta would know all about branch stacking. She knows what sort of people are attracted to her party, as she's attracted them. She is a disgrace. But it does not end there. The Labor Party is trying to play the race card. It is interesting to look at the record of the Premier* [Bob Carr] *who, as usual, is absent during this important debate ... The Premier's attitude to certain key tenets of One Nation policy is interesting. One thing that comes through loud and clear from One Nation is its abhorrence of Australian immigration, which it constantly attacks ... Interestingly, the Premier espouses a key tenet of One Nation policy, that all our problems will be solved by cutting the migrant intake.*

This is typical of so many debates in state and federal parliaments since the advent of One Nation.

In Victoria, Liberal Premier Jeff Kennett played ethnic politics when he entered the minefield of the Greek–Macedonian divide. But playing the race card is primarily Labor's game. So ingrained is the strategy that Labor continued as if nothing changed after the 1996 election. Labor's spokesman on Aboriginal affairs, Daryl Melham, repeatedly accused the federal government of 'racism', just as his predecessor, Robert Tickner, did before he lost his seat in Parliament. Then there was Senator Nick Bolkus, an inveterate ethnic player. He once told reporters: 'Part of the portfolio was to attend religious functions and on average I attended about ten every weekend because you knew if you weren't there the Opposition would be.' In Opposition, Senator Bolkus, during one speech by the new Minister for Aboriginal and Torres Strait Islander Affairs, kept repeating: 'Why do you hate blackfellas?'

A full year after the most disastrous rejection in the history of Labor governments, the party's leaders had still not been able to metabolise the real cause of its defeat, which it attributed to fatigue in the electorate after thirteen years of Labor, combined with Paul Keating's pungent personality. The truth was much worse. The depth of community anger at being ignored, and divided showed in the depth of Labor's descent: a mere 38.8 percent of the primary vote. At the 1996 elections Labor was seeking to run a country it had come to patronise.

Paul Keating's response to the challenges of the Howard

government would have been interesting, but he was soon gone. Also gone was the Australia that existed when Keating had first spoken in Parliament twenty-five years earlier.

> *It is true that we are experiencing full employment but this does not mean that our families are enjoying a standard of living which the wealth of this country should allow. The real challenge which the government must face is how to control inflation. There is only one effective answer—control over prices and services ...*
>
> *I believe that the Commonwealth can control prices by setting up a statutory prices authority to fix prices for all goods and services used by Australian people. The authority could include representatives of producers and consumers and would be responsible to Parliament. The authority should determine the requirements of an average family. It should inquire into an average family's needs in respect of clothing, food, recreation, entertainment, housing and health. From all this information it should recommend a wage adequate to provide a standard of living determined by the authority. This wage would be set by an Act of Parliament and varied from time to time ...*
>
> *Family life is the very basis of our nationhood. In the last couple of years the Government has boasted about the increasing number of women in the work force. Rather than something to be proud of I feel that this is something of which we should be ashamed. The*

> *short-sightedness of the Government's policy was borne out by the headlines in this morning's newspapers. The number of unfilled jobs has increased six percent while the unemployment figure has fallen by ten percent. How can we have national growth without people? How can we survive without a population? Is this Government doing anything about child endowment? Is it doing anything to put the working wife back in her home? It is not.*

So much changed, but some things remained the same. The upstart young member spoke for twenty-five minutes in a wide-ranging, magisterial, cheeky address filled with references to social justice and jibes against the Liberals, with a bucketing for the Country [now National] Party as 'a political reactionary Siamese twin of the Liberal Party'. Some things about Keating's New South Wales Labor Right faction never change either. The struggle to replace him in the seat of Blaxland was marked by a formal complaint of 'gross irregularities' in the preselection contest by a national official of the Australian Workers' Union.

Keating's last speech to Parliament could not have been more different from his first. It was made on 30 November 1995, a speech which no-one at the time (except perhaps Keating himself) realised would be his valedictory address. By tradition, the speech by the Prime Minister before the Christmas adjournment is the time when he thanks all the people, great and small, who make the Parliament run. Paul Keating spoke for thirty minutes and thanked them all, including the parliamentary switchboard staff, Marlene, Margaret, Pam and Gaylene.

It was a long, good-natured, nonpartisan speech and a touchingly prescient farewell to the Parliament that had sustained him for twenty-five years:

> *Public life is a passing parade. Anyone who thinks otherwise is deluding themselves. We can only be on the stage for a while, hopefully usefully to be able to do some things. The good thing about the parliamentary system is that we are all first among equals. If you rise to Cabinet or prime ministerial rank or if you do not, the Caucus is where the weight and the responsibility is—the sense, the touch with the community and picking up the plasma of Australian democracy.*

These would have been the perfect words to end his brilliant parliamentary career. But Keating, typically, delivered his last comments for Hansard a few minutes later, as an interjection, during a speech by his old sparring partner, John Howard. Thus, the final words of Keating's parliamentary career were:

'I'd like to be a fly on your wall, mate.'

To which Howard replied, 'I bet you would, mate.'

7
THE BILLION DOLLAR BLUFF

ON 30 AUGUST 1997, THE PRESIDENT of the Australian Labor Party, Barry Jones, said the unsayable. In a speech to the annual conference of Australians for an Ecologically Sustainable Future Population, the former federal minister gave some frank views on the subject of immigration and population policy. Midway through his speech, Jones entered Labor's no-go zone:

> *The handling of it by the previous* [Labor] *government was, I'd have to say, less than distinguished. Partly because, I think, immigration was seen as very important, a tremendously important element, in building up a long-term political constituency ... There was that sense that you might get the Greek vote locked up, or, from other party-political points of view, you might get the Chinese vote locked up.*
>
> *As a result, the idea of bringing groups of people to fulfil family reunion requirements and so on was seen as being a real advantage to the party in power at the time.*

Bang! After I quoted this statement in *Among the Barbarians* and it was picked up in several newspapers and prompted a parliamentary question, Barry Jones got up in Parliament on

28 May 1998, and denied saying what I and several hundred others had heard him say: 'The words attributed to me are a very rough paraphrase of what I said. As quoted, they completely misrepresent my position.'

Oh really? Then let's go to the official version of the speech, the one which Jones edited himself, of which I have a copy, complete with the editing changes in his own handwriting:

> *The handling of the population issue, I'd have to say, by the previous Government was less than distinguished. Partly because immigration was seen as a tremendously important element in building up a long-term political constituency. There was a sense that Labor might get the Greek vote 'locked up' or the Liberals might get the Chinese vote 'locked up'. The idea of bringing people to fulfil family reunion requirements was seen as something that was a very real advantage to the party in power at the time.*

What, you might ask, is the difference? The key point here is Jones's admission that immigration was regarded as a key tool in building up electoral support. That's why Labor stuck to an immigration policy dominated by family reunion. That's why it poured unskilled non English speaking background migrants into the big cities even after it could see the evolution of an immigrant underclass. That's why it tolerated depression-level welfare dependence among some immigrant streams. That's why it ignored the opinion polls on immigration.

And that's why Barry Jones got up in Parliament again, on

24 June 1998, after I had challenged his denial, and kept bluffing:

> *The article by Paul Sheehan in today's* Sydney Morning Herald ... *compounds his misrepresentation of my position on immigration and multiculturalism ...*
> *Sheehan used my remarks as the peg on which to attack multiculturalism and the ALP.*

No, this book is not an attack on multiculturalism, it is, among many things, an attack on the betrayal of multiculturalism. It is an attack on the billions of dollars of public funds spent building up a political constituency through direct community grants, government patronage and welfare benefits.

This book explains the anger in the electorate caused by more than a decade of economic rationalism combined with racial politics, a highly combustible combination.

It examines the hypocrisy of those who are now leading the outrage against Hansonism as if they had nothing to do with creating the phenomenon.

And it challenges the biggest and most successful bluff of all: that those who criticise multiculturalism are racist and those who criticise immigration policy are anti-immigrant.

Governments make mistakes. Bad outcomes often come from good intentions. No-one is immune from blunder. But it is the cynical use of threats and smears and hidden agendas that is worse than any mistake.

It wasn't as if Barry Jones was the first or the last Labor politician to talk about the dangers of Labor's ethnic strategy. In a symposium held soon after Labor's 1996 electoral debacle, the blunt-spoken Labor frontbencher, Laurie Ferguson, said:

> *The two big negatives for the Keating government were the question of migration and multiculturalism. Unfortunately, the party became convinced that dancing polkas and going to the mosque mean that some Iman can deliver 20 000 votes to you the next morning.*

Another Labor frontbencher, Mark Latham, in his 1998 book, *Civilising Global Capital*, described major problems with Labor's immigration strategy:

> *Australia's recent experience, particularly through the large family reunion program in the late 1980s, has shown that poorly skilled migrants are unlikely to avoid the problems of economic exclusion and welfare dependency. For instance, five years after their arrival in Australia in 1989–90, one in four of the 58 000 settler migrants registered for unemployment benefits. The level of welfare dependency has, in some cases by place of origin, been even higher—such as a seventy-one percent unemployment rate over the five year period for arrivals from Lebanon, and seventy-nine percent from Turkey.*
>
> *Migration policies such as these—which, perversely enough in the public arena, are often cast in the name of social justice—simply add to the extent of underclass neighbourhoods in Australia's major cities. In the new labour market there are virtually no jobs available for unskilled migrants ...*

Latham, who represents a western Sydney electorate in the thick of this evolving problem, advocates a fundamental change in Labor's policies:

> *The recent history of unskilled migration to Australia has added considerably to the extent of downwards envy and the declining legitimacy of the public sector. The ALP, in advocating the policies of a learning society, needs to fundamentally alter its thinking on immigration.*

A 1998 paper by immigration scholars Bob Birrell and Byung-Soo Seol, 'Sydney's Ethnic Underclass', fleshes out the same argument:

> *Sydney is increasingly divided on ethnic, class and residential lines ...*
>
> *Over the decade to 1996, there was a major contraction in manufacturing employment in Sydney of 41 000 jobs, thus diminishing opportunities in what was once a major provider of entry level jobs for NESB migrants ...*
>
> *There is a bigger picture which has not been recognised properly by commentators. This is the growing concentration of diverse NESB birthplace groups within a relatively tightly bound region of Sydney's south-west ... Immigration and multicultural advocates tend to deny that concentration is occurring at all ... or suggest it is a temporary phenomenon.*
>
> *However, the Census data is unequivocal. There is a growing concentration of low income families in*

> Sydney's south-west which is primarily derived from
> NESB countries ...
>
> The concentrations identified are acute by any standards. In the case of Fairfield, Canterbury and Auburn, seventy percent of all adult male residents aged 25–64 by 1996 were overseas-born, in each case predominantly from low-income NESB backgrounds. Moreover, these concentrations are increasing.

Another former senior minister in the Hawke–Keating governments, Graham Richardson, warned on his radio show about ethnic politics and Labor's reckless ethnic branch-stacking.

Yet another former Labor minister, Peter Walsh, has become extremely angry about the entire subject:

> Politicians across the spectrum have played ethnic politics, including ethnic branch stacking, for perceived political gain to themselves, their factions or their party. In this cynical self-serving exercise they are joined by opportunists who claim to represent the ethnic groups from which they come. Together they constitute the multicultural industry, which claims to be indispensable to creating and maintaining a tolerant society. The reverse is closer to the truth.

In the decade prior to 1996, Labor and its surrogates cultivated a policy of ethnic alliances in growing NESB communities. As part of this policy, Labor assiduously ignored the electorate on immigration until it reached the point in the run-up to the 1996 election where roughly seventy percent of Australians wanted lower migration and only about three percent wanted higher migration. It was an absurd disconnection from the public mood, and it came at a high price.

Yet the strategy worked, up to a point.

In the federal election landslide of 1996, the only section of the electorate which held firm for Labor were the urban electorates with the heaviest NESB immigrant populations. Under Labor, these electorates had received a steady flow of federal largesse. We also know, thanks to neutral grassroots activists like Sheila Christofedes, who worked extensively in Sydney for the No Aircraft Noise Party, that Labor successfully targeted the NESB news media, which operate below the radar screen of mainstream media scrutiny. 'When I was door-knocking,' Mrs Christofedes said, 'I could tell that Labor propaganda was really working with migrants who had little English skills. A lot of them told me, "We only vote Labor." They believed that if John Howard was elected that Medicare would be in jeopardy, that immigration would be in jeopardy, that Howard's policies would actively discriminate against ethnic minorities. This is what Labor's foreign-language election material said.'

After Labor's defeat the multicultural industry scrambled to contain the damage and keep control of the debate. When the election was followed, six months later, by the first rush of Pauline Hanson into the national headlines, there was apoplexy in the multicultural industry. At its darkest hour of political defeat, it had been given a lifeline.

At the height of the news media's Hansonmania in late

1996, I attended the monthly meeting of the Ethnic Community Council of New South Wales. The meeting began with the chairperson, Angela Chan, holding up a copy of the *Bulletin* with a photo of Pauline Hanson on the cover and the headline: POLL SHOCK: AT LEAST FIVE SEATS. The latest opinion poll had found that if Hanson formed her own party it would win five seats at the next Senate election.

'She is a danger to Australia,' said Chan, who had campaigned vigorously during the 1996 federal election, warning that a Coalition victory could mean 'the death of multiculturalism'. When she handed the meeting over to her vice-chair, Josie Lacey, Lacey continued the rhetoric. 'If the Human Rights Act is weakened, this country is lost.'

Attendance at the meeting was larger than usual, about forty people, because lawyers from the Human Rights and Equal Opportunity Commission had come to talk about proposed changes to the Racial Hatred Act.

'How long does it take before she [Pauline Hanson] goes to jail?' Josie Lacey asked the lawyers.

When told that Hanson could not go to jail under existing laws, she said the Act needed amendment. This led to a discussion about the Act's effectiveness. It soon became obvious that everyone in the room (other than me) wanted to get rid of the section which stated that 'a fair and accurate report' in the news media was exempt from prosecution as an act of racial hatred.

'The British invented the concept of race and used it to rule the world,' said Dr Anthony Pun, a vice-chair of the

Council, who would replace Angela Chan as chairperson the following year.

It was not exactly a gathering of civil libertarians.

Although the Federation of Ethnic Community Councils of Australia is nominally a federation of hundreds of community-based organisations around the nation, its real power lies with government, which provides all the funding, and with the news media, which relish accusations of racism. Peter Walsh, another former minister in the Keating government enjoying the luxury of freedom and writing robust columns for the *Australian Financial Review*, now attacks the multicultural lobby he once helped feed:

> *The inability to speak English is another leading indicator of migrant unemployability. The suggestion during the election campaign that migrant points should be skewed more towards English speakers induced a threat from Angela Chan to send its proponents off to the Human Rights and Equal Opportunity Commission's thought and speech police for re-education or punishment.*
>
> *Chan appears not to have noticed that the High Court pulled the HREOC's teeth a couple of years ago. But, if her point is to be taken seriously, she has unwittingly demonstrated how stupid we have been in enacting highly subjective, open-ended clauses in the Race Discrimination Act.*
>
> *Chan is, of course, a paid-up member of the multicultural industry ... Such people have bluffed governments*

> *out of doing sensible things before. Governments have swallowed claims that they represent their ethnic community; if the government upsets them, then the community will vote en bloc against it. This always doubtful proposition has been demolished by two [studies] ...*
>
> *If the government is smart, then it will recognise the multicultural industry as another paper tiger.*

Long before the costly thought-policing by the multicultural industry, Australia was radically broadening its immigration base, enfranchising the Aboriginal population and expanding links to Asia.

The shift that would eventually divide Australia took place in several stages, under both Labor and the Coalition. The first stage was the appointment by Gough Whitlam of Al Grassby as Minister for Immigration, who imported the term 'multiculturalism' and practised a brand of overt ethnic politics.

The second stage was the arrival of Malcolm Fraser's Coalition government. Senior immigration officials of the time, and scholars like Professor Warren Hogan, saw the Fraser Government shift away from assimilationism toward the embrace of cultural differences, a shift that was inevitable. Fraser's government created the SBS network, allowed a dramatic increase in refugees from Vietnam, Cambodia and Laos and oversaw a change in the immigration program from an emphasis on skills to emphasising humanitarian concerns. (This change was accompanied by policy tensions between the Department of Immigration and the Department of Labour, which wanted to retain a program focused on skilled immigrants.)

When Labor took Government again in 1983 it had been in power in Canberra for only three of the previous twenty-five years. It quickly began to expand the public sector, creating new categories of grievances and needs. Among the chief beneficiaries of these reforms were the lawyers and white-collar political activists who had become the party's new lifeblood.

This was the new breed of Labor that had so alarmed the old Labor warhorse, Arthur Calwell, Whitlam's predecessor as Labor leader. In his 1972 memoir, *Be Just And Fear Not*, Calwell wrote:

> *There is another faction in the Labor party today which consists of aggressive, assertive, philosophical, way-out people whose purpose is certainly not to promote the well-being of the party or of society; it is to create an agnostic, hedonistic society based on Freudian philosophy, even if that philosophy is largely discounted today.*
>
> *... the time is coming when we will either be a socialist party or we will finish up as a muddle-minded, middle-class, petit-bourgeois, status-seeking party.*

They might have been aggressive, assertive, agnostic, hedonistic, middle-class, status-seeking and petit-bourgeois, but the new Labor elite was not muddle-minded.

Whereas the Coalition parties have the private sector as their cash cow and regenerative source of money, talent and ideas, Labor, confronted with shrinking trade unions, had to rely on an expanded public sector as its other cash cow. Columnist Max Walsh put it bluntly: 'Thirteen years of Labor has seen political patronage spread to every nook and cranny of the public sector.'

This patronage oiled the wheels of a billion dollar public sector program directed at Labor's own rapidly changing electorates. Labor's disregard of the opinion polls on immigration pointed to its new priorities. The melding of Labor and new ethnic blocs was a process of osmosis as unskilled migrants poured into areas of low-cost housing—traditionally Labor seats—and as Labor politicians and union officials formed a thousand marriages of convenience.

This process was then given ideological shape by what Mark Latham describes in *Civilising Global Capital* as Labor's 'drift towards interest group capture':

> *In this way, policies for gender equity come from the women's committee; policies for multiculturalism and immigration come from the NESB committee; and so it goes for each interest group activity ... For those who do not closely identify with one segment or another ... perceptions of neglect and misplaced priorities inevitably arise.*

These interest groups did not give up their agendas lightly, especially after they have been placed inside the public-sector power structure.

After Labor lost office, its surrogates inside the bureaucracy conducted a guerilla war against the new Howard government, and strategic leaks claimed at least four ministerial casualties and embarrassments. From the day it lost office, Labor and its surrogates inside and outside the bureaucracy, notably multicultural and indigenous activists on the public sector payroll, kept up an incessant din about 'division' that became self-fulfilling.

For example, the Human Rights and Equal Opportunity Commission, packed with members of the multicultural industry was shrill in the wake of Labor's defeat. Zita Antonios, the Race Discrimination Commissioner, wrote in her 1996 report:

> *This new wave of racism has been bubbling under the surface for some time but has erupted in the past year quite publicly. It manifests itself in the view that policies, legislation and even funding for Indigenous Australians and people of non-English speaking background have 'gone too far'.*

Note: criticism equals racism. The same tactic is used again and again. Ms Antonios was mild compared with Mick Dodson, the Aboriginal and Torres Strait Islander Social Justice Commissioner, whose analysis of the 1996 election in the same report showed apoplectic outrage that a conservative government had been elected:

> *A wave of resentment and racism began to take form during the lead-up to the March 1996 election, and has washed across this country and the national media ever since. The defining political climate is a disturbing culture of disrespect, disregard, resentment and vilification.*

Not surprisingly, the Howard government tapped Mick on the shoulder and told him his services would not be needed when his term as commissioner expired in January 1998. The government also slashed the Commission's budget. No more junkets to Paris. It also introduced the Human Rights Legislation Amendment Bill 1996 aimed at curbing the Commission's ideological excesses.

Peter Walsh admitted in his memoirs, *Confessions of a Failed Finance Minister*, that the Labor government had suppressed or ignored the costs of high-immigration policies.

> *In short, migration adds more to demand than it does to supply, ipso facto it blows out the current account deficit. (Apologists for immigration, such as the BIMPR [Bureau of Immigration and Multicultural Population Research] either deny this fact or claim it applies only in the short term. This could be true for a once only immigrant intake, but not for an ongoing program.) ... an immigration program of 140 000 a year had an adverse current account effect between four and six billion dollars.*

Those billions of dollars helped underwrite Labor's electoral strategy. This was not the sort of information the Labor government wanted to disseminate. Instead, it set up and expanded a government agency, the Bureau of Immigration and Multicultural Population Research, which came to be regarded as so politicised that the Howard government shut it down within its first year in office. The BIMPR did not give Australians the sort of new immigration analysis that began emerging in the United States in the 1990s.

Immigration has been, and remains, essential to Australia's survival as a nation, but national problems have been caused by shoddy management and by the racial politics played by the Labor Party and its surrogates in the multicultural industry. The negative effects of large-scale unskilled immigration revealed by substantial new research have been largely left out of the national debate. For example, the Australian public has not learned about the research of Harvard economists Larry Katz, Richard Freeman and George Borjas, who concluded that immigrants, for their first twenty to twenty-five years in a new country, are a net fiscal drain on society. After studying the impact of immigration at the local level, they found native-born workers responded to immigration by moving out of high-immigration areas or by not moving into them. The same trend is occurring in Australia.

The Harvard economists also found that immigration had a major impact on twenty million native-born high-school dropouts who were competing with unskilled immigrants. Between 1979 and 1995, the average hourly wage of American males who hadn't finished high school fell from

$12.22 to $8.92 (in constant 1995 dollars), a drop of thirty percent.

A 1998 report on the positive effects of immigrants to Australia, by the Centre for Economic Policy at the Australian National University, found that migrants generated more jobs than they took. On average, immigrants brought $20 000 to Australia, money which created economic activity.

This positive news is qualified by research into the impact of unskilled migrants conducted at the University of Michigan, where George Johnson studied the impact of ten million unskilled migrants to America between 1980 and 1995 and estimated that ninety-eight per cent of increased output in the economy went to the migrants themselves, resulting in a 'trivial net gain to domestic residents'.

Another Michigan economist, William Frey, found an America divided by immigration, with a historic level of out-migration by unskilled Americans from the areas of high unskilled immigration—California, New York, Texas, Florida and Illinois. He found immigration patterns which undermined the melting-pot theory and were creating a social geography in which America was increasingly divided into areas either dominated by younger, multicultural populations, or by an older, white and alienated population.

A comparable trend is taking place around the area of Australia's greatest immigration flow—Sydney. In their 1998 paper, Bob Birrell and Byung-Soo Seol wrote:

The Australian-born leaving the south-western suburbs appears to be relocating in outer suburbia, notably in

> *Penrith and the northern coastal area of Gosford-Wyong. These growth areas have remained predominantly Australian-born.*

These two growth areas also became fertile ground for One Nation, which was recording between fourteen and twenty percent support in the wake of the 1998 Queensland election, according to polling in these two areas by the Liberal Party. The Central Coast, with its high population of Australian-born retirees, has become a hotbed of conservative politics.

Australia has the fastest-growing population among the wealthy OECD nations, yet the immigration scholar John Atchison was moved to write an essay in 1997 entitled, 'The Sad State of the Immigration Debate', bemoaning the absence of academic rigour from the public immigration debate. The biggest oversight is that about one-third of those entering Australia as immigrants do not stay for the long term. 'At a time when some 37 000 persons leave Australia annually on a permanent basis, this is a healthy corrective to easy judgements about the immigration phenomenon.'

Atchison has also written about what he calls 'the latent fascism' in the constant accusations of 'racism' in the Australian immigration debate. The rhetoric of 'racism' is certainly the weapon used to protect vested political interests. Within a year of Labor losing office, the new government began to clamp down on welfare abuse, immigration abuse and lax spending, and quickly extracted savings of more than one billion dollars a year. It wasn't long before the accusations of 'racism' began to flow from the Opposition.

Anthony Albanese, a federal Labor MP from Sydney and notorious factional activist, charged that there were 'strong racist overtones' in the government's attempts to crack down on false marriages. Senator Nick Bolkus, always reliable, simply described the government as 'racist'. His usual baiting was moderate compared with the speech in the House of Representatives on 16 June 1997, when Laurie Brereton stood up and for twenty minutes bucketed the historian Professor Geoffrey Blainey:

> It was Blainey who started it all off. He was the person who lit the fuse in that fateful speech in 1984 when he proclaimed his arguments for a racially discriminatory immigration policy.
>
> In words which have an eerie contemporary resonance, he declared the pace of Asian immigration to Australia to be well ahead of public opinion and warned of conflict and turmoil in the suburbs of our nation. The reaction to those remarks was explosive. By speaking as he did, Blainey fuelled the community fears on which he put so much weight.
>
> More than that, he gave credibility and legitimacy to some of the more ignorant and sinister of the Australian community who quickly found new inspiration and voice ... It was Blainey who unquestionably mapped out the

intellectual terrain, prepared the ground for the Member for Oxley and her racist One Nation Party.

Thus spoke Laurie Brereton, the man who introduced to the federal public service the Equal Opportunity-mandated categories of 'PWD' (People With Disabilities), 'NESB1' (Non-English Speaking Background, first generation), 'NESB2' (Non-English Speaking Background, second generation) and 'ATSI' (Aboriginal and Torres Strait Islanders).

Why couldn't Professor Blainey just shut up and let the Labor Right, that paragon of virtue and ethics and electoral probity, set the national agenda?

So effective were the tactics of smear and denial over so long a period, and so ingrained is the imposed orthodoxy, that even the incoming Liberal Minister for Immigration and Multicultural Affairs, Philip Ruddock, continued the process of disinformation. In the aftermath of Pauline Hanson's maiden speech to Parliament in September 1996, and the ensuing media frenzy, Ruddock wrote a newspaper article headlined TRUTH AND IMMIGRATION, published on 25 October 1996.

Presumably the article was prepared by senior officials within the Department of Immigration, which has a vested interest in making Australia's immigration policy look like a paragon of virtue and efficiency. Ruddock had an arduous assignment of cleaning up the system keeping open the flow of genuine immigrants, while reducing the flow of people who go straight on to welfare. He had moved to tackle fraud, streamlined the Immigration Review Tribunal, which Senator

Bolkus had stacked with political appointees, and had been careful not to antagonise any ethnic sensibilities. Ruddock was one of the quiet successes of the Howard government.

However, the complexity of this task did not explain why a federal minister would put his name to an article such as 'Truth and Immigration'.

> *Statistics show that people from the many countries that make up the Asian continent comprise only 4.5 percent of Australia's total population. Based on recent immigration patterns, the projection is that by 2031, the Asian-born might be about 7.5 percent. This hardly constitutes an invasion.*

Misleading. More than forty percent of all immigrants from Asia (the Asian continent includes the Middle East) settle in just one place—Sydney. Not only do the majority of Asian immigrants concentrate in just two cities, Sydney and Melbourne, they concentrate in clusters *within* these two cities.

The statement that the 'Asian-born' population might be only about 7.5 percent is disingenuous. It ignores the large and rapidly growing numbers of Asian-Australians born *in Australia.* Various demographic projections have placed the Asian-Australian population at around twenty percent of the total population within a generation. This twenty percent figure is borne out by a major study of immigration trends, *Immigration and Ethnicity,* by demographer Charles Price, published in 1996. Professor Price used Australia's long post-war immigration history and the ethnic composition of immigrants from 1983 to 1995 to project the population in twenty-five years. 'The work of Charles Price remains absolutely essential for anyone wanting to appreciate the social and demographic processes of integration, especially on marriage patterns,' wrote John Atchison in 'The Sad State of the Immigration Debate'.

Price's study projected the Asian-Australian population (which includes Middle-Eastern) at 19.5 percent in the year 2025, plus one percent ethnic Pacific Islanders. This level has already been reached in large areas of Sydney. According to the New South Wales Health Department, one in four births in central Sydney and one in five births in the south-west are to Asian-born mothers.

There is nothing wrong with this trend. But there is a great deal wrong with pretending that such a major demographic shift is not underway. This shift is the product of social engineering, and the highest population growth among advanced nations.

Ruddock went on:

Research has consistently indicated that a properly balanced immigration program has a neutral effect on a number of the key aspects of economic life ...

Wrong. Broad, bipartisan community support does exist for a properly balanced immigration policy, but as Australia did not have such an immigration program under Labor, there was no broad community support, a fact confirmed by poll after poll. Nor did Ruddock acknowledge the growing environmental dimension of immigration, a dimension now of concern to a majority of Australians.

> *A long-term survey being undertaken by my department shows an unemployment rate of twenty percent eighteen months after arrival for migrants in the Preferential Category, covering spouses and children.*

Wrong. This twenty percent figure is bad enough, but it carefully understates the problem. The journal *People and Place* has repeatedly found astronomic unemployment numbers among some immigrant groups, including an overall long-term unemployment rate of 24.3 percent among settler arrivals entering the workforce in 1988–89. Among immigrants from Vietnam who entered the work force in 1988–89, the majority, 55.3 percent, were receiving Jobsearch or Newstart payments five years after their arrival. The figures were even worse for settlers from Lebanon, 71.1 percent, and Turkey, 79.1. In contrast, the extremely low rates of long-term unemployment among settlers from Hong Kong, 2.4 percent, and Malaysia, 5.5 percent, who arrived in 1988–89 illustrate the huge disparities within the diverse 'Asian' immigration stream to Australia.

Are we really importing criminals as some would have us believe?

Yes. Check the prison statistics. Check the drug trade.

Apart from Aborigines, who are exponentially over-represented in the prison populations, four immigrant groups stand out, per capita, in the prison population: those from

Vietnam, Lebanon, New Zealand and the former Yugoslavia. These same groups tend to be negatively over-represented across the spectrum of official statistics. Yet Ruddock has claimed it is 'unfair' to use small statistical groups like prison figures. Far from being unfair, these statistics are signposts to wider illegality.

The Department of Immigration, despite its best intentions, unwittingly helped to create Australia's largest-ever drug market in Cabramatta. In the face of a multitude of quality control problems with Australia's immigration stream is a Department of Immigration so cautious it cannot even bring itself to charge those illegal overstayers who are actually caught. A 1997–98 report by the Australian National Audit Office (ANAO) expressed dismay at the department's habits:

> *People detained or removed from Australia are legally liable to pay for the cost of this action. However, in 1993–94 the ANAO observed there was very little recovery of costs by DIMA.*
>
> *Three years after the previous audit, 0.1 percent of nearly $10 million in compliance costs of people who were removed was recorded as paid before departure on the computer compliance system ...*
>
> *ANAO was advised of instances where people who had breached their visas and were being removed from Australia had substantial liquid assets with them and yet did not pay for their detention and passage.*

The ANAO also expressed disapproval of the department's poor record in clamping down on passport rackets:

> *In 1993–94, the ANAO noted limited progress in DIMA's investigation of a significant rate of 'lost' passports in Australia amongst a particular class of entrant. The ANAO saw a need for vigilance on misuse of passports more generally.*

Immigration rorts do not sit well with the electorate, and the empty denials that these rorts are widespread does not help. Though most Australians continue to support economic growth through immigration and non-discriminatory politics, the majority are tired of being patronised on the realities of immigration racial politics in Australia.

Belatedly aware that immigration problems had cost Labor dearly in 1996, Labor under Kim Beazley began quietly supporting immigration reform. It allowed the Howard government to impose a ban on welfare payments to immigrants in their first two years in Australia, supported measures which allowed the government effectively to almost abolish the immigration of parents, a category that was slashed by ninety percent. Labor also allowed the imposition of English tests for the family program. Bob Birrell of Monash University, wrote an article asking: 'How did such radical changes get through Parliament? What happened to the previously influential lobby groups who had helped prompt governments to put out the welcome mat?' It was a rhetorical question. He knows the multicultural industry is, with a few exceptions, a surrogate for Labor.

It will take at least a decade to dismantle the problems caused by the potent cocktail of economic rationalism coupled with large-scale, low-skill immigration. Structural reform is already under way. Quietly.

Even so, attempts to clean up some blatant abuses of the system have been blocked by the Labor Party. As a result, the immigration appeal system is growing out of control. The number of applications for Protection visas exploded from around five hundred a year in the late 1980s to 11 000 a year in the late 1990s, to the point where immigration cases now make up sixty-five percent of Federal Court administrative law cases.

'The misuse of the courts has had a corrosive effect the immigration system,' Mr Ruddock said. 'It is clear many people are making fictitious claims, to test and retest the system. The Protection visa system is being abused by people who simply want to prolong their stay in Australia, or obtain work rights, or gain access to Medicare, or seek financial assistance as an asylum seeker. The processing time for cases has trebled in three years. It is appalling.'

The Labor Party does not regard it as appalling. Having given undertakings to various interest groups, it has sought to block and blunt reform of the immigration review process, and then call in its debts at election time, which it did again in 1998. Consider this headline in a 'special edition' inserted into Chinese-language newspapers in Sydney: AUSTRALIAN-CHINESE COMMUNITY SUPPORTS THE

AUSTRALIAN LABOR PARTY, FEDERAL ELECTION 1998.

The supplement, designed to appear like editorial copy, was not identified as an advertisement. It contained 'articles' such as one by Mr Jun Young, who wrote:

> *This is the first time the 40 000 Chinese students will be eligible to vote. But whom to vote for? To answer this question we only have to think who allowed us to stay in this beautiful country, who has stirred up racism and who has implicitly tolerated it.*

The headline for this article was: A FAVOUR OF A DROP OF WATER SHOULD BE RETURNED IN A FOUNTAIN. PLEASE GIVE YOUR SACROSANCT VOTE TO LABOR. The 'special edition' was put together by the Deputy Lord Mayor of Sydney and Labor Party activist, Councillor Henry Tsang, whose photograph appears on nearly every page. The funds for the supplement were raised at a fund-raiser attended by Labor leader Kim Beazley, Premier Bob Carr, shadow minister Martin Ferguson, state MP Helen Sham-Ho, who had recently deserted the Liberal Party, and about six hundred members of the Chinese community. The function raised $120 000 for the Labor Party.

Not everyone liked the published claim that 'the Chinese community supports the Australian Labor Party'. 'Who are these people claiming to speak for the entire Chinese community?' asked Ms Pamela Loo, a former president of the Australian-Taiwanese Friendship Society. 'These people are self-appointed leaders,' she told *The Sydney Morning Herald*. 'This is exactly the sort of race-based advertising that damages multiculturalism'.

And raises money and votes for the ALP.

On 28 May 1998, Philip Ruddock, was asked during Question Time in the House of Representatives about abuses in the immigration program. In his answer, Ruddock quoted Barry Jones's remark that in the previous Labor government 'immigration was seen as a tremendously important element in building up a long-term political constituency'.

> PHILIP RUDDOCK: *Let me say that it confirms, I think in a very graphic way, what I have been saying about the way in which the immigration program which we inherited was seriously out of balance—where seventy percent of the migration program was represented in the family stream ... We have now redressed the balance.*

Ruddock revealed that since measures aimed at curbing the widespread sham marriages had been introduced, the number of applications for spouse or fiancé visas had plunged thirty percent. He also said the family reunion program had been scaled back to fifty percent of the total intake, another major policy shift.

After Question Time, an angry Barry Jones rose to speak.

> BARRY JONES: *Mr Speaker, I wish to make a personal explanation.*

> SPEAKER: *Does the honourable member claim to have been misrepresented?*
> JONES: *The material from Paul Sheehan's book* Among The Barbarians *attributed to me ... is a significant misrepresentation.*

I have his comments on tape. I was at the conference when he spoke. I have the official transcript he edited himself. His comments were unambiguous. Far from being a rough paraphrase, the quote is taken off the tape.

The most effective rebuttal of Jones's transparent bluster comes from his own mouth. During a speech at the Royal Melbourne Institute of Technology on 27 March 1996, this is what he said about his own government:

> *I have maintained a judicious silence about some policies pursued by the outgoing government with which I disagreed. However, I will break my resolve a little to say that I was profoundly disappointed by the government response to the Report of the House of Representatives Long Term Strategies Committee on Australia's Population Carrying Capacity ...*
>
> *The draft government response was essentially 'No worries, we have plenty of room'. The specific environmental issues we raised were completely ignored ...*
>
> *I warned that if the government response was tabled in Parlimanent I would have to attack it. In the circumstances, it was withdrawn ...*
>
> *However, in December, the government published a response to the Report of the United Nations*

International Conference on World Population and Development, held in Cairo in 1994. The Cairo conference called for a world population policy and urged countries to adopt their own. Both ideas were contemptuously rejected by Australia. This exhibits a pathetic short-sightedness and self-interest from people who have made their careers out of immigration.

This pathetic short-sightedness and self-interest, has caused damage to the cohesion of Australian society. The time has come for a closer look at what Barry Jones was alluding to, but would not name.

8
A KICK IN THE TEETH

VOTER FOCUS GROUPS RUN by the major parties in 1998 found that most people weren't sure what the word 'multiculturalism' meant, but didn't like it whatever it was.

According to Emeritus Professor Jerzy Zubrzycki, the person who imported the word to Australia was Al Grassby, Minister for Immigration in the Whitlam government, who brought 'multicultural' from Canada in 1973. 'The term has been a subject of misunderstanding and confusion ever since,' said Professor Zubrzycki.

Ah yes, Al Grassby. Given Grassby's fondness for historical allusions, and given his key role in the introduction of 'multiculturalism' to Australia, it is worth revisiting the final chapter in his public career. In 1986 the Nagle Special Commission of Inquiry, conducted by John Nagle QC, examined the aftermath of the 1977 assassination of anti-drug crusader Donald Mackay in Griffith, New South Wales, a country town in Al Grassby's former federal electorate. In the course of his inquiry, Nagle examined certain actions by Albert Jaime Grassby. Nagle gave a damning summation of Grassby's behaviour in his final report. He found that Grassby had distributed an anonymous document, obtained from highly dubious sources, containing 'scurrilous lies' that grossly defamed the family of Donald Mackay. The document suggested that Mackay had been murdered by his wife and son after a family argument. It also suggested that the family solicitor was an accessory after the fact.

Nagle said the writing style in the document was characterised by a 'sneering nastiness'.

He said the document 'appears to be written as a parliamentary speech'.

He said none of the accusations withstood factual examination.

He rejected Grassby's defence of his actions—that he was trying to prevent the 'racial defamation' of the Calabrian Italian community in Griffith over the disappearance of Donald Mackay:

The Commission makes only one comment—that no decent man could have regarded the attacks on the Calabrians as justifying him in propagating the scurrilous lies contained in the anonymous document.

He described Grassby's behaviour as a witness during the hearings:

He was long-winded, dissembling, and unconvincing, and was constantly driven to uneasy claims of defective memory ... [Grassby] was, at the best, less than frank about, and at worst concealed, what he knew about the origin of the documents ...

He claimed to have no memory at all of the parliamentary speech which he handed to Maher.

A KICK IN THE TEETH

The now infamous document had first surfaced in July 1980 when Grassby, by then long voted out of office, gave it to a New South Wales State Labor MP, Michael Maher. At their meeting in Grassby's office, Maher found two men and a woman with Grassby, who, on behalf of this group, gave him twelve pages containing the allegations about the Mackay family. Grassby also gave documents to the *Sun-Herald* newspaper. In August 1980 a story in the *Sun-Herald* claimed Michael Maher was about to make allegations in Parliament on the Mackay case. The story ran under the front-page banner: NOT THE MAFIA ...?

Wrong. During the Nagle inquiry, Grassby's barrister suggested to Maher that Grassby had merely suggested he 'raise' the matter in Parliament. Maher strongly disagreed:

> *My recollection is that he said 'read' because he became quite heated—more emotional than I had ever seen him before.*
>
> *He* [Grassby] *said: 'If they stop you, keep going, if they take a point of order, keep going.'*

Maher also said Grassby had told him he had given the document to the then shadow Attorney-General in South Australia, who would read it in State Parliament. Maher, far from reading the document in the New South Wales Parliament, gave it to the New South Wales police. Nagle would describe Maher's evidence to the Inquiry as 'cogent and convincing'.

Grassby, and others, were later charged with conspiring to pervert the course of justice. He was cleared of the charge after a five-week court hearing. After the Nagle Inquiry report was released, the Labor Premier of New South Wales, Barrie Unsworth, accepted Grassby's resignation from his $48 000-a-year job as Special Adviser to the Premier on Community Relations. The job, worth more than $100 000 a year in today's dollars, had been created for Grassby by the previous Labor Premier, Neville Wran. In the New South Wales Supreme Court on 12 March 1987, Grassby apologised to the Mackays and to their solicitor, Ian Salmon. He was ordered to pay them $5000 damages. In making his apology, he accepted that the document he wanted read in Parliament 'makes the most serious allegations imaginable'.

The Mackays sued Grassby for criminal defamation. In 1991 a jury found Grassby guilty on three charges. Supreme Court Justice Allen, in fining Grassby $7000, said he had considered jailing Grassby but had decided not to because, 'There must be hurt in having a lifetime of public service crowned not with honour but with disgrace and humiliation'. The following year the jury's verdict was overturned by the New South Wales Supreme Court.

The greatest mystery in this episode is why Grassby would choose Michael Maher, a famously honest man, as the target for an attempt to defame the Mackays and abuse parliamentary privilege. When I asked Maher in 1997 why Grassby had chosen him, he replied: 'Because I had the biggest number of Italians in my electorate. I had big concentrations of Italians in Haberfield, Five Dock, Concord, Drummoyne and Chiswick.' He thought he could play the Italian vote:

> *At the start of the meeting he suggested that I could represent him on some overseas trip. I think it was to the Middle East. I just dismissed that. He then produced the document. I was appalled. I thought, 'That poor woman [Mrs Mackay]'.*
>
> *I clearly remember how agitated he became. I refused to even read it. This document could not be read. He was certainly acting for forces in Griffith who wanted to damage Mackay. I sent it to the police.*

That was effectively the end of Al Grassby's political career, but the episode set a precedent for the tactic of personal abuse and the claim of 'racial defamation' of entire ethnic groups. The political self-interest behind the rhetoric of tolerance, all these qualities remained at the heart of the multicultural industry's methods as it grew large in the decades 1973 to 1996.

The central fantasy of the multicultural industry is that Australia should be a cultural federation. But Australia has a distinct, dominant, cohesive, assimilative, blended culture that has been painstakingly built through trial and error. There is an enormous difference between the self-evident diversity of Australia's multiracial society and the big protective tent under which this diversity is thriving. Take away that big tent—Australian culture—and this diversity curdles into state-sponsored tribal animosities.

These animosities are helped by the well-oiled machinery of complaint and victimisation. The New South Wales Anti-Discrimination Board, for example, actually celebrates the growing litigiousness it is fostering, as if this were a measure of community health. The Board's 1994–95 Annual Report gushes:

- *1994–95 was a fantastic year for the Aboriginal and Torres Strait Islander Outreach Program. The number of complaints that we received rose dramatically ...*
- *The Labor government is ... committed to extending the grounds of unlawful discrimination in New South Wales to include more types of discrimination.*

One of the jewels in the bureaucratic crown of the multicultural industry is the national broadcaster SBS, which started with laudable goals and bipartisan support but, having to please a babel of constituencies, has been plagued by endemic in-fighting. The following leaked memo from an SBS manager was the quote which opened the 1996 story, 'The multicultural myth':

... the following remarks were [allegedly] made in the context of an application for the job of [a management position]:

- *There is no way I'll accept having that woman in the job. We don't need someone from that sort of background, an Anglo.*
- *An Anglo shouldn't be given that job; it should go to an ethnic. We don't need people like that.*
- *How can she know what the ethnic community needs? She's an Australian.*

A KICK IN THE TEETH

If you transpose the words Anglo and ethnic, I believe it is immediately clear that these comments were racist.

When the job of general manager of SBS became vacant in 1997, the successful applicant was Nigel Milan, who had a long history of successful senior media management and had also come to Australia as an immigrant. He was the wrong choice according to members of the multicultural industry for reasons that had little to do with media management. A New South Wales Liberal politician, Jim Samios, even complained publicly that two of the failed candidates—Angela Chan, who runs her own immigration consultancy, and the chairman of the New South Wales Ethnic Affairs Commission, Stepan Kerkyasharian—'would have excelled' if they had been chosen. Why? Neither Chan nor Kerkyasharian had any experience as senior managers or entrepreneurs in the media business. The big problem with the successful applicant appeared to be that he had migrated from the wrong country—Britain.

In his 1997 book, *Liberal Racism*, the American author Jim Sleeper argues that modern liberal orthodoxy has placed racial identity as the 'central organising principle of our public life', a process that divides the infinitely complex community into rigid racial groups and reflects a 'primordial' desire to classify people according to their skin colour. In 1996 Australian multicultural ideologues produced a book entitled, *The Teeth are Smiling,* subtitled, *The Persistence of Racism in Multicultural Australia.* One of the book's coeditors was Stephen Castles, Director of the Centre for

AMONG THE BARBARIANS

Multicultural Studies at the University of Wollongong, who appeared earlier in this book's chapter 'It Wasn't Luck' with his description of Australia's past as racist, sexist, elitist and genocidal. His co-editor, a sociologist at the university, wrote a chapter entitled 'Dialectics of Domination: Racism and Multiculturalism,' which describes the 'loss of identity' felt by many Anglo-Australians 'because they feel they have lost their hegemony over the cultural and geographical spaces they once controlled'.

As an example of this sense of loss, the sociologist quotes the poet, Les Murray:

> *They are creating an Australia that is exclusive. Multicultural, they call it. But they are discriminatory, they exclude. 'They' are not just the Australia Council; they are the ruling elite of today's Australia: the cultural bureaucrats, the academics, the intellectuals ... They are excluding people like me from their Australia—the country people, the rednecks, the Anglo-Celts, the farming people—they have turned their backs on us. They act as though they despise us ... We Old Australians, not always Anglo but having no other country but this one, are now mostly caught and silenced between the indigenous and the multicultural.*

The sociologist then comments:

> *This is a fairly articulate lament from someone who feels*

*he has lost his sense of hegemonic identity within the
cultural scene. It is instructive to know that Murray has
formed the Australia Council Reform Association with
Mark O'Connor who is a leading member of Australians
for an Ecologically Sustainable Population, a well-known
organisation whose anti-immigration discourse is part of
a broader racist rhetoric.*

Note what is going on here. She presumes to find Les Murray 'fairly articulate'. She also presumes to call him, by association, a racist. The logic is that anyone who wants lower immigration is pursuing a racist agenda. This allegedly includes groups such as Australians for an Ecologically Sustainable Population, an organisation which is part of 'a broader racist rhetoric'.

I attended the 1997 national conference of Australians for an Ecologically Sustainable Population (as a reporter not a participant). It was opened by the Premier of New South Wales, Bob Carr, and a key speaker was Labor Party President Barry Jones, who would tell the truth about immigration and politics under the Labor governments. There were six other speakers, all scholars, and one of them, Associate Professor Frank Stilwell of Sydney University, touched on the big issues latent but largely unspoken beneath the stresses in Australian politics:

*The delicate balance between diversity and social
cohesion is at the heart of the matter ...
Size itself is not a crucial variable on economic matters*

> *... In any case, there is no possibility of competing with our regional neighbours in terms of absolute scale ...*

Speaker after speaker said Australia would no longer become stronger and better by simply bulking up its population. Then came Barry Jones, MP, who warned:

> *... that an exaggerated emphasis on immigration, in isolation, was potentially very divisive, with migrants then becoming scapegoats, being blamed for a cultural threat.*

Jones also warned of the danger of an aging, declining population:

> *I spent some time in Bulgaria last year. Bulgaria was very striking, a country with a very sharp population decrease. You become conscious that Bulgaria is, to a very large extent, a culture of death ... the lack of new life contributes to the sense of decay, ruined buildings and a sense of fatalism and the sense that nobody's going anywhere.*

The conference room was packed. The audience listened carefully to Barry Jones's warnings that immigrants are easily scapegoated for society's problems. Few if any of the predominantly middle-class people in the conference hall believed that such scapegoating was fair or useful.

The defining picture of Australia at the end of the twentieth century was being told at this conference. On any given day so many different stories were flowing into each other like the tributaries of a single large river. Take, for example, the reports from a newspaper on 5 June 1996.

AUSTRALIA PLACES JOBS BEFORE OZONE
The Federal Government has vowed it will not sacrifice tens of thousands of jobs by agreeing to inequitable greenhouse gas reduction strategies.

GUN REBELS FORCE GOVERNMENT TO RETALIATE
Alarmed by the growing backlash against the proposed gun law reforms, the federal government is planning a nationwide campaign to try to stem revolts from conservative voters.

WE'RE WRONG: SYDNEY SHOULD BE CALLED WEERONG
If Dr Tim Flannery's dream is fulfilled, Sydney will be given back its Aboriginal name, Weerong, Sydneysiders will be called Cadigals, the Harbour will be called Cadi and Botany Bay Cameera.

TOUGH JOB AHEAD TO REIN IN THE DAMAGE
The first attempt to fully document the economic and social importance of Australia's environment and its health has revealed that the nation is facing vast ecological challenges from pollution, land degradation, irrigation and deforestation.

OUR 'BREADBASKET' IS IN BIG TROUBLE
The economic importance of the Murray-Darling Basin and its precarious health makes the waterway, which

drains four states, one of Australia's most important environmental issues, according to a report released yesterday.

PERMIT SYSTEM URGED TO SAVE TOURIST ICONS
Some of the most fragile and beautiful parts of Australia—including the Great Barrier Reef and Tasmania's World Heritage areas—are being loved to death, a national study has found.

ANGER AS TWO FACE CAB MURDER CHARGE
Family and friends of a murdered taxi driver and the supporters of one of the accused clashed outside Bankstown Local Court yesterday. Davina Leaituaalesi, 19, and Julius Graff, 19, were refused bail by the magistrate when they appeared on a charge of having murdered Mr Youssef Chmeis on May 25 at Riverwood.

VET POO-POOS TINNED PET FOODS
There are 6.8 million pets in Australia, and they produce 1.7 million kilograms of excrement a day, three times the volume of the excrement which would be produced if they were eating natural foods, such as meaty bones, and it is sticky, putrid and contaminated with bacteria. 'It gets into waterways and causes environmental havoc,' said vet Dr Tom Lonsdale.

UN WARNS OF BIG DRY TO COME
Most cities in the developing world will face extreme water shortages by 2010, according to the opening paper at the United Nations human settlement conference.

A KICK IN THE TEETH

CHINA: POLLUTION CRISIS
AS ECONOMY GOES INTO OVERDRIVE
Beijing—China's pollution woes continued to mount last year despite strenuous efforts to tackle its environmental problems, according to a government report.

JAKARTA SHIPPING PLAN SPARKS ANGER
Australia and Japan are deeply concerned about Jakarta's plan to limit the passage of military and commercial shipping to three sea lanes running north-south through the archipelago state. The curbs could add million of dollars to the cost of shipping between Australia and Japan.

39 FACE TRIAL IN IRIAN JAYA
Thirty-nine people are to be tried in Irian Jaya for taking part in riots in March in which four people were killed.

SYDNEY'S ALIEN NATION
Few of the early Chinese settlers saw Australia as home but those families who stayed endured hardship and discrimination that have spanned five generations.

QANTAS STEADY
Qantas Airways is adding a second flight to Ho Chi Minh City beginning in July.

Connect the scattered pieces and a single portrait emerges. The mosaic of news depicts a tolerant, advanced, prosperous and democratic country enduring social and environmental stress, the side effects of economic growth, high and undisciplined immigration, racial politics, a growing divide between city and the bush, a growing awareness of the magnitude of the Aboriginal issue, and a nation increasingly interdependent with an Asia whose economic growth carried costs as well as benefits.

The people of the bush, those closest to the ethos on which Australian culture and mythology was built, feel so marginalised by the new dominance of urban politics that many believe they are being thrown on the historical scrap heap. Rural Australia, while still having thousands of successful farms and a significant export industry, also has dying country towns, large areas of shrinking job prospects and growing crime. In some rural towns up to eighty-five percent of people are living on some form of assistance. The levels of crime in many country towns is endemic. This sense of siege in the bush provided the white heat in the historic Wik debate on native title.

On 11 December 1997 the *Sydney Morning Herald* ran a front-page banner headline, 500 000 CHILDREN ON BREADLINE based on new figures from the Centre for Population and Urban Research at Monash University which showed that Australia's working poor are concentrated in the bush. On the same day the newspaper also carried a front-page headline, THE GREAT SYDNEY GRIDLOCK, a story about increasing 'traffic paralysis' in Australia's largest city. It was a perfect juxtaposition of two separate yet linked trends: country drain and city strain. The stress of increasingly crowded big-city streets showed up in a 1997 survey by the insurance company AAMI, which found that fully two-thirds of drivers said they frequently encountered what we now call 'road rage'. The survey found that young women had become as susceptible to road rage as men.

The collective unease caused by these underlying stresses erupted on 2 March 1996 when a powerful government was thrown out of office. The Keating government was humiliated despite twenty consecutive quarters of economic growth, low inflation, high business confidence and sound economic management. Despite all this, the ruling Labor Party was suddenly reduced to a rump thirty-nine percent of the primary vote. No election since Federation has combined such a benign economic environment with such a savage electoral rebuke. The deafening silence imposed on debate cloaked the real issues of concern during the election campaign—the politics of intolerance masquerading as tolerance.

Speaking of which, within months of the publication of *The Teeth are Smiling*, which sank without trace in the public debate, Les Murray's new collection of poems, *Subhuman Redneck Poems,* became a best-seller with more than 20 000 copies sold, extremely rare for a book of poems in Australia.

Where will Australia be held?
Ethnics who praise their home ground
while on it are called jingo chauvinists.
All's permitted, though, when they migrate;
the least adaptable are the purest then,
the narrowest the most multicultural.

From 'The Suspension of Knock', *Subhuman Redneck Poems*

Murray is a provocateur, a bush eccentric, a man of feuds, ideologically uncompromising. His poems about multicultural orthodoxy are not written to make people feel comfortable. His work is included here because he has been smeared and because, like all original artists, he does not fit the prevailing artistic orthodoxy. One of his primary targets is this new orthodoxy which, having largely swept away the old Eurocentric, male-dominated value system, has settled into some of its own intolerant rigidities.

> *Our one culture paints Dreamings, each a beautiful claim.*
> *Far more numerous are the unspeakable Whites,*
> *the only cause of all earthly plights,*
> *immigrant natives without immigrant rights.*
> *Unmixed with these are Ethnics, absolved of all blame.*

From 'A Brief History', *Subhuman Redneck Poems*

Les Murray is a writer with an international literary reputation whose fans include the 1996 Nobel Laureate for Literature, poet Seamus Heaney. *Subhuman Redneck Poems* won the 1997 Victorian Premier's Literary Award for poetry. It was one of the three finalists for the 1997 New South Wales Premier's Literary Award for poetry. Several months after being smeared by multicultural zealots, Les Murray won the T.S. Eliot Award, one of the most important poetry prizes in the world.

9
IN THE FOOTSTEPS OF ALEXANDER

COMPLAINANT WITNESS: *... It was only after the fifth century that they [Macedonians] gradually became part of the wider Greek world, but there's no doubt that scholars have found that linguistically and religiously they were part, they were Greeks. They shared the same language and religion as the other Greeks.*

COMPLAINANT COUNSEL: *They worship the Gods of Olympus?*

WITNESS: *Yes.*

DEFENCE COUNSEL: *I object at this point, Mr Chairman. It's now too far from anything raised in cross-examination. I didn't cross-examine about the Gods of Olympus.*

COMPLAINANT WITNESS: *... The opposing argument always refers to the Greek politician Demosthenes who's probably the most famous orator of antiquity, who hated Philip very much. But most sources ... refer to the fact that in Athens when Demosthenes was attacking Philip there were also two others ...*

AMONG THE BARBARIANS

DEFENCE COUNSEL: *I object, Mr Chairman. There has to be a limit drawn to this! It's an expensive exercise.*

Limits? Costs? This is the Equal Opportunity Tribunal. This is the Anti-Discrimination Act. The case of Hellenic Council of New South Wales v Macedonian Youth Association is too bizarre not to warrant a close look, especially as one of the most dangerous trends in Australian democracy would be to allow foreign animosities to be played out in the Australian legal system under the guises of multiculturalism and anti-discrimination.

The dispute, which took more than five years to resolve, began when, in the wake of the creation of a Macedonian state in the break-up of Yugoslavia, a full-page ad was placed by Greek cultural zealots in the *Sun-Herald* on 1 March 1992 under the headline MACEDONIA IS GREEK. Among the more provocative statements in the ad were:

Nobody took the notion of a 'Slav' Macedonia seriously because the whole world knew that Macedonia was always Greek and could be nothing else.

We encourage the Skopian community both abroad and here in Australia to search their rich and beautiful Slavic history for the appropriate naming of their new independent nation. However, continued usurping of the name 'Macedonia' will firm the resolve of Greeks and Phil-Hellenes around the world to defend this glorious heritage from further plunder and rape.

IN THE FOOTSTEPS OF ALEXANDER

It came as no surprise when, two months later, in a full-page ad in the *Sun-Herald*, zealots from the Macedonian community returned the provocation, under the headline MACEDONIA—LAND OF LEGENDS! LAND OF GLORY! BUT *NEVER* GREEK, along with a map of a barbed-wire-enmeshed greater Macedonia.

> *Had the misguided Greek community known the truth of their history, they would never have infected Australia with the elements of a cancerous European epidemic known as nationalism, thereby transforming 'The Lucky Country' into another arena for foreign dispute ...*
>
> *The Macedonians (tall and fair) were in Europe long before the beginning of time itself, and were referred to by the Achaeans (short and dark) as 'Endopi', which means 'Old Settlers', inferring that etymologically Macedonia was a name borne by the Macedonians before the Achaeans had even arrived in Europe ...*
>
> *Well, no more! We can only take so much. Fellow Australians, you have read the facts, now it's time we stood up to these hostile fascists. It's these radical community sects which entangle our politicians within the labyrinth of foreign policy, translating foreign issues into domestic ones ...*
>
> *Always remember: 'Phillip II, Alexander the Great and Aristotle were Macedonians.'*

This, in turn, prompted the Hellenic Council of New South Wales, to lodge an action with the Equal Opportunities Tribunal of New South Wales in May 1992. They also made a claim to the Press Council. The existence of the Anti-Discrimination Tribunal and the Anti-Discrimination Act provided an avenue to sue. Even so, when the case was about to begin after a four-year delay, the plaintiffs had still not lodged a statement of claim, and sought an immediate postponement. This prompted exasperation from the chairman of the Anti-Discrimination Tribunal, Michael Bieddulph: 'I'm talking about a statement of claim in the Supreme Court ... It was ordered to be filed. The tribunal relies on the points of claim. It was never filed.'

If this nonsense had taken place before one of the dragons on the bench of the New South Wales Supreme Court, the Hellenic Council case would have been over before it began. Instead it was allowed to lurch ahead, and in its own unintended way it illuminated nearly every dubious trend in the fetish for tax-supported 'cultural diversity'.

For Australians, a disturbing statement appears in a book by an American anthropologist, Loring Danforth, who quotes the then Greek consul in Melbourne as stating: 'Australia is the first line of defence in the battle for Macedonia.'

In 1992 there were mass demonstrations by Greeks in Australia and one of the speakers at these demonstrations was federal Labor MP Andrew Theophanous, a product of the left-wing ethnic 'Greek' Labor branches in Melbourne. According to the *Age* of Melbourne, Theophanous told the crowd that Slavic people were the most recent arrivals in the region of ancient Macedonia and had no right to misrepresent history by monopolising the name. This was exactly the same line propagated at the time by the then government in Athens which, in addition to the stated reasons of cultural defence, used the emergence of a Macedonian state to deflect attention from several domestic scandals.

A Greek scholar received death threats after publishing her work on Slavic speakers in Greek Macedonia. The censored book, *Fields of Wheat, Hills of Blood*, challenges the official Greek government line that there is no Macedonian minority in Greece. So does Loring Danforth's book, *The Macedonian Conflict: Ethnic Nationalism in a Transnational World*, published by Princeton University Press. Danforth first came to Australia in 1988 as a guest of the Melbourne Greek community. He was later disowned when he deviated from the official line:

PLAINTIFF WITNESS: *By adopting the name Macedonia, Macedonians automatically aspire to adopt the history of ancient Macedonia, thereby creating confusion in the man in the street. The man in the street associates Macedonia with Alexander the Great, whereas Alexander the Great and ancient Macedonia are part of the history of Ancient Greece and no serious scholar can dispute that.*

Loring Danforth points out that neither the household of Alexander the Great nor his Greek contemporaries regarded him as Greek. He argues that the melding of the two hostile and distinct cultures began only centuries later under pressure from a common enemy, Rome, and even then Macedonia was regarded as marginal. Macedonian identity, he argues, has largely been fostered by Greek oppression. He lists in elaborate detail the long and often brutal suppression of minority rights in Greece, a record which explains why the two groups in Australia have fought each other in soccer riots, fire-bombings and insulting newspaper ads.

The Anti-Discrimination Act states that 'a public act, done reasonably and in good faith ... for public purposes including discussion or debate' cannot be rendered unlawful. This means it was always going to be a difficult case for the Hellenic Council activists to win, or to win more than a token or symbolic victory.

It was not clear what exactly the Hellenic Council was trying to achieve with this case. Was the council trying to remind people that there is an independent state called Macedonia? To remind Australians that Greece has practised suppression of minorities? The author and journalist Robert Kaplan, writing in the *Atlantic Monthly* in 1997, was brutally succinct in depicting how the modern Greek state was formed: 'Greece is a stable democracy partly because earlier in the century it carried out a relatively benign form of ethnic cleansing, in the form of refugee transfers, which created a monoethnic society.'

Is that what the Hellenic Council wanted to revisit? Or did it want to reopen the issue of irresponsible meddling in Australian affairs by the Greek government? Or examine the links between the Australian Greek community, the Greek government and the federal Labor government? If so, Hellenic Council of New South Wales v Macedonian Youth Association succeeded on all fronts.

PLAINTIFF'S COUNSEL: *Would you agree that following FYROM* [Former Yugoslav Republic of Macedonia] *seceding from Yugoslavia that the Australian government made a decision ... that your type of Macedonia would hereafter be classified as a Slav-Macedonia? And that decision annoyed you?*

DEFENCE WITNESS: *I didn't see that as to the interests of multiculturalism in Australia. I saw it as an attack on the principles of multiculturalism ... I saw it as an attempt to deny our right of self identification and self determination. A right that all other Australians enjoy ...*

PLAINTIFF'S COUNSEL: *You realise that by being called Slav-Macedonians the government of this country was entertaining the idea, at any rate, that, that there could be other types of Macedonia like Greek Macedonians and Bulgarian Macedonians?*

DEFENCE WITNESS: *Well, from the conversations that I had with Prime Minister Keating, Foreign Minister Gareth Evans, and Multicultural Minister Nick Bolkus, the reason for the decision was pressure from within the Greek community.*

It was inevitable that the name of Nick Bolkus would turn up eventually. This case was another window into the career of Senator Bolkus, whose brand of ethnic politics was also placed under a microscope by scholar Ernest Healy in *People and Place*, the journal of the Centre for Population and Urban Research at Monash University:

Recent decisions by the Minister for Immigration and Ethnic Affairs, Senator Bolkus, raise serious questions about the Minister's preparedness to tolerate open debate about immigration and multicultural issues, and about measures he has taken to control the debate ...

During 1993 Senator Bolkus appointed Stephen Castles as Chairman of the advisory council and included Mary Kalantzis as a member—both have written disparagingly of Australia's past ...

The role of ethnic blocs as tools in Labor politics found its most naked expression in the large Greek community of Melbourne, which was allowed to set up fourteen 'community language' branches. These branches, in turn, formed the bedrock of power of the Socialist Left of the Labor Party. This regressive move was justified in terms of Labor's support for multiculturalism. It legitimised the rampant ethnic branch stacking that had taken place. Greek activists within the Socialist Left faction argued that these stackings were countermeasures against the Labour Unity faction recruiting from the Turkish and Macedonian communities.

In 1994, a year of sustained ethnic violence in Australia as Greek and Macedonian nationalists waged a campaign of demonstrations, threats and bombings against each other, Senator Bolkus gave his closest Victorian ally, Andrew Theophanous, the role of directing the community access program by the Office of Multicultural Affairs. This program produced a document, *Our Nation*, which advocated changing the Australian Constitution to incorporate 'multicultural principles'. These and other measures were among the reasons for the Labor government's emphatic rejection by the electorate in 1996.

By 1997 the legal battle between the Greeks and the Macedonians in Hellenic Council of New South Wales v Macedonian Youth Association was still working through the legal system.

> PLAINTIFF'S COUNSEL: *Mr Chairman, there is somebody swearing behind me ... It has happened on three occasions. I decided to ignore it on the first two occasions.*
>
> CHAIRMAN: *All right, I will ask that gentleman withdraw himself from the court and remain outside. [Pause]*
>
> CHAIRMAN: *No, outside, and remain outside the precincts of the court.*

Finally, on 25 September 1997 the Equal Opportunity Tribunal handed down its judgement. The Hellenic Council lost. In dismissing the complaint, the tribunal found that

> *... the Macedonian Youth Association showed that they had an honest belief in the statements within the article, and believed the article itself to be a reasonable response to what had already been published by the Greek community. The Tribunal accepts this submission and finds that the public act was done reasonably and in good faith, for academic and research purposes and for*

other purposes in the public interest, including discussion and debate about the Macedonian issue.

Freedom of speech may have won in this case, but the matter had dragged through the system for five years and four months. It cost the respondents $15 000 and the Australian taxpayers much more than that. It revealed the weaknesses of the anti-discrimination, equal opportunity and racial vilification legislation.

The great majority of Australians do not care about the arguments raised in this case. What they do care about is any meddling in Australian domestic politics by foreign governments. They do care about free speech, and they do care about having to pay thousands of dollars to subsidise ancient alien disputes such as this case, which managed to portray one of Australia's most successful migrant groups—a smart, educated, diverse, entrepreneurial community—as if it were a foreign enclave whose heart is 10 000 kilometres from home.

10
THE VOTE EATERS

AUSTRALIA'S FIRST assassination of a political figure occurred at 9.30 on the night of 5 September 1994, when a member of the New South Wales Parliament, John Newman, was murdered at his home in western Sydney.

Newman had been warned. A Labor member of the New South Wales Lower House he had been campaigning against the burgeoning Cabramatta drug market since his election to State Parliament in 1986. Death threats started in 1991, followed by a bullet through the window of his electoral office. A warning was left on his answering machine: 'You dead, Newman. We kill you.' The voice had a heavy Vietnamese accent. The brazenness of the warnings increased. Newman's car was splashed with white paint, a standard warning. On the night he was killed, he was in the driveway of his home, putting a cover over his car to prevent further paint daubings.

He was shot twice in the chest at close range. The murder was carried out in front of his fiancée, Lucy Wang. After an investigation lasting three years and a coroner's inquiry, on Friday, 13 March 1998, three men were charged with Newman's murder. One of them was the most well-known member of the Vietnamese community in New South Wales, Phuong Ngo, a local councillor and operator of the Mekong

Club in Cabramatta. The other two men charged with murder, Tuan Van Tran and Quang Dao, were both associates of Ngo and worked for him at the Mekong Club.

Phuong Ngo had come to Australia as a Vietnamese boat refugee in 1982. Five years later he became the first Vietnamese to win political office in Australia when he was elected to Fairfield City Council. Over time, he developed a fierce political rivalry with John Newman, the state parliamentarian whose electorate included Cabramatta. Ngo wanted to enter Parliament. Newman wanted to destroy his career.

The trial of Phuong Ngo, Tuan Van Tran and Quang Dao had not begun when this book went to press and there is a huge difference between being accused and convicted.

The assassination of a political figure is a frontal assault on the democratic system and Australia had been miraculously free of such an assault throughout its democratic evolution. Newman's killing may prove to be a political aberration, but a more insidious assault on the democratic system—electoral fraud—was also carried out that same year by Vietnamese and their Australian allies inside the union movement. The election fraud took place, ominously, inside the major mail centres, which have predominantly immigrant workforces, especially Vietnamese and Filipino.

More than 1000 workers had their votes manipulated or improperly gave their ballot papers to fixers. It was a major fraud. A key element in the rorting of the system was ethnic politics, specifically the manipulation of workers with poor

English skills who were culturally susceptible to pressure from ethnic group leaders. Prominent among the people who illegally collected blank ballots and intimidated voters were a group of Asian fixers. The Australian Federal Police obtained the names of a number of those believed to be responsible for illegal vote gathering, and many of them were Vietnamese. But the police were not brought into the case until long after the events. None of the fixers was ever prosecuted or reprimanded.

The year 1994 was not a good one for grassroots democracy in Australia. Not only was John Newman assassinated, but the election for the postal workers branch of the Communications Electrical Plumbing Union (CEPU) was found to be so tainted that it was declared void after a court challenge before Justice Michael Moore of the Industrial Relations Court of Australia. The electoral irregularities took place within a culture of bureaucratic inertia that worked to the advantage of the then federal Labor government, which was aligned with the same Right faction controlling the CEPU.

Justice Moore expressed dismay at the problems which escaped the notice of Australia Post, the Australian Electoral Commission and the investigating arms of the government.

In fact, of all the hundreds of union elections that took place during all the years of Labor government, I was not able to find evidence of a single prosecution for union election manipulations.

Control of the postal workers union has always been one of the prizes of intra-Labor fighting. Control translates into

Labor Party delegates and factional power in Cabinet or Shadow Cabinet. For political zealots, political power in mail centres means some degree of potential influence, however small, in all elections.

Australians believe their basic institutions, like the postal system, are free of political influence. They are not. They are, and always have been, a one-party state. It is revealing to see what befell the two men who, through their court challenge to the 1994 election, successfully revealed the scandal.

One of them was an ordinary postman, Quentin Cook, working in the Blue Mountains west of Sydney. In the midst of what would prove to be a successful court challenge that would eventually lead to reforms of the entire Australian system of industrial elections, Quentin Cook was sacked by Australia Post. Cook was handed his dismissal papers in front of his family, at the front door of his home. The reason given was 'insubordination'. He continued to fight his election court case but, broke, living on debt and his wife's earnings and no longer employed by Australia Post, he could not afford his union dues for several months. When the new election was held in 1996 to replace the one he helped overturn, he was barred from standing for office by the Australian Electoral Commission because he had been an unfinancial member for several months. So the man who helped expose the tainted election was barred from standing in the new one.

Cook sued Australia Post for unfair dismissal and won a delayed but emphatic victory. Judicial Registrar Joan Locke, in her 1997 judgement, scorched Australia Post management:

The response was so out of proportion, ill-founded, unjust and illogical that by independent, objective standards it was tantamount to capriciousness and spitefulness.

The other key figure in exposing this fraud was a veteran and colourful union organiser, Noel Battese, also known as 'Cementhead'. He, too, would be abused for his role in the affair, this time in federal Parliament. At 7.20 p.m. on 12 September 1996, Senator Stephen Conroy, a member of the Labor Right faction in Victoria, also a former official of the Transport Workers' Union and a key figure in the Victorian branch-stacking wars, stood in Parliament and began defaming Noel Battese:

Justice Moore has exposed that supporters of the Cook-Battese team were involved in electoral fraud. Was there any indication of who might have been involved with this? ... A member of the Cook-Battese team has pointed directly at who is responsible. Yet Battese is the instigator of the challenge to the election on the grounds of electoral fraud. One of his own team has given him up.

Senator Conroy knew, or should have known, that the judge, while making no finding as to who might be responsible, had noted that the faction which controlled the union, the Labor Right, Conroy's faction, was overwhelmingly the beneficiary of the tampered ballots. Senator Conroy made his speech on the eve of the new union election campaign, the one held to replace the rorted election. Within twenty-four hours of his speech, thousands of copies of the Hansard record were printed and distributed anonymously around the mail centres under the heading 'The Cheat Team'. A second version of the speech was printed in Vietnamese.

Noel Battese challenged Senator Conroy to repeat his claims outside the Senate.

Silence.

Another member of the Right faction, Leo McLeay, swung into action on 31 October 1996. Mr McLeay's most famous episode in a long parliamentary career is receiving $60000 in taxpayer-funded compensation for falling off his bicycle. McLeay stood in the House of Representatives and repeated the same attack on Noel Battese that Senator Conroy had made in the Senate the previous month.

At least the matter was given an airing in Parliament by the Minister for Workplace Relations, Peter Reith, on 11 September 1996.

> MR REITH: *The electoral fraud consisted of multiple voting by a limited number of persons. The court found that members of the union had been approached by other members to hand over their uncompleted ballot papers, which had been completed by a limited number of other persons ... In all, some 930 ballot papers were tampered with in this fraudulent election.*
>
> MR [JOHN] HOWARD: *Any motorbikes?*

MR REITH: *All in good time, Prime Minister. The court ordered a new election ... The [CEPU] is a big union. It has 187 000 members. The relationship between the former government and this union is on the public record. For example, in 1992–93 the former Labor government granted to this union $100 000 directly and in return the CEPU donated to the ALP $140 000.*

—*Opposition members interjecting*—

MR REITH: *We have got plenty of time. The last point to be made is that the CEPU has been run by the New South Wales Right, and of course there are close links between some of the leading affiliated unions in the New South Wales Right and current members of this House, including former ministers for communications, including the member for Dobell, and there are others who may similarly be named. We are concerned about these matters, and investigations are under way.*

The federal police encountered a wall of silence. When they interviewed one CEPU official whose handwriting had been identified by a forensic expert, he arrived for the interview accompanied by a junior barrister, a solicitor and a QC. He then declined to make a statement. When a TV crew went to the CEPU office, officials hid from view.

By the time a vigorous examination of the CEPU election rort was finally conducted, the trail had gone cold. The union official who police believe helped organise the rort, Jalal Natour, had died of a brain haemorrhage. He was buried with full honours in 1995, and his funeral was attended by a long list of dignitaries from the Labor Right, including a federal minister.

But a window had been opened. The public inquiries into the Newman assassination and the CEPU election revealed some of the extent and the interconnectedness of the branch-stacking, vote-rigging and ethnic vote-trading operations inside Labor politics. At one point in the coronial inquiry into John Newman's murder, after repeated testimony about relentless ethnic branch stacking by both Newman and his rival, Phuong Ngo, the coroner, Jan Stevenson, asked, does talent have anything to do with succeeding in the ALP?

The inquiry revealed that on the day Newman was shot, Phuong Ngo had lunched with John Della Bosca, general secretary of the NSW Labor Party, and a union official, Jalal Natour (who would later come to the attention of police over CEPU election irregularities).

No-one has ever suggested Della Bosca is even remotely connected with the Newman murder. But the investigation into Newman's death did reveal many links between the New South Wales Right, which Della Bosca heads, and ethnic politics in the ALP. All three of the men charged with Newman's murder were ALP members. All were nominally members of the Right faction. Two of them had run for office under the Right's ticket.

The luncheon came to light during police evidence before the coronial inquiry. Phuong Ngo was first interviewed by police on 14 September 1994, nine days after the murder. Two detectives were waiting at Sydney Airport when he returned from a trip to Taiwan. That same day, Ngo gave a two-hour videotaped interview to police, which was later played during the coronial inquiry in February, 1998.

Asked about his movements on 5 September 1994, Ngo told the detectives he had spent most of the day at his office at Cabramatta. 'I left to have lunch in the city with the Labor Party people.'

Where?

'At a Chinese restaurant in Chinatown.'

Who with?

'John Della Bosca.'

Who is he?

'General Secretary of the Labor Party.'

Who else?

'Jalal Natour, assistant secretary of the Communication Workers Union [now part of the CEPU].'

Anyone else?

'Just the three of us.'

Why did you meet?

'I helped the union, which had just had an election and many members of that union were Vietnamese, working in the mail centres. I helped them in campaigning for their ticket, through my newspapers, and through my community connections. And they got elected, so we had lunch to thank me for my help for the union."

This election was the same one later voided during the inquiry by Justice Moore.

It was not the first time officials involved in this election had been embroiled in controversy and it would not be the last. In April 1998, accusations began flying in a preselection battle that was wild even by the standards of the ALP. The battle was for Lindsay, a crucial marginal federal seat on the western edge of Sydney. I received thirty-five pages of leaked ALP letters, memos and statutory declarations which portrayed the Lindsay preselection as a farce. There were phantom meetings, phantom members, an entire phantom branch, missing minutes, questionable records and standard branch stacking.

A dozen people signed statutory declarations alleging manipulation of the preselection process. Some of the allegations smelled. Literally. Statements referred to the smell of glue. *'It was clear the pages had only a short time before been pasted into the book. I felt the pages and the paper where the glue had been applied was still damp and there was a distinct odour of wet paste.'* The glue was used to insert pages into minute books, such as lists of new members and alleged meetings.

Those accused of the manipulations were CEPU officials of the same Right faction which won the controversial 1994 election. Once again, a large number of Asians were involved on behalf of the faction, mostly Filipinos, including many rank-and-file members of the CEPU. Formal challenges were made at the NSW Labor headquarters, but they were voted down on factional lines by the Right.

It was a skirmish in a generalised factional war which saw an estimated 8 000 names added to the ALP's membership lists in a single year after new rules were pushed through by the Right at the 1996 ALP state conference. The stacking wars were concentrated in the south-west of Sydney, the area of heavy unskilled, non-English-speaking migration. The rules were later tightened when the branch stacking veered out of control, but the 8 000 new names, most of them stacked, were allowed to stay.

In Melbourne, it was almost the same, and the extent of the problem was exposed by reporter Paul Ransley and the Channel 9 network's *Sunday* program, which spent months investigating the story. Predictably, as it was nearing completion, a warning was sent on 23 April 1998, by the State Secretary of the Victorian ALP, John Lenders:

> *Based on the information we have received, your program is in danger of stepping over the line of professional journalism. It has certainly created the perception within some ALP branches that it is acting in a politically biased, if not racist, way and the ALP State Office has been asked to consider whether there have been breaches of racial discrimination or privacy laws.*

The *Sunday* program ignored this hoary threat, which had been used for years as an intimidatory tactic by the ALP and its surrogates. The story went to air loaded with hard detail:

> **Dean Mighell, Victorian State Secretary, Electrical Trades Union:** *Bus loads or car loads of ethnic, non-English-speaking people were basically driven or bused into the centre and an arm would go around the person by their leader or one of their peers and they'd be escorted in to be shown how to vote the right way.*

AMONG THE BARBARIANS

Graham Hudson—political science lecturer [and Melbourne University doctoral student]: *Five thousand dollars can buy you a seat. That buys you I think about three-hundred members if that's the game you're in ... Head office of the Labor Party did a survey of the memberships and it may well be that about thirty percent of branch members in Victoria do not pay their own dues.*

Eddie Micallef, Victorian MP: *When I tried to door knock some of them with some Cambodian-speaking people, they said they had been visited by a member of the Cambodian Association and given their orders on how to vote.*

Statutory declaration by a Salvation Army worker: *I found it was common knowledge that people approaching the Cambodian Association for welfare assistance would be expected to join the ALP.*

The program went for an hour, fact after fact, and Senator Stephen Conroy cropped up again, introduced as 'the key numbers man on the [Right] ... We have no evidence to suggest Conroy is directly involved in some of the questionable ethnic branch-stacking practices but he has certainly been a man who has worked hard, behind the scenes, to establish the Right's dominance in Victoria.' Senator Conroy did not stay behind the scenes when the CEPU was having trouble with its elections up in New South Wales. He used parliamentary privilege to tip a bucket of abuse on the two men who had exposed the election rorts.

THE VOTE EATERS

An increasing number of Labor politicians have begun to question this style of warfare and its effect on the character and intrinsic values of the party. After Labor's defeat in the 1998 federal election, Gary Johns, a former minister in the Keating government, described a structural fault line that had emerged inside Labor:

> *Labor branch numbers ... are overwhelmingly middle-class. If not middle-class, then they are stacked with people who cannot speak English and whose support is traded among factional leaders for preselection. Is Labor's special responsibility for the working class, or its new support from the middle class, proving too great a divide? The wonder is that it has kept the show together so successfully for so long.*

Johns thus joined a growing list of former and current Labor politicians—Mark Latham, Peter Walsh, Graham Richardson, Laurie Ferguson, Rod Cavalier—openly questioning Labor's grass roots value system, a system whose flaws were revealed in the 1998 federal election campaign when Labor lost crucial marginal seats.

There was bad news in the marginal seats in the two great battlefields of Sydney and Melbourne. Among the worst news was up in Robertson, on the coast above Sydney. Despite a big infusion of funds, despite Kim Beazley promising fifty million dollars for local freeway development, and Premier Bob Carr announcing a twenty-four million dollar sports complex, and heavy radio spending, and a blizzard of mailings, plus the support of a local newspaper in which John

Della Bosca is an investor and director, and despite the great advantage of the GST bogy—*You will pay a GST on your train fare*—the Liberals held this marginal coastal seat, defeating the more heavily-financed Labor candidate, Belinda Neal, who just happens to be the wife of John Della Bosca.

After the election, the dean of the Canberra press gallery, Alan Ramsey, surveyed the battlefield and thundered:

> *Reality will not be long in coming.*
>
> *It has arrived already for the faction-ridden State ALP machines of both New South Wales and Victoria ...* [which] *delivered a pathetic five or six seat gain between them ...*
>
> *The recrimination will be fierce, particularly in New South Wales. While both state machines are now little better than crude factional patronage operations for head office loyalists, their poor campaign discipline and professionalism has not previously been so thoroughly exposed.*

Among those exposed were the branch-stacking, glue-sticking factional operators who had delivered preselection in the seat of Lindsay to the partner of a CEPU official. If Labor could not win Lindsay, which only needed a 1.6 percent swing to fall, then Labor could not win the election.

And they couldn't do it. In the midst of a national swing to Labor, and widespread fear of a GST, the factional warriors from the CEPU could not get even one percent of the electorate to switch their vote to Labor.

PART THREE

'People need to see how their tax dollars are being pilfered on an enormous scale—every conceivable rort and deception is used to beat the system. Medicare rorts, dealing in prescription drugs, obtaining multiple identity papers, milking the social security system, even stealing electricity.'
New South Wales Police Commander

11
STRIP MINING

DR RICHARD BASHAM seems normal. He is not. He deals with murder, blackmail, organised crime, gangs, prostitution, human smuggling, immigration fraud, tax evasion, welfare abuse and racism. Strange, because Dr Basham is a teacher, with an office on the lovely main quadrangle at Sydney University. He gives classes, marks students' papers, attends committee meetings. He is the former head of the Department of Anthropology at Sydney University. But Richard Basham leads a double life. He spends a lot of time talking to cops. He is one of Australia's leading authorities on the links between crime and culture. He advises the New South Wales Police Commissioner.

He is also worried.

Organised crime, drugs, gangs, extortion, tax evasion, fraud, these have now reached a level where they are damaging the national economy. What has happened at Cabramatta is just the tip of the iceberg, but it often seems that anyone who dares to talk about Asian crime in this country is shouted down as a racist.

Richard Basham lives at an interesting cultural intersection. He speaks Thai and teaches courses on South-East Asian societies. He is an immigrant to Australia and an advocate of Asian immigration, yet he investigates abuses of the system by immigrants. He is an academic anthropologist, yet has deep knowledge of crime and corruption. He is American but has spent the bulk of his career in Asia and Australia. He has a Thai wife and a Eurasian daughter, both now Australian citizens, and both have experienced racial prejudice. Even so, he is passionately opposed to using race as a tool for political censorship:

> *Racial prejudice against Asians in Australia is real. It hurts. My own wife has experienced it. But to use charges of racism as a moral skewer to silence discussion of ethnic-based crime is arrogant and, ultimately, dangerous. Censorship has divided this country. All crime has its cultural base and it is foolish to pretend, for example, that Asians don't dominate the hard drug trade in Australia.*

The police agree with him. 'Australia has never had anything like Cabramatta before,' one New South Wales police commander told me, requesting anonymity. 'The gangs have got guns, and the violence within the Indo-Chinese community is noticeably higher than in other communities. They are very confronting. European-style cops do not represent much of a threat ... Cabramatta has the highest homicide rate in Australia. It has the highest number of foot soldiers in the drug trade. It has the largest number of people who die in the streets from heroin overdoses. It has the highest concentration of cases of hepatitis C. It has the highest incidence of drug-related arrests. Fifty-seven percent of drug-related arrests in New South Wales are Indo-Chinese ... Cabramatta is the largest retail outlet for heroin in Australia. Nothing competes with it ... People go to Cabramatta because it is the purest dope. It can be cut [diluted and on-sold]. Roughly two-thirds of the drug abusers also deal. They come to Cabramatta in taxis to pick up stocks ... We arrest them, and they are soon back on the streets ... When security cameras went into Cabramatta, we discovered street-level violence—bag-snatching, drug-dealing, assaults, and multiple heroin deals—were far worse than we had realised. A real eye-opener.'

Cabramatta is the extreme, but many of the same characteristics are evident on a smaller scale in pockets of the west and south-west of Sydney. In Melbourne, the heavy concentration of Vietnamese in Springvale was followed, as in Sydney, with this enclave also becoming a drug centre. Vietnamese gang activity has now spread from Springvale, Footscray and Richmond to parts of at least eight other Melbourne suburbs, and continues to spread.

Cabramatta and Springvale became the focus of the urban drug trade not because many of the Vietnamese who congregated there were criminals—exactly the opposite is true—but because poor bureaucratic oversight had allowed many hardened criminals into the country among the inflow of Vietnamese refugees after the Vietnam War. Hundreds of criminals arrived. They formed the original Cabramatta gangs, and the 5T gang was the prototype. The five Ts stand for *tinh* (love/sex), *tien* (money), *tu* (prison), *tu* (death) and *toi* (criminal convictions). Over time, the 5T gang was gradually worn down, but Vietnamese have emulated the gang style. 'Once the Vietnamese learned the networking originally used by the Chinese they just replicated it,' the commander told me. 'The Vietnamese have now supplanted the Chinese in retailing. They took over by offering the highest quality at the best price.' Increasingly, Vietnamese drug importers are also cutting out the Chinese wholesalers, importing heroin through Vietnam in vertically integrated operations.

Each year, between 2000 and 3000 kilograms of heroin are sold and consumed in Australia, and most of it goes undetected. 'We're only getting about ten percent or a little less,' said Peter Lamb of the National Crime Authority, adding that police seize about 220 kilograms of heroin a year. While Vietnam has emerged as a major transhipment route for heroin to Australia, Vietnamese authorities have offered little cooperation because of a mixture of incompetence, corruption and lack of resources. The ethnic Chinese remain the big money players. 'The major heroin dealers are in Chinatown,' said Federal Agent Ray Tinker of the Asian Organised Crime Group. 'Cabramatta is the end of the chain. The major heroin dealers are in Chinatown because that's where all the orders and brokers are. The amounts that are dealt with down there leave Cabramatta for dead.'

'Organised crime in Australia is different to the traditional Mafia-style where you're in a permanent family arrangement,' said Assistant New South Wales Police Commissioner Clive Small. 'Groups do their own thing but come together when it's mutually of benefit to them.' The new Asian crime operations follow the lead established by traditional Australian criminals, a loose group of mainly Australian-born criminals which the National Crime Authority calls the 'East Coast Milieu'. The backdrop to all this is a disturbing upward curve in crime in Australia, particularly violent crime. In her 1997 study *Rising Crime in Australia*, Lucy Sullivan gives the problem its historical perspective:

> *Violent crime more than doubled between 1981–82 and 1993, and increased by a factor of seven, or seven-hundred percent, between 1964 and 1993, attesting to the accuracy of public perceptions of the growth in, and people's growing fear of, personal violence ...*
>
> *Our penal system, also overtaken by the escalation in crime, has allowed the 'economic' rewards of crime to rise markedly.*

Gang crime is Australia's biggest criminal growth area. The arrest of Chinese and Vietnamese for heroin importation has become routine. Typical—it was a minor news item—were the arrests made on 19 December 1997 after raids by police on several Sydney homes yielded 21 kilograms of heroin with a street value of around thirty-two million dollars. All those arrested in possession of the heroin were Chinese. One of those arrested came to Australia from China as a political refugee. He was unemployed and had been receiving government welfare benefits.

'Let's not deceive ourselves,' the New South Wales police commander told me. 'It does not help or serve the victims of Asian crime when we are not frank with our problems. The overwhelming majority of victims of Asian crime are Asians. Yet a lot of the decision-makers in this state are intimidated by the issue.'

It is not difficult to see why. The New South Wales Police Commissioner, Peter Ryan, was set upon by the Thought Police when he dared to wander into the no-go area of ethnicity and crime. Commissioner Ryan's sin was to make the following remark in an interview with a British police magazine:

> *Here* [in Australia], *the crime is partly Lebanese-based, partly from the old Soviet Union, Hong Kong, Vietnam and China.*

The political pain was immediate and it was personal. 'I am disgusted, I am not happy at all,' responded Helen Sham-Ho, a Liberal member of the New South Wales Upper House. 'For the past eight years I've been trying to persuade police not to identify even suspects by race. Now the top man in the force comes and reverts back to the old ways ... You have to back up claims with evidence.'

Franca Arena, a Labor member of the same Upper House, called the Commissioner's remarks 'pathetic'.

Angela Chan, a spokeswoman for the Federation of Ethnic Community Councils of Australia, said the Police Commissioner's comment 'stereotypes people as criminals on the ground of race and in today's climate, with all this anti-Asian sentiment and racism debate going on, it just adds fuel to the fire'.

In the wake of these and other public rebukes, Commissioner Ryan and the police went quiet on the issue of ethnic crime. Dr Basham regards this climate of censorship as dangerous:

> *The charge of racism is being used to suppress information. The comfort level of Asian criminals in Australia is now very high. It is almost as if they have political protection. This imposed silence is one of the reasons why Australia now has Pauline Hanson. Australians have to realise that attempting to cope with crime among people living in different cultural worlds without trying to understand those worlds is not only foolish but a waste of resources. What is unacceptable practice in Australia can be regarded as acceptable in much of Asia. Common violations of Australian law, such as tax evasion, immigration abuse and money laundering, are often not really viewed as criminal at all. This extends to bonded servitude, which is found in China, Thailand, Cambodia and Burma.*

In a 1997 graduation speech at Bond University, delivered before a large audience including many Asian students and their families, Basham praised the self-evident vitality that Asian immigration has brought to Australia but also challenged those in the media who were exploiting Pauline Hanson while expressing outrage about her:

> *In contrast to Australia, no Asian society genuinely prohibits racial discrimination in immigration or before the law. Indeed, racial discrimination is so deeply imbedded in the moral premises of Asian societies that it often goes*

> *unnoticed. While someone of Asian ancestry who is born in Australia can expect citizenship, the same cannot be said for someone of Caucasian ancestry born in Malaysia or Japan.*

This is not the sort of stuff that usually comes out of Australian universities. Richard Basham's personal world has seen too much struggle between life and death in recent years for him to care about political convenience. For a decade he watched his wife slowly dying.

> *We had ten years living under a death sentence; it changes the way you live your life. My wife, Charoen, was diagnosed with leukaemia in 1981. It was chronic myeloid leukaemia, for which there was no cure. The average survival rate was three-and-a-half years. All the other people who were diagnosed at the same time have died.*

Today, Charoen is alive and well.

> *We don't know how she lived so long until the technology existed to cure her. But she took a Buddhist response. She wasn't afraid of death. She hung on until new drugs were invented which permitted her to undergo a bone-marrow transplant using marrow from her sister, who did not even have the same blood type. At that time, no operation involving such a mismatch had been successful in Australia. The odds were bad. But the doctors gave their all for her.*

STRIP MINING

By the time Charoen Basham was out of danger, Richard Basham had stripped his own life down to the fundamentals.

He knew there were big problems with Australia's immigration program and he wasn't going to be intimidated by politicians and political activists with racial agendas. Because his web of contacts and experience allowed him to see not merely the vitality and talent that Asian immigration is bringing but also the problems seeping into Australia from countries where corruption is endemic, Basham became much more active in his work with the police, helped by a doctorate in psychological anthropology from the University of California, Berkeley, and expertise in cultural psychology, inter-ethnic relations, Asian business practices, and the cultural elements of organised crime.

From this vantage point Basham believes one of the greatest threats to Australia's long-term stability is complacency about the rise of international crime syndicates, the dark side of capitalism's rise in Asia and the former Soviet Union. He sees the rise of these syndicates as afflicting the entire region.

Police intelligence believes the Hong Kong triads are diversifying beyond heroin, gambling and protection rackets into food importation and property portfolios.

Home invasions, almost unknown in Australia prior to the arrival of triads and criminals hidden among the legitimate refugees from Vietnam, are occurring in Sydney at a rate of three a week, according to the Bureau of Crime Statistics and Research. An unknown number of home invasions go unreported. An attempt by New South Wales police to break the code of silence in the Asian community was met with only limited success. 'Home invasions and extortion are real barometers of Asian crime in Sydney and if they are going up we are in for trouble,' said Dr Basham. 'If they are left unchecked, then kidnappings become more common. If police cannot provide protection against home invasions and kidnappings, then people will seek out those who can.'

Gang crime, modelled on the triads, has penetrated the schools. 'There have been numerous instances of extortion attempts involving Asian school children,' said Detective-Inspector Tom Sharp, who ran the Oak Investigation Unit into Asian organised crime. 'It's happening at a lot of schools. We have had some prosecutions ... Some people have paid up, and some people have withdrawn their children from school in Australia ... We always have a lot of trouble finding people to come forward in all crimes.'

Many of those targeted have been from Hong Kong, where the most wealth is generated and where most expatriate children are from. Triad-style influence is evident in the recurrence of the number 36, a traditional triad number, in school extortions. 'If they say 36, they mean $360, if they say 360, they mean $3600,' said Inspector Sharp. 'The triad traditions have mostly gone, but the numbers have carried on. The leader is the 489, the "dragonhead". His deputy is 438. The fighters are 426. The messengers are 432. The chief of staff is 415. The number four means death.'

Asian organised crime is so widespread it has even replicated elements of the coastal piracy practised in South-East Asia. Vietnamese gangs are operating a large-scale black market trade in abalone, a shellfish delicacy highly prized in Asia and now being poached from Australian waters.

Richard Basham sees all this as part of the evolution of what he calls 'parallel moral universes' in Australia. 'I have spoken to so many Australian businessmen who are just stunned when their supposed Asian partners have robbed them blind. In my business consultancy I tell companies they should forget about signing contracts at first, they are better off with a memorandum of agreement, because in much of Asia a contract will bind the Westerner while leaving the local partner free to behave as he likes.'

Exactly the same warning is given by Reg Little and Warren Reed in their 1997 book, *The Tyranny of Fortune*. They buttress Richard Basham's argument that 'parallel moral universes' are developing in Australia. 'We don't just have a crime problem,' said Basham. 'The reality is that there are all kinds of immigration, taxation and welfare rorts in the Asian communities and a lot of them are simply seen by Asians as using the system that exists. On arrival in Australia, many immigrants, often so-called "students" from countries such as China, will be forced to work at a number of jobs to repay debts upwards of $15 000. Failure to repay will invoke serious sanctions.'

Many Australians have come to believe, wrongly, that the growing prevalence of violent and drug crime among some immigrant groups in Australia is the product of a criminal mentality. This is not true, and it is dangerously misleading. There are a number of logical antecedents for crime problems among immigrant groups:

AMONG THE BARBARIANS

(1) Geography. The Golden Triangle lies between southern China and Indo-China. If the remote mountainous opium fields lay in Australia, native-born Aussies would no doubt be lining up for a piece of the enormous profits.

(2) History. Triads and triad-style groups have an ancient history in Chinese communities and in some ways evolved to fill the role filled by the police in Western society. Although this role mutated into crime, many protection rackets do operate as a (warped) form of police, keeping restaurants and businesses safe from other criminals.

(3) Culture. Some immigrant groups simply have a different value system to the one prevailing in Australia. This division breaks down with the second generation.

(4) Familiarity. The people who suffer most from immigrant crime are other immigrants from the same ethnic group, especially business operators. They are the ones robbed and extorted.

(5) Politics. The Immigration Department, under political pressure from the multicultural industry, has allowed criminals and parasites into the country by the thousands. Abuse of the immigration system has been integral to the penetration of Australia by criminal groups. 'The Family Reunion Program has been widely abused, and the Migrant Business Program has been widely abused,' says a Chinese adviser to the Asian Organised Crime Unit set up in 1997. 'To get a business visa, many people took loans and paid them back after they came to Australia. Gangsters came into Australia this way. Of course, they had access to plenty of money.'

(6) Inadequate police resources. 'The thing about the Viet-

namese criminals who came as refugees is that they quickly understood that Australian law can't really touch them,' said Richard Basham. 'So the payment of protection money in Cabramatta has become so routine that it's almost ritualised.'

As long ago as 1988, Carmel Chow, senior investigator with the National Crime Authority, said that Chinese 'triads' had a near monopoly on heroin importation into Australia. He also said Hong Kong police expected many triad members to migrate to Australia in the decade prior to the Chinese takeover in 1997. He was proved right.

In the real world, it is a fact that one of the engines of growth in crime in Australia is the high levels of crime among some immigrant groups. In New South Wales, the state with by far the most immigrants, as well as a raging crime problem among young Aborigines, assaults surged up to twenty-six percent in 1996, accounting for most of the national increase. Break-ins were up twelve percent, three times the national average. The problem is particularly acute among young Indo-Chinese, mostly Vietnamese, whose numbers in the prison and juvenile detention systems rose dramatically in the 1990s.

When I compared statistics from two very different New South Wales government documents—the 1996 green paper, *Building on our Cultural Diversity*, and the 1996 *New South Wales Inmate Census*—I found that the Vietnamese-born prison population was between three and four times over-represented compared with the per capita Vietnamese population in the state. The strong anecdotal evidence from police of heavy Lebanese and Turkish involvement in the illegal drug trade was also borne out by these statistics. The proportion of Lebanese-born prisoners was double the per capita Lebanese-born population. Turkish-born prisoners were also doubly represented, per capita, although their number was small. Drug arrests accounted for most of the Lebanese, Turkish and Vietnamese in the system. Other sharp disparities showed up in the per capita representation of various immigrant groups. New Zealanders, for example, were over-represented on a per capita basis.

One disastrous by-product of the heroin abundance was the rapid spread through already vulnerable Aboriginal communities after young Aborigines in juvenile detention centres mixed with young Vietnamese gang members. Aborigines were once rarely seen in the Cabramatta hard drug market, but that changed. Detective-Sergeant Debbie Wallace of the Cabramatta police watched it happen. 'We are seeing a lot of Aborigines in Cabra now, and we never used to see them here.'

An anthropologist who spent years studying the heroin subculture, Dr Lisa Maher, foresees enormous costs to the health care system. Dr Maher found that patterns of teenage addiction began with smoking heroin in cigarettes or cannabis but progressed to addiction and injecting within three months. She found about forty percent of young addicts were females. She also found most heroin dealers were heroin users. Another disastrous by-product has been the flowering of gang culture based in immigrant communities with extremely high unemployment and low English-language skills.

STRIP MINING

It takes courage to raise, as Richard Basham does, the issue of widespread abuse of the immigration and welfare systems in Australia because anyone who does so in the past has routinely been vilified as a racist. Dr Basham, clearly, is not a racist. 'It is interesting to see how many people fail to make a distinction between criticism and racism,' he says. A growing number of people are voicing informed concern about what amounts to the strip mining of Australia.

'The problems have been exacerbated by silence,' says Basham. Intercepting criminals at Australian airports has been made more difficult since the rules were changed preventing immigration officers from selecting incoming passengers at random. An exasperated secretary of the Australian Federal Police Association, George Nichols, says the practice of random searches was stopped 'because certain groups started claiming they were being victimised'.

'We have our heads in the sand,' says Mark Craig, a former intelligence analyst with the Queensland police who at the time of publication was being eased out of the force for his outspoken views:

The Immigration Department suppresses certain issues. The human smuggling trade is very big, much bigger than people realise. Immigration also doesn't like to talk about which provinces in China the overstayers come from. In most cases, it is Fujian.

Craig said a boatload of 139 illegal Chinese entrants was picked up in Queensland and nobody from the Immigration

Department called the police. 'They were all from Fujian. They all had Queensland driver's licences. We didn't get a call. It was an immigration matter. They sent 135 of them home, and kept four. They spent $360 000 flying them to Port Hedland. And they didn't get any information out of the entire group.'

On 14 October 1998, on an obscure beach near Port Macquarie on the north coast of New South Wales, police intercepted a heavily-laden boat wallowing in the surf. They removed thirty-one bags, each weighing 14 kilograms, each filled with 700 gram blocks known as 'Thai units', of high-grade heroin. They also recovered a Glock semi-automatic pistol. The 434 kilograms of China white was by far the biggest drugs seizure and by far the most valuable illicit cargo ever seized in Australia. Federal Police Commissioner Mick Palmer said the heroin was enough, when cut for street sales, for twenty million sales worth about four hundred million dollars.

The boat had come onto the beach from a mothership, the *Uniana*, standing offshore. The *Uniana* operated out of China and Hong Kong. After police and customs officers boarded the 40 metre *Uniana* and arrested the eighteen crew members, it was found that the ship, which on the outside was an old, scrubby coastal freighter, was fitted with new engines, huge additional fuel tanks for long range, a steel hatch to conceal the delivery boat, and a hidden steel hatch large enough to conceal half a tonne of heroin. The *Uniana* was a drug ship, and it had been making regular visits to Australia for several years. Because heroin has a shelf-life of about six months, the raw opium pulp would have been processed to order before being trucked to port. The drugs were loaded in China or Burma.

Four men, all from Hong Kong, were arrested near the beach rendezvous on the New South Wales coast. Hong Kong police, who had given the original tip-off that led to the operation, raided six addresses in Hong Kong. The head of the police sting operation, Federal Agent Ray Tinker, said the shipment had been organised by a crime group operating from Hong Kong, China and Sydney. The amount of potential street heroin intercepted was so valuable that police were concerned the interruption to supply might flow through to higher street prices and greater property crime. They were also concerned the flow of heroin into Sydney was so great the seizure might make no difference at all.

'Australia really needs to wake up to what is going on,' says Richard Basham. 'I'm very much in favour of Asian immigration, which I think has enhanced the texture of Australian life, but we need to select carefully the people we are taking in.' He regards curbing abuses as important to preserving an open immigration system and preserving Australia's proven cultural commitment to equality, which he believes has been dragged through the mud by the Australian media. Like all courageous people, he refuses to wallow. He concluded his 1997 graduation speech at Bond University with these words:

> *Far from being pessimistic about Australia's racial future, I hold out great hope for it. I cannot but be*

reminded of my family's return to Australia from a trip to Thailand late one night in January. Exhausted, the three of us, my Thai-born wife, my Eurasian, Australian-born teenage daughter, and I, with my distinctive American accent, approached the immigration officer and handed him our passports. After stamping them, he handed them back to us with a warm and genuine smile and said, 'Welcome home.'

RICO

The resource gulf between police and drug traffickers is growing, not narrowing. The drug trade generates so much cash that dealers can buy sophisticated electronic equipment and discard cellular phones like wrapping paper. Police surveillance is becoming increasingly difficult.

But there is a powerful American weapon that could be adapted: the Racketeer Influenced and Corrupt Organization Act, known as RICO. The groups that would most fear RICO's arrival are crime gangs and corrupt unions. The law was devised in the United States when it became obvious that existing laws had failed to stop the virulent spread of the Mafia. RICO proved a formidable tool against the Mafia, and Mafia control of the Teamsters union. It has now become the primary weapon against Asian crime syndicates.

'RICO has made a huge difference in the United States,' says Dr Richard Basham. 'The beauty of RICO is that it introduces the notion of collective responsibility for crimes to an entire criminal organisation. Since an entire gang can be charged with crimes its members commit, previously untouchable bosses go down with everybody else. So it's more difficult for gangs to intimidate informers.'

The first hint of RICO's power against the code of silence came in 1985, when twenty-seven members of the Ghost Shadows were sent to jail on charges including murder, robbery, kidnapping, extortion and running a racketeering enterprise. The Ghost Shadows had previously been the largest and most feared gang in New York's Chinatown.

Since that victory, more than a dozen major RICO prosecutions have succeeded against Asian gangs. In 1991, a single murder investigation by the Federal Bureau of Investigation led to the unravelling of the Green Dragon gang, ten of whose members were charged on thirty-six counts, including seven murders, extortion, robbery, bribery and running a racketeering organisation. Nine of the ten went to jail. The tenth, the leader of the Green Dragons, fled to China. In 1996 the former head of Tsung Tsin Association in New York, one of the largest and oldest civic associations in the Chinese diaspora, was sent to jail on RICO charges.

'Australia is going to have to do something,' says Dr Basham. 'The level of police resources to tackle organised crime is pathetic. The existing laws aren't enough.'

12
THE BIG NOWHERE

EACH JANUARY IN THE annual initiation rite when young people around Australia receive the final results of their high school careers, newspapers carry photographs of happy students who have received the ultimate result—perfect scores. One joyous front-page picture in 1997 showed some of the best new faces of Australia: Denise Lee, Johnny Wong, Sanushka Mudaliar, Philippa Webb, all Asian or Eurasian, part of a regenerative immigrant surge from Asia that the country needed and continues to need.

The impact of Asian intellectual muscle was affirmed the next day when the top 5000 Higher School Certificate results were published. The list confirmed, yet again, the role that Asian students, mostly ethnic Chinese, are playing in boosting the standards of excellence in Australian education. More than 1800 Asian names were on that list, far out of proportion with the per capita numbers of Asian-Australian students in New South Wales, by a magnitude of around five hundred percent.

The list of Asian-Australian and Asian students who topped or shared the top place in the state was a long one: Johnny Wong in Mathematics 4 Unit; Anna Lam in English 3 Unit; Louisa Chan in Mathematics 3 Unit; Vidian Choi in

AMONG THE BARBARIANS

Music (Board) 3 Unit; Kenny Chan in Physics 2 Unit; John Lee in Chemistry 2 Unit; Colin Tan in Geography 2 Unit; Sarah Cheung in Accounting 2 Unit; Raymond Lam and Saurabh Kumar in Business Studies 2 Unit; Anita Chandrasekaran in Economics 2 Unit; Ju-Lee Ooi in Agriculture 2 Unit; Po-Tsang Chui in Electronics Technology. Asian students—again, mostly ethnic Chinese—dominated several disciplines.

It was much the same again in 1998. When the list of the forty-two top students in New South Wales was released, seventeen of them—forty percent—were Asian-Australian. The two students who scored a perfect 100 on their tertiary entrance rank were Ju-Lee Ooi and Kavita Enjeti.

This is a social revolution. Asian academic success in Australia has become part of the social fabric. The large number of talented Asian school students has flowed through to disproportionate success in the university honours lists, especially in medicine, science and mathematics. Although many of these students return to their home countries, the majority of them are Australians whose high productivity has begun to flow through the system.

Australia benefited from the economic surge in Asia in the past thirty years, when East Asia accounted for the bulk of the growth of Australia's exports. The growing blends of Asian influences in Australian culture and cuisine, and the growing number of young interracial couples, are happy by-products of this evolution. A pro-Asian immigration policy is not merely the best policy for Australia, it is the only viable immigration policy.

It is important to the country's economic, cultural and moral future.

But while newspapers were showing the happy, and heavily Asian face of perfect graduation success, the front page of the *Daily Telegraph* did exactly the opposite in 1997 with a headline THE CLASS WE FAILED, and the Year 12 class picture of Mount Druitt High School, representing the bottom of the graduation success scale. Mount Druitt is a suburb named often when demographers talk about the formation of ethnic enclaves with high socio-economic problems. The *Daily Telegraph* was sued for its troubles. Lawyers donating their services argued that the front-page photo and accompanying story caused the students to be embarrassed and ashamed, and the newspaper had breached the privacy of the students. The New South Wales Teachers Federation described the story as 'appalling'. The claim for damages was denied in court.

But if someone comes first, someone also has to come last. The school system, always the front line of cultural cohesion, has shown clear signs of social stress as Australia's booming trade and cultural links with Asia, the Middle East and the South Pacific have percolated through society. A national survey of high-school teachers in 1996 found that half the teachers said immigration levels should be reduced because of high unemployment. The inflow most identified by the teachers as causing social stress came from Asia and the Middle East. Replicating the experience of France, the United Kingdom and the United States, Australia's immigrant flow in the 1980s and 1990s has brought extremes of social behaviour. At the high end, the great majority of immigrants are contributing to their new country, especially the thousands putting in the long, slogging hours of small businesses. At the low end, groups within this diverse immigrant stream are overrepresented in welfare abuse, extortion, drug importation, gang crime, marriage rackets, visa abuse, insurance fraud and tax avoidance.

'There are immigration and welfare rackets of all kinds, and some of them are organised by government officials in Asia,' says Richard Basham. 'Since the moral authority of the larger society is often rejected by Asian immigrants, and since people may have lied to its agents—in immigration, social services, and the taxation department—there is always the fear of being turned in if they cooperate with authorities. So there is a silence, an opaqueness, between the mainstream society and the Asian societies within it.' In the context of their own cultures, he says, they are merely continuing the ancient habits of self-interest, thrift, family commitments, group ties and fear of the oppressive central authorities. 'I'm very much in favour of Asian immigration, but I think our naivety is dangerous.'

David Reid resigned from the Department of Social Security because he believed the system, for political reasons, was winking at a lot of rorting by immigrants.

'The abuse is extensive, it is upsetting, I resigned on principle,' said Reid, a former determining officer handling sole-parent claims in a Sydney social security office serving a largely Vietnamese population:

> *The system is biased in favour of people who lie. Most of the people I saw were hard-working people, survivors, opportunists. But they regard the social security system as a source of income, not a safety net. When the Vietnamese claim a sole-parent benefit, the first thing they usually do is give a separate address for the wife and the husband. I have run those addresses through the computer and found up to six so-called separated husbands listed at the same address ... When they are denied benefits, they appeal. They sign statutory declarations. They back each other up. When I challenged people, they retreated behind the language barrier. This was a standard practice.*

The most extreme example he encountered was a Vietnamese family who lived in a North Vietnamese enclave in inner Sydney:

> *They were a family of seven: mother, father and five daughters. Three of the daughters had children, and two were receiving sole-parent benefits. The third daughter was on unemployment benefits. Her boyfriend was also on unemployment benefits. A fourth daughter was working in a cake shop but got paid in cash and was claiming unemployment benefits. The mother was on unemployment. The father was on unemployment. Six of the seven family members were receiving benefits. The seventh was at school. There was an industrial sewing machine in the home. It was going all the time. They all worked. The piecework was never declared as income for tax purposes.*

AMONG THE BARBARIANS

The widespread combination of unemployment benefits and illegal garment industry work is well known as an integral part of the Vietnamese black economy. The combined income from welfare payments, based on sole-parent benefits and the range of unemployment benefits extant at that time, was $1745 a fortnight. Plus the income from illegal garment industry piecework. All tax-free. Black money.

'They were all keen to get their Australian passports and get the whole scheme rolling again for their relatives,' David Reid told me.

> *The worst individual case I saw was a Vietnamese girl who was already married, in a Buddhist ceremony. She went to Vietnam and married a second man, for a fee. She brought him to Australia, and moved back with her husband. She went on unemployment benefits ... Her second husband went on the dole. After they officially split up, she applied for the single-parent benefit. On the same day she claimed the sole-parent benefit, her real husband came into the social security office with her to claim unemployment benefits.*
>
> *Another classic was a Lebanese woman who told us her husband had left her two weeks before. She got the benefit. Then she left for Lebanon. She would come back each year to maintain her single-parent benefit. She wasn't a single parent at all. Her husband was in Lebanon. She was able to keep this up for two-and-half years until she stayed away for more than a year, then came back to Australia with a return ticket to Lebanon.*

David Reid's stories are supported by other sources including, most importantly, official statistics. A Monash University researcher, Ernest Healy, pointed out in 1995 in the journal *People and Place*: 'An exploitative informal labour market based on the clothing industry, and related to social security fraud, has assumed major proportions.' The New South Wales Minister for Fair Trading, Faye Lo Po, confirms that tens of thousands of Asian immigrants are working in illegal sweatshops in the garment industry in Australia.

A common estimate of the size of the illegal garment industry is about 100 000 workers. The head of the School of Industrial Relations at the University of New South Wales, Professor Michael Quinlan, says the outworkers include children. 'It comes about,' he said, 'because they are on such low pay. They have no choice. It becomes a question of survival.'

Another former Social Security officer, an Asian woman then working as a review officer specialising in Asian clients, told me David Reid's comments were consistent with her own experiences. 'Most of the clients I see treat the system as a piggybank. They test the system for what they can get.'

If these various claims were wrong, the social security statistics would show no significant per capita variations among ethnic groups. But the official statistics do show extreme disparities. Checking David Reid's comments on Vietnamese single-parent claims, I found the latest figures available—for 1996—showed that Vietnamese-born comprised 1.8 percent of sole-parent beneficiaries, but were only 0.8 of the Australian population. The per capita discrepancy is thus more than a hundred percent. In contrast, immigrants from

Malaysia and Hong Kong put very little strain on the social security system, much less so than among people born in Australia. At the other extreme, welfare usage is endemic among immigrants from Lebanon and Turkey.

> *I never had a decision overturned by a review officer,* David Reid told me. *'Because I was an ASO-4* [Administrative Services Officer, grade 4], *I didn't have authority to look at addresses in the computer. I had to get an ASO-5 to do it. But when we ran addresses through the computer we found the same addresses coming up repeatedly ... I referred blatant cases to review officers, but I found the regional office often did not check them. Social Security cannot enter a person's home. If they make a home visit, which is rare, and the person is not there, they must leave a card requesting an interview.*

A third former Social Security officer, from Melbourne, wrote to me describing his experiences in the late 1980s:

> *Many of our files indicated that migrants of some groups had decided to come here because of the benefit payments ...*
>
> *Prosecution of some really blatant abuse of the system was discouraged in the case of some migrant groups.*

What most exasperated him, he told me, was the lack of resources or powers to attack abuse of the system, compounded by a fearfulness of accusations of discrimination when these abuses involved migrants.

The multicultural industry is particularly vigilant on the

matter of allegations of rorting among immigrant groups. All three former Social Security Officers said the department's culture was completely intimidated by accusations of discrimination. 'If we push too hard in Cabramatta, they go to the welfare rights people,' said the former review officer.

> *Our officers used to live in terror of the Welfare Rights Centre,* said Reid. *The Welfare Rights Centre automatically assumes the recipient is always right and we are discriminating against them ... Local staff are not supposed to imply that any particular ethnic group are disproportionately accessing the system. The department discourages the compilation of such statistics, saying it breaches the nondiscriminatory ethic of the department.*

The Department of Social Security confirms this. 'We select people for examination on the basis of risk factors, not ethnicity,' said a spokesperson. The department does, however, practise active discrimination in other ways. Its staff is carefully divided, in accordance with the equal opportunity-mandated categories, into 'PWD' (People With Disabilities), 'NESB1' (Non-English Speaking Background, first generation), 'NESB2' (Non-English Speaking Background, second generation), 'ATSI' (Aboriginal and Torres Strait Islanders) and 'Women'.

Social Security had explanations when asked about the extreme variation among ethnic groups. Turkish migrants are high welfare users and receive disability pensions at a rate three times higher than Australian-born because they are primarily engaged in manual labour and heavy industry. The

Turkish category also contained Kurdish war refugees and refugees are often severely disadvantaged. Similar reasons were given for Lebanese being similarly over-represented. As for the high number of Vietnamese-born sole-parent beneficiaries, Social Security provided a written response.

> *SPBs born in Vietnam represent around 1.8 percent of the SPB population but Vietnamese-born people represent only 0.8 percent of the total Australian population ... The Vietnamese-born community may contain a higher proportion of women of child-bearing age ... The Vietnamese-born community may have been particularly affected by negative experiences often associated with refugee immigration: for example, the death of a partner ... The experience of immigration and re-establishment may have been particularly difficult for Vietnamese couples ...* [and] *led to separation while in Australia.*

These are important explanations, but although they account for much of the steep discrepancies between various immigrant streams they certainly do not contradict the observations by the former Social Security officers.

'It is basically a refugee problem, not an immigration problem,' said David Reid. 'The refugees are the people who are most exploiting the system because refugees bypass the normal checks in the immigration system.'

Although eighty-five percent of refugee applications are found to be unsustainable, an applicant with good legal advice can string the system out for years, staying and working in Australia while appealing through the Refugee Review Tribunal and then the court system.

Le Geng Jia arrived in Australia from China in 1991, on a one-year permit. Twenty-two days later, he applied for refugee status claiming he would suffer persecution if he returned to China because he had been involved in the Tiananmen Square riots. Refugee status was denied. He appealed. It was denied. He was then subject to a deportation order. In the interim, in 1993, Jia was convicted of rape and sentenced to a six-year prison term. Released in 1997, Jia appealed against his conviction. The appeal was dismissed. He then applied for legal residence in Australia under new criteria which had been introduced while he was in jail. His application was rejected. He then appealed to the Migration Internal Review Office. The appeal was rejected.

He then appealed to the Administrative Appeals Tribunal. The deputy president of the tribunal decided that Jia was of good character and should be allowed to remain in Australia permanently. He also noted that the woman Jia had raped was 'an attractive but manipulative and argumentative person, quite able to stand up for herself'.

The Minister for Immigration, Philip Ruddock, overruled the tribunal and cancelled the visa. Jia appealed to the Federal Court. The appeal was dismissed in 1998. As the law stands, he is able to appeal again and was planning to do so. It is little wonder that immigration cases now make up sixty-five percent of the administrative law cases before the Federal Court.

AMONG THE BARBARIANS

The reality is that there are all kinds of immigration rorts and welfare rorts and crime in the Asian communities, says Richard Basham. *Everyone knows it. On arrival in Australia, many immigrants, often so-called 'students' from countries such as the PRC [People's Republic of China], will be forced to work at a number of jobs to repay debts upwards of $15 000, debts which while unpaid attract usurious rates of interest. Failure to repay such debts will invoke serious sanctions. I saw a case of a Sino-Thai who had actually been kicked out of Australia. He bought a new identity from a 'Tiananmen refugee' who had gone back to China, and he came back to live in Australia with a new identity.*

The Australian embassy in Beijing backs up these claims. In 1997 the embassy complained to Canberra about chronic visa abuse by Chinese. 'The current overstay rate by Chinese nationals is unacceptably high,' said Todd Frew, the top immigration official in Beijing. He said a large number of applicants for tourist, student or business visas end up working in restaurants or sweatshops. The Australian diplomatic missions in Beijing, Shanghai and Guangzhou granted visas to 54 000 Chinese visitors in 1996, a fifty percent surge on the previous year. The diplomatic missions cannot cope with the increase in demand, a fact exploited by immigration consultants in Australia and China, who often create bogus job offers in Australia. The Beijing embassy also conceded that obtaining false Australian passports by switching identities was a common practice.

Once in Australia, the evolving culture of abuse and opportunism among some immigrants feeds a variety of illegal schemes, such as the underground trade in stolen Medicare cards, which are sold to new immigrants who are not entitled to benefits under stricter new government rules.

A former principal of Randwick Primary School, which has a large Asian enrolment, says she interviewed many newly arrived Asian families who immediately asked for letters that could be given to welfare agencies to establish residency requirements. She remembers instances where 'the child was enrolled, the letters written, and within a day the child removed from the school'.

The owner of a Vietnamese restaurant in Sydney was even more damning about tax avoidance than the Social Security officers. 'It's very hard to keep staff because they want to work the social security system or the tax system or the immigration system. We are always losing staff because they only want black money. It's lucky my wife is such a great cook.'

The luckiest place in New South Wales is Cabramatta-Fairfield, according to the New South Wales Racing and Gaming Commission. These adjoining suburbs are the biggest source of Lotto winners. In a period of seven years, Cabramatta residents won fourteen first prizes. Cabramatta's winning run has little to do with luck and everything to do with gambling fever, tax avoidance, money laundering and the black money that dominates Cabramatta's economic life. Direct buses operate between Cabramatta and the Sydney casino. The Cabravale Ex-Servicemen's Club, in the heart of the Vietnamese enclave, has so much money flowing through its poker machines that it borrowed nineteen million dollars to expand and paid the money back within ten months. The 'casino rooms' at the Cabramatta Inn, the Stardust Hotel and the Kookaburra Hotel in nearby Canley Vale are all thriving.

'When we investigated organised crime, we found Asians were using the casinos as money-laundering operations,' says retired Justice Athol Moffitt, QC, who headed the Moffitt Royal Commission. 'We found that some of these so-called Asian high rollers were bringing drug money and Asian crime syndicate money into the country,' he told me. 'The [federal Labor] government wasn't interested.' So concerned about the rise of organised crime is Justice Moffitt that he believes sweeping new law enforcement powers are essential. He advocates giving police greater power to seize the assets of drug carriers by the imposition of a much less onerous civil, rather than criminal, burden of proof in asset seizure cases. Drug dealers have benefited enormously from the often impossible burden of proof required in criminal cases.

Millions of dollars in profits from the Vietnamese black economy of cash-skimming restaurants, illegal garment-making outlets, welfare rorts, unregistered businesses, gang activities and the booming drug trade are laundered through gambling.

'A tremendous amount of money is going out of the country through the gold bullion exchange,' said a source in AUSTRAC [Australian Transaction Reports and Analysis Centre], the agency which tracks money transactions into and out of Australia, and which estimated that criminals laundered about 3.5 billion dollars overseas in 1995. 'The Vietnamese buy gold off dealers and pay cash. They buy less than $10 000, so it doesn't have to be reported to AUSTRAC.'

The practice of making multiple deposits of less than $10 000 to avoid currency controls is known in America as 'smurfing' and the term has come to Australia. In March 1997 the National Crime Authority arrested a group of Vietnamese money launderers who used to drive around Sydney in a Tarago filled with packets of cash, making $9000 deposits to numerous bank accounts in various branches, then transferring the money overseas. The NCA believes these Vietnamese smurfs sent twelve million dollars overseas in 1200 transactions in the year prior to their arrest.

Cash is king in Cabramatta and the surrounding suburbs where more than half Australia's 160 000 Vietnamese live. 'When I worked in Cabramatta,' said an officer with the Commonwealth Bank, 'I saw an unbelievable amount of cash. Most of it wasn't in accounts. It was in bags put on the table in front of me by people making applications for property loans. I used to wonder where the money came from. They had these pyramid and savings schemes that people contribute to, but I still wondered where a lot of the money came from.'

The theme of tax avoidance also recurs repeatedly among the ethnic Chinese immigrants interviewed by Sang Ye in *The Year the Dragon Came*.

> *I've already reached the $30 000 mark. A few people have couriered most of it back to China for me. You never know when there's going to be a change in*

government policy. This way the tax department won't catch up with me either.

The biggest immigration scheme of all is phoney marriages. 'So many Asians are working the marriage racket that the price for a marriage has plummeted in the past year,' says Dr Basham. 'The price has dropped from $35 000 to less than half that, and a lot of people are ticked off. I know a restaurant chain that is routinely involved in marriage scams. It has dozens of illegal workers who arrived that way.'

Bob Birrell of Monash University, writing in *People and Place*, argues that spouse migration was the largest single component of Australia's immigration program, and the most abused.

With spouse migration now accounting for forty percent of the immigration and likely to grow in size, especially with the prospective PRC [China] flow, questions about its economic costs and benefits need to be asked.

We know that very high proportions of recent spouse arrivals from countries like Turkey, Lebanon and Vietnam are dependent on unemployment benefits ...

For example, there was a total of 1518 arrivals from Lebanon in 1991–92, of whom 770 were spouses. Many of the others were children and elderly persons. Yet as of May 1994, according to Department of Social Security files, 553 of them were receiving unemployment benefits. The availability of our welfare benefits (generous by the standards of most Third World countries) is a standing inducement to spouse migration. As a spokesperson for the Arab Community Welfare Centre stated in October 1994 of Lebanese spouses: 'A lot of them don't want to work. They want to be on the dole. ... It is not clear that the [tough] new rules have discouraged fraudulent applications ... It may be that those whose prime objective is to utilise marriage for immigration purposes have simply moved offshore to make their applications. By doing so they can avoid any serious evaluations of the bone-fides of their marriage ... the number of spouse/fiance visas issued offshore has increased [since the tough new rules] *from 17000 to over 19000 a year ...*

It seems likely that some migrants have taken advantage of the system. The best data source is the pattern of divorces. In the case of PRC, there have been a large number of successful onshore marriages (937 in 1989–90 and around 500 a year since). The number of Chinese-born persons involved in divorces has since increased sharply from 533 in 1990 to 1390 in 1993.

'There are 120000 marriages a year in Australia and an astonishing proportion of these, about thirty percent, involve offshore spouses,' Birrell told me. 'China and Vietnam now provide the two largest flows of offshore spouses ... A substantial number of these people do not have the wherewithal to cope in Australia. Many go straight to the Social Security office.'

The high ratio of divorces to marriages among Chinese is part of the worst kept secret in the immigration business—the widespread abuse of the system by immigrants from the PRC. Using Australian laws to advantage has been openly discussed in numerous Chinese-language articles and books, such as *My Fortune in Australia* and *I Married a Foreign Woman*, published in China, and *The Year the Dragon Came* and *Bitter Peaches and Plums*, in Australia. Many of the Chinese immigrants interviewed in *The Year the Dragon Came* are blunt about using the system:

> *As soon as I got to Melbourne I arranged a phoney marriage. It cost me over $10 000 but I got PR* [permanent residence] *out of it ... Now I realise that if I'd stuck it out I would have been able to stay on humanitarian grounds.*

Another man in *Dragon*, a librarian, expressed pain at the general attitude of his fellow immigrants from China who, he said, were always trying to take advantage of loopholes and were 'outraged' if they were refused.

The Department of Social Security does engage in a ceaseless effort to sift the welfare roles of abusers, conducting three million data checks a year. The department compares databanks from the Australian Taxation Office, other departments, and other compensation payers looking for discrepancies, a process known as data-matching. The number of reviews more than doubled in the five years to 1993–94, then really took off when the Howard government and its budget razor gang arrived in 1996. In the first full year of administration by the new government, 1996–97, the number of reviews of social security payments rose twenty-eight percent; the number of payment cancellations or reductions increased forty percent, and the amount of debts recovered soared forty-seven percent, all producing net savings to the system of $1.5 billion without any important change in policy.

The cumulative effect of all the small and large abuses of the social security net, the immigration system and the tax system is a huge black economy which mingles with the black economies from money laundering, drug profits, organised crime, extortion rackets and human trafficking. Richard Basham has warned police they should treat documentation from Asian consulates with caution because of corruption among consular officials in some countries, and proceed with caution in information shared with some Asian police forces, including Vietnam. 'Australians can remain naive for only so long,' he said. 'At a certain point it becomes dangerous. I think we have reached that point.'

9
LOVE AT FIRST SIGHT

HANSARD, HOUSE OF REPRESENTATIVES, Tuesday, 10 September 1996:

> MR ACTING SPEAKER: *Before I call the honourable member for Oxley, I remind the House that this is the honourable member's first speech. I ask the House to extend to her the usual courtesies.*
>
> MS HANSON (Oxley) (5.15 p.m.): *Mr Acting Speaker, in making my first speech in this place, I congratulate you on your election and wish to say how proud I am to be here as the Independent member for Oxley. I come here not as a polished politician but as a woman who has had her fair share of life's hard knocks.*

Pauline Hanson spoke for twenty minutes, concluding her speech at 5.35 p.m. Within minutes, the switchboard at Parliament House began to light up. People were calling asking for copies of Hanson's speech. The density of the phone traffic was highly unusual and unprecedented for a political novice.

The news media's immediate reaction to the speech was to fixate on one sentence: '*I believe we are being swamped by*

Asians.' Although clearly the best bite to take from the speech, Hanson's statement immediately beforehand, rarely quoted, was even more important to understanding her rise to prominence:

> *Immigration and multiculturalism are issues that this government is trying to address, but for far too long ordinary Australians have been kept out of any debate by the major parties. I and most Australians want our immigration policy radically reviewed and that of multiculturalism abolished. I believe we are in danger of being swamped by Asians. Between 1984 and 1995, forty percent of all migrants coming into this country were of Asian origin.*

It did not matter whether people loathed her or loved her or used her, the key to Pauline Hanson's rise in Australian politics are these words—'for far too long ordinary Australians have been kept out of any debate by the major parties'. Prior to the arrival of this unpolished politician in 1996, an anger had built up in the electorate over the furtive, bipartisan dissembling by politicians and the press over the issue of social cohesion. So strong and so ruthlessly imposed were the protocols constraining discussion of racism, discrimination, affirmative action and immigration, it would be a foolish person who smashed through and express, with undisguised resentment, the unpleasant fears felt in much of the electorate. Pauline Hanson was that foolish person. That's why the phones lit up at Parliament House.

LOVE AT FIRST SIGHT

'It all soon became like a fan club, a personality thing,' said the man who helped draft that maiden speech, John Pasquarelli, Hanson's chief political adviser at the time, who was later sacked amid spectacular discord. 'Barbara Hazelton [Hanson's office manager] started telling her all the time she could become Prime Minister. She thinks she's doing an Eva Peron.'

* * *

One of the ANZACS who landed at Gallipoli in 1915 was Frederick Charles Webster. He was wounded in action. Shot in the chest, he lay on the battlefield surrounded by dead soldiers. In her 1997 biography, *Pauline—The Hanson Phenomenon*, Helen Dodd (an Ipswich pharmacist with a PhD in biotechnology) writes that the young soldier was found by a Turkish doctor who saved his life. After he returned to Australia he married Alice McKee and they had a daughter Nora, who in turn had a daughter, Pauline.

Pauline Lee Seccombe was born on 27 May 1954 near Brisbane. Three of her grandparents had migrated to Australia from England prior to World War I. The fourth, her maternal grandmother, Alice McKee, was the only Queensland-born. Pauline left school at fifteen, got a job as a clerk, worked most nights at her parents' hamburger shop, married at age seventeen to Walter Zagorski, a Polish immigrant, had two children, divorced in 1977 after six years. She married Mark Hanson at age twenty-five, had two more children, and divorced again after six years. By then she was Pauline Hanson, living in Ipswich.

Her bridge to politics was Rick Gluyas, a friend whose influence led her to run for Ipswich City Council as an independent in 1994. She won a seat in an anti-Labor swing against the council, but her friendship with Gluyas did not survive this development.

Hanson's success in gaining Liberal preselection was not seen as a great prize. Oxley was a safe Labor seat, needing a mammoth 14.7 percent swing to change hands. Any Liberal candidate would likely be cannon-fodder. Hanson did not even last until the election before her preselection was stripped away. The catalyst for disendorsement was a letter she wrote to the *Queensland Times*, published on 6 January 1996, in which she wrote of indigenous Australians:

> *How can we expect this race to help themselves when governments shower them with money, facilities and opportunities that only these people can obtain no matter how minute the indigenous blood that flows through their veins, and this is what is causing racism. Until governments wake up to themselves and start looking at equality not colour then we might start to work together as one.*

The letter became her unintended campaign manifesto, especially after the sitting Labor member, Les Scott, refused to appear on the same podium with her at a pre-election debate. Local Aboriginal elders Elsie Geebung and Gladys Graham described Hanson as 'ignorant as a pig in mud'. This, like Les Scott's boycott, merely served to enhance her cause. On election day, 2 March 1996 Hanson won a 19.3 percent swing, the biggest in the nation. The *Queensland Times*, in noting her resounding success in ending 'the unspectacular career of Les Scott', also saw the key element in her victory:

> *While some supported her comments, others simply supported her right to speak out on the issue and still others admired her for the bravery of her convictions in the face of the party machine.*

Within days of her victory, a complaint of racial discrimination was lodged with the federal Human Rights and Equal Opportunity Commission. Thus began the surreal political phenomenon of Pauline Lee Hanson. Right from the start, it was propelled by a ferocious level of attention from the media, which accorded her the news status of a redneck Princess Diana. 'There's no doubt the media attacks were magnificent for her,' John Pasquarelli told me. Denis McCormack, a leader of Australians Against Further Immigration and the Australia First Party, also shared the belief that the international attention on Hanson was in large part a media phenomenon.

> *She is on centre stage completely because of the news media. Pauline is straight out of the movie* Being There. *She is the Chauncey Gardener of Australian politics.*

Privately, her career was marked by incessant feuds and a stream of personal casualties. The first to go was her campaign manager, Maurie Marsden. 'Ten years of friendship just went out the window,' he told me in 1997.

> *It was playground stuff. I was told not to come back to the office. She said she felt I was disrupting her office ... They didn't like being told problems. They only wanted to be told they were wonderful ... The situation became ridiculous. Pauline can't take criticism. She was taking notice of strangers. People came in from nowhere wanting to run the show ... I see a lot of our work on important issues going down the chute. She hasn't got policies. The whole thing is turning nasty. She's fighting with everybody. All the original grass-roots campaign organisations are going down. I've seen a turn against her in Ipswich.*

John Pasquarelli didn't last long either. He had come to her office on the recommendation of the anti-immigration crusader, federal MP Graeme Campbell. Pasquarelli tried to play Svengali with the inexperienced, inarticulate Hanson and it blew up. He was fired within a year.

> *Nobody ever goes away a friend, he told me. They all go away enemies. I used to have to tell her to ring people to thank them. It never occurred to her ... There was a big element of curiosity value about her, but it's basically a sideshow. She can't carry the big arguments ... The one thing that may save Hanson as a political force, at least in Queensland, is black racism. Australians will resent*

> *reconciliation if it's rammed down their throats. If this
> happens, people may be prepared to overlook Pauline's
> inadequacies.*

Pasquarelli was sacked on 9 December 1996. Sacked on the same day was Jeff Babb who had barely arrived. Pasquarelli sued for unfair dismissal in the Industrial Relations Court, his claim was settled out of court.

Several early grass-roots organisers also angrily broke with Hanson, notably Bruce Whiteside, founder of the Pauline Hanson Support Movement, and Vic Piccone, who headed the movement in north Queensland.

In 1997, the main adviser in Hanson's life became a Sydney Liberal Party activist, David Oldfield, a bachelor in his early thirties who met Hanson after defending her from a shouting abuser in a Canberra restaurant. Hanson's new adviser did little to hide his long-term desire to win a seat in federal Parliament. He also brought in a friend and professional fund-raiser, David Ettridge, to run the new Pauline Hanson's One Nation party.

For a new political party dealing with the highly loaded subjects of racial discrimination and immigration, Hanson's new principal political adviser brought plenty of emotional baggage. Oldfield came from a home indelibly printed with scars left by Japanese atrocities in World War II. 'My father is a decorated gunnery officer,' Oldfield told me.

> *He served all through Indonesia. He was shot down
> by the Japanese in October 1944, and was a POW for
> seven months. He came close to being murdered many*

times. His bomber crew was held for interrogation, moved six or seven times, and never put in a camp with other POWs. They were beaten, tortured. My father was fourteen stone when he was captured, and six and a half stone when he was released. He was bashed so violently he had to hold his eyes open. They would line them up and say, 'We are going to decapitate you'. He had two friends lopped during the war. They would also line them up and put them in front of firing squads, and simulate an execution. The Japanese killed all the bomber crews and they were planning to kill my father's crew when the war ended. My father would not say anything about the war until the 1980s, but we weren't allowed to have anything in the house that was made in Japan.

David Oldfield did not arrive at Hanson's office in time to save his new boss from her greatest debacle, the book *Pauline Hanson—The Truth*. Nearly everything about the book was amateurish, paranoid, mean-spirited, and fifth-rate. No serious politician could have put their name to it. 'People say she received bad advice about the book,' said Maurie Marsden, 'but she was the one making the decisions. The copyright is in her name. Her name is on the cover. So she is responsible for what's in the book. She can't just walk away.'

The book, with its comments about cannibalism among Aborigines and its parody of a future Asianised Australia run by a lesbian Asian who was partly genetically engineered, was nominally by Hanson but its true authorship soon became secretive after controversy erupted immediately after publication.

'The media created her,' said Bruce Whiteside. 'She was a small target while she was the member for Oxley. She could be nicely naive, inarticulate. That even worked in her favour. But when she became leader of a party she became a big target. She needed a lot of help, but she won't accept help. She's ego-driven.' In 1998, Barbara Hazelton departed through a trapdoor as quickly as she had arrived, in yet another bitter passing. Even Helen Dodd, Hanson's benign biographer, fell out with Hanson–Oldfield soon after. Once gain, more public pain.

By the time Hanson made her rise from battler to national figure she had left in her wake a formidable list of estrangements—Walter Zagorski, Mark Hanson, Rick Gluyas, Maurie Marsden, John Pasquarelli, Jeff Babb, Bruce Whiteside, Vic Piccone, Barbara Hazelton, Helen Dodd, and even, for a few years, her eldest son, Tony. 'She will never run a happy ship,' predicted Maurie Marsden.

* * *

On Australia Day 1998, the world champion sprinter and one of Australia's most beloved public figures, Cathy Freeman, was named Australian of the Year. The award recognised the moments of national communion she had given Australians at the 1996 Atlanta Olympics and the 1997 World Championships when, after brilliant performances, she had carried the flags of Australia and Aboriginal Australia with pride and dignity on an international stage. Several days prior to Freeman being honoured, a Vietnamese-born, twenty-year-old Melbourne law student, Tan Le, was honoured as Young Australian of the Year for her work with immigrants and refugees. Tan Le herself had come to Australia as a refugee, but in accepting the award she described herself as 'an ordinary Australian'.

Pauline Hanson told a radio station that while she had 'no problem' with either woman, the awards smacked of tokenism and the honouring of Cathy Freeman was meant to make Australians 'forget about the Wik, forget about the stolen generation and I think appointing the young Asian lady, the government's been pushing us to become Asianised and I'm totally against becoming Asianised ... I think it's all very political. I'm not very impressed by it whatsoever. I think the majority of Australians will know what I'm talking about.'

When this was passed on to the Prime Minister, John Howard, he responded later that same day: 'Her remarks were not only inaccurate, they were stupid, they were petty, and they're very divisive remarks to be made on Australia Day.' Nothing more needed to be said.

Pauline Hanson's crusade, however, asked some questions that the political heavyweights had been ducking for years, and she attracted some heavyweight critics. Henry Reynolds, a distinguished and influential historian, expressed outrage about the racist references to Aborigines in *The Truth*.

Henry Reynolds is the same historian who has argued, with great impact and moral authority, that Australians had tried to sweep the dark side of their history out of the collective memory. He is right. Yet he also, in effect, says it is acceptable to pump up the moral volume with claims of white 'genocide' and 'holocaust' but not acceptable to play the tough rhetorical game of references to routine violence and endemic clan hostilities even though scholarly literature is filled with dispassionate references to brutal practices among the indigenous peoples. Henry Reynolds, it should be remembered, is the man who led the charge to try and destroy the professional reputation of Geoffrey Blainey. In 1985, he told *The Australian* that Blainey had 'lost the respect of practically the whole profession' over his views on immigration. He and other historians had joined together to put 'the jackhammers' to Blainey's work. 'What you've got to expect if you engaged in this kind of public controversy is that you are going to be shot at.'

Kenneth Maddock, a visiting professor of anthropology at Macquarie University, was prompted to write a rebuttal to Reynolds in April, 1997. In raising the issue of double standards and selective history, Professor Maddock brought into focus perhaps the most important issue that spun out of the entire Hanson debate:

> *What we are seeing is a struggle for the high moral ground using the method anthropologists call the politics of embarrassment. The aim is to soften up your opponents by making them feel bad about themselves or their ancestors. This puts them in a mood to make concessions. Indigenous groups have become adept in these*

> tactics. The trouble is the method is not particularly useful for identifying problems, let alone solving them. But it is being resorted to so often that it would be hypocritical to raise an eyebrow just because a popular but unfashionable politician uses it.

Exactly. Within a year of Hanson's arrival in federal Parliament, she had unwittingly rewritten the language of political debate in Australia. Her name became the standard weapon with which to bludgeon opposition. Labor's defeat in 1996, and the vulnerability of the enormous grievance industry it had left behind, saw an escalation of shrill rhetoric and an assault on the middle ground from those who had lost power. As for the news media, Helen Dodd wrote of their relationship with Hanson:

> Styled as the 'race debate', it was never a debate among average Australians. It was written, orchestrated and performed by the media. The media have peddled the idea that Australia is a racist country so widely that our Asian neighbours are beginning to accept this twisted reporting as fact [and] the media have now placed Australia in a precarious position.

This comment, by an educated non-journalist, reflects a dismay widely felt in the community at the media's combination of shedding crocodile tears over the divisions Hanson was creating while at the same time fomenting these divisions. For the media, the story was simple. It was black and white, good versus evil, middle-class enlightenment against redneck prejudice. There was more than a touch of class war—focaccia and cappuccino versus fish and chips. Even Zita Antonios, the federal Race Discrimination Commissioner, expressed disgust at the class condescension that lay behind many of the attacks on Hanson. 'I get so angry about some of the criticisms of Pauline Hanson,' she told *The Australian* in 1998.

> *Whatever one thinks about her position on any of the issues that she speaks about, it is supremely offensive to me that she is ridiculed because she lacks a formal education, or because her grammar is poor, or because she struggles over reading speeches, or indeed that she is a fish and chip shop owner. I grew up with fish and chip shop owners. It's symptomatic of the very things we are arguing against ...*

Trevor Watson, a former head of ABC Radio, crystallised the problem at a conference on the Australian news media in 1996. 'Today the emphasis seems to be on conflict and sensation. The objective doesn't seem to be to inform the public any more, it seems to be to entertain the public through some sort of conflict.' He described Australia as a tolerant, non-racist country but a very different impression was given to Australia's Asian neighbours by the media's coverage of the Hanson debate. The Hanson public relations disaster for Australia in Asia was largely media-made.

Above all, the media declined to investigate the fire that lay beneath the smoke of Pauline Hanson. Thrashing Hanson as a racist and a fool is no substitute for actually doing some work. Moral outrage does not explain what caused the widespread unease that found expression in the 1996 federal election and the huge swing Hanson received in that election. The collective attitude of the press pack was that this complex issue was actually simple: white racism was still common in Australia.

The possibility of community anger at political duplicity never seemed to enter the equation.

This softness is not merely an Australian phenomenon. The Harvard economist and immigration scholar, George Borjas, expressed dismay at the bias of the American media, led by the *New York Times*, when they covered a major report on immigration in 1997.

> *The big news, which was not in the headline in* The Times, *is that there is a growing consensus among economists that the gains from immigration are small. Overall, the National Academy of Sciences report is not as favourable as the press made it out to be, and I'm sort of stunned by the way it was spun by the press.*

He should not have been stunned. The news media, whether in the United States, Britain, Canada, Australia or Western Europe, is extremely leery of reporting negatively on immigration or ethnic crime or non-white racism. The only racism it feels unconstrained in reporting is white racism. Anything else produces a professional rash. John Cassidy, economics correspondent for *The New Yorker*, a journal as liberal as it is prestigious, confronted this problem in an article on immigration published in July 1997.

> *According to opinion polls, about two-thirds of Americans now believe that immigration should be restricted, yet support for an open-door policy is virtually a badge of respectability among the political and media elite* [even though] *immigration may also be affecting internal migration patterns in ways that undermine the notion of the melting pot.*

Cassidy then cited the distinguished demographer, William Frey, the scholar who first identified 'white flight', who is now writing about what he calls the 'Balkanisation' of America.

Similar concerns are expressed in Australia by Pauline Hanson's One Nation Party. Hanson herself says she is opposed to racial discrimination in all its forms. When she was running her seafood shop, she employed a young Laotian immigrant, Lilly Vichitthavong, who says she enjoyed working for Hanson. 'Everyone in the shop was spoken to at the same level,' she said. 'I never heard any racist comments at all.' Hanson's maiden speech contained numerous references to racial equality, few of which were ever quoted by the media:

> *Paul Hasluck's vision was of a single society in which racial emphases were rejected and social issues addressed. I totally agree with him, and so would the majority of Australians ... Reconciliation is everyone*

recognising and treating each other as equals, and everyone must be responsible for their own actions ... I do not consider people from ethnic backgrounds currently living in Australia anything but first-class citizens, provided, of course, that they give this country their full, undivided loyalty.

Hanson's general ineptitude meant that these comments were dismissed as disingenuous. The video address she recorded in November 1997 to be released in the event she was assassinated—'Fellow Australians, if you are seeing me now it means I have been murdered'—further enhanced her reputation for paranoia.

But another reality of Australian politics is that Pauline Hanson has been spat on, subject to numerous threats, her younger son has been stalked and she has received a torrent of racist abuse from Aborigines. One Nation's opponents covered themselves in disgrace in 1997. Hundreds of people were subject to a gauntlet of insults and projectiles as they attended One Nation meetings. Many were threatened, some were beaten. A docile news media and Labor Party both watched as a systematic assault on freedom of speech and freedom of assembly took place—in the name of tolerance. The violence culminated, inevitably, with a serious assault when Keith Warburton was bashed by three goons calling him a 'Nazi' as he came out of a One Nation meeting in Dandenong, Victoria. He had attended the meeting out of curiosity. 'I'm just an individual without political leanings,'

Warburton said later. Political curiosity carried a high price in Australia in 1997.

For much of that same year, the formal complaint of racial discrimination made against Pauline Hanson after her election victory was working its way through the Human Rights and Equal Opportunity Commission.

Hanson's former chief adviser, John Pasquarelli, gave his version of this dispute in his 1998 book, *The Pauline Hanson Story*:

> *On Monday, March 4, 1996, just two days after Pauline Hanson was elected, the* Australian *newspaper ran an article headlined 'Liberal reject proclaims a victory for the 'white community'.'*
>
> *... From the day I arrived in Pauline's office until the day I was thrown out of it, there was a barrage of correspondence from the Human Rights Commission demanding that Pauline attend at their Sydney headquarters to enter into a process of reconciliation with the aggrieved parties ...*
>
> *The Human Rights Commission subpoenaed the audio tape from the* Australian *and was obliged to release a copy to Pauline—which it did ... In the verified transcript, a full stop did not follow after 'Aboriginals and Torres Strait Islanders'. There was a comma, and further comment by Pauline ... Her plea for 'everyone to be equal' and her desire for 'everyone to work together as one' puts an entirely different interpretation on the very damaging, selective quote used by the journalist ...*

AMONG THE BARBARIANS

> *The final act in this mini-drama ... was played out on October 24, 1997, when Commissioner Sir Ronald Wilson found that Hanson's comments about Aboriginals and Torres Strait Islanders, taken in the context of the entire interview, did not constitute racial discrimination as defined by the Racial Discrimination Act.*
>
> *This finding took a long, drawn-out eighteen months ... We should not hold our breath waiting for the published apologies.*

Meanwhile, back in Parliament, Pauline Hanson, though greatly discredited and diminished, was still able to ride the silences that had brought her to power. During question time on 30 October 1997 she asked a question which produced a stunned silence from both sides of the House and muffled applause from sections in the public gallery:

> MS HANSON: *My question is to the Prime Minister. Would the Prime Minister please explain how his government can justify making available to Indonesia what may be as much as 1.7 billion dollars when we already give approximately ninety million dollars in foreign aid, eight million dollars of which is for their defence forces? Has the government considered that perhaps it is more appropriate for President Soeharto to help bail out his own people with some of the billions he and his family have profited from during his time in office? Is it the policy of this government to prop up questionable and militaristic regimes with appalling human rights records?*

LOVE AT FIRST SIGHT

The most discomforting thing about this question is that it was a good question. Leaving aside that the government's decision to help Indonesia was the right thing to do, everyone in Parliament knew that the Indonesian ruling elite was a deeply corrupt military plutocracy which had funnelled away billions of dollars for its own enrichment, especially the enrichment of the extended Soeharto family. Everyone knew that the Indonesian economic system was collapsing under the weight of unchecked cronyism.

The Prime Minister responded:

MR HOWARD: *I think the question raised by the member for Oxley deserves a serious and considered response.*

The measure that I announced was designed not to prop up a regime but to help the Indonesian people ... a demonstration of regional neighbourliness; I describe it as regional mateship.

... it is a situation where it is in Australia's national self-interest to have a strong Indonesia capable of buying goods and services from Australia ... It would be a very short-sighted and narrow-minded Australian government that passed up the opportunity to extend a strong hand of economic support in a time of difficulty to a friend and neighbour.

Despite East Timor, despite all the corruption, despite the destruction of the rainforests, despite the burning of hundreds of Christian churches, despite the growing threats toward the

Chinese minority in Indonesia, Howard's answer was the only possible answer. Australia and Indonesia must be allies, not enemies. There was, however, a time when the left wing of the Labor Party would have been willing to ask such morally pointed questions, but that time has passed. The historian Geoffrey Blainey had warned, accurately, that the silences being imposed on Australian political debate had become dangerous:

> *Democracy in Australia is not quite as healthy as it should be. There is a strong view, reinforced by a section of the media based in Canberra, that certain topics are too dangerous to be handed to the people for decision at election time. Immigration is one topic ... We hear, again and again, that the Australian people themselves cannot be trusted to vote on immigration ... Aboriginal affairs is another topic not to be trusted to the people. The press joined with Mr Keating in wiping it from the agenda at the 1993 Federal election. And of course the Native Title Bill was deliberately introduced to Parliament without any chance of members of the public seeing that Bill, and a strong attempt was made to push it through as quickly as possible ... It will remain a smouldering topic in Australia for many years to come.*

The coalition that imposed this silence was formed by Labor, the multicultural industry and the selective news media, three heavily overlapping constituencies, especially at the ABC and SBS. This coalition created a vacuum in Canberra. The vacuum was filled.

14
THE BIG PINEAPPLE

15 June 1998.

Pauline Hanson's One Nation has just won eleven seats in the Queensland Parliament.

The editorial cartoon of *The Australian* depicts dead Asians hanging from trees and hillbilly lynch mob, armed with shotguns and pitchforks marching towards the Queensland border.

* * *

7 August 1998.

A crowd of several hundred has gathered on the steps of the Ipswich Civic Council. TV crews are filming and their lights are bright among the crowd, heightening the tension.

Pauline Hanson is standing on the steps, about to speak. One Nation is holding the rally on the steps because the council will not let the party use the town hall. She begins to speak. Demonstrators begin to chant:

AMONG THE BARBARIANS

Migrants are welcome, racists are not
Migrants are welcome, racists are not

Pauline Hanson raises her voice, and acknowledges the demonstrators:

They are having their protest. It's a shame that they don't realise the democratic way to do it is at the ballot box. Not on the streets of Ipswich. Not on any Australian streets at all. But at the ballot box ...

And hopefully a lot of these people are unemployed and what I'm saying here tonight is that I want to get Australia up and going again. I want to get jobs and certainly jobs for a lot of the rabble over here who hasn't even got jobs. Who rely on the rest of society to support this.

The chanting continues:

Asians are welcome, racists are not
Asians are welcome, racists are not

Some people begin jeering the demonstrators, who are drowning out the speech for many in the crowd. The police stand ready. The lights of the TV crews scan the scene.

Pauline Hanson begins to shout above the din:

I am not going anywhere! You won't get rid of me! The only people that are gonna get rid of me are my constituents, the people that vote in the ballot box. Not you! Never, never you!

Look at your own damn signs. Asians are welcome

here and I have always said that. Stop and listen to what I'm saying. Not listening to biased reporting from the media.

Migrants are welcome, racists are not
Migrants are welcome, racists are not

The TV cameras are focused on the angry figure of Pauline Hanson:

You're so ignorant. If you were to keep quiet for a while you might learn the truth of what One Nation and what I stand for ...

I see one of those placards says 'The Socialist Worker'. You have no idea because you support the government in Cuba ... that believes in communism, where half a million people are trying to leave their country because they have no freedom and no democracy.

I feel sorry for you—you have no idea.

They will not allow me to have access to our facilities. As the ratepayers of Oxley the facilities belong to us, not the council.

The people who came out here after the Second World War carved out a future for themselves and their families ... but by God they feel they're more Australian than some of the bloody rabble that's here tonight.

The scenes receive airplay on all network evening news programs.

AMONG THE BARBARIANS

* * *

11 August 1998.

The sickly sweet air of 'the crush' hits as soon as you leave the airport. It is the smell of the cane-crushing season. It is also the smell of political insurrection. The National Party has just been decimated in Queensland and it has been ugly inside the party room in Canberra.

De-Anne Kelly, the first woman ever elected to federal Parliament for the National Party, was shredded in Canberra the week before for her outspoken dissident views about Coalition policy. 'It was extremely distressing hearing people stand up for two-and-a-half-hours telling you were an idiot and they were ashamed of you. It wore pretty thin.'

It was Kelly's federal seat of Dawson, anchored by the sugar coast, which delivered one of the most potent electoral messages of the 1998 Queensland election—a thirty percent primary vote for One Nation, higher than any of the major parties, and enough to win two seats in the State Parliament. Only the region around Gympie, the land of the Big Pineapple, polled higher for One Nation. The Hansonites took five seats from the Nationals and six from Labor.

> *This is not Left versus Right, or liberal versus conservative,* Kelly says. *Australian politics now is defined by the struggle between winners and losers. It's ordinary people versus big global corporations. People now have a way to protest against the political establishment.*

> *People are pretty tired and disappointed. They are fed up with reform. They are telling me they are treading water. Now that socialism is dead and capitalism is the driving force, it isn't turning out as we expected. The multinational corporations and national chains are taking over and working conditions are being degraded. We are approaching a new period of servitude for working people.*

She is friendly and quietly-spoken but not given to understatement: 'Deregulation and globalisation—this is a monster roaming rural Australia.'

After the Queensland election, the Nationals believed One Nation could win at least ten Lower House seats and hold the balance of power after the next federal election. De-Anne Kelly didn't wait for John Howard's announcement. She went straight into election mode. 'If the results of the Queensland election were repeated in Dawson, I would finish third in the primary vote, and this is one of the safest National Party seats in the country.'

The first thing she did was distance herself from Canberra. 'I am amazed at the extent to which Canberra is not listening to the electorate ... I'd love to see the Coalition agreement rewritten. The one we've got now isn't worth a warranty on a washing machine.'

On this day she puts on her Akubra hat, gets into her car, and drives up the Pioneer Valley, a beautiful, industrious, prosperous place, the living embodiment of the National Party ideal of rural communalism and capitalism. The road curves through canefields and past the belching smokestacks of the sugar refineries. The effect is softened by the smell of molasses and the giant fig trees, the crimson poinsettias, the flame trees, foxtail palms and mango trees.

This forty-four-year-old woman, her blonde hair streaming in a ponytail from beneath her hat, stops at each village along the 80 kilometres of the valley—Marian, Mirani, Gargett, Pinnacle, Finch Hatton, Eungalla. She walks along each main street greeting those who know her and meeting those who don't. At lunchtime she stops for a beer and a pie at the Pinnacle Hotel.

'It's a shame the catalyst for change had to be Pauline Hanson,' says one of her constituents, Noel Venton, an egg farmer. 'But something had to happen.'

What were the people talking about in the Pioneer Valley?

'Telstra, anger at Government, guns, losing the sugar tariff while textiles, clothing and footwear were let off,' says Kelly. 'Problems of small business. Waste in payments to Aborigines. Concern about the GST.'

Guns. Two years after John Howard's sweeping gun-control reform, the gun issue is still reverberating outside the cities, a strength of feeling which is difficult for city Australians to understand. 'It was an insult,' she says.

I don't think Howard and the Libs really understood what they were doing. It really struck at the heart of what it meant to be a rural person. It really cheesed me off, and I am not a gun-toting Annie Oakley. You grew up learning to handle a gun because there are poisonous

> snakes, because your stock get injured and you need to put them down humanely. You spend a lot of time by yourself and you want a sense of protection.
>
> To say to people, 'We know you've had those guns all your lives but we don't trust you' was a real slap in the face. It cut at the core of what it meant to be in a rural and isolated area. The farmers are still upset about guns. We lost Burdekin to One Nation because of guns and the sugar tariff. And now we have to face the same electorate and sell a GST.

Even Kelly's staff is hostile toward Canberra because they have had to deal with the GST mess. 'Canberra has spent ten million dollars on educating people about the GST and it was wasted,' says staffer Marcella Massie. 'When they set up a hotline people didn't even know about the cuts in the tax rates that would offset the GST. The toll-free hotline was staffed by people who knew nothing. It was clear the people didn't want a GST on food. It was a shambles.'

De-Anne Kelly's anti-Canberra stand generated a big increase in publicity, which she maintained with a series of public disagreements with the Coalition leadership over the sale of Telstra, gun policy, and deregulation.

> A lot of businesses will be ruined by deregulation and I think it's quite immoral. People are not merely consumers. They are also producers and job-creators and parents and members of a community.
>
> Mackay is a prosperous area because it is highly regulated. If you want to see the effect of deregulation on

rural Australia, just look at the beef towns in western New South Wales. Dusty, empty streets, high unemployment, youth suicide. Very dispirited towns. My father started the Cattlemen's Union back in the 1970s, when you could sell a deck of bullocks for $100. People were going broke all over the place. It's happening again now.

Though some in her party and in the media may disagree, De-Anne Kelly is not an idiot. She graduated from the Engineering Department of the University of Queensland. She built, with her husband Roger, a successful manufacturing business employing forty people. They run a successful small farming operation, a mix of cane and cattle. While raising a son and running a business, she worked hard inside the National Party.

She smiles a lot. She is telegenic, hyperbolic and honest.

Would she give her preferences to One Nation?

'Probably. [She did.] I'm not going to ignore my electorate. I'm not going to be a dead hero.'

Would she consider becoming an independent?

'That would be a real act of treachery to our thousands of supporters. I'm not Cheryl Kernot.'

When a virulent attack against her attitude toward guns was published in *The Australian*, her staff made 4000 copies of the article and mailed them to gun supporters in the electorate. Her response was yet more evidence that media attacks and attitudes were providing much of the oxygen for the political insurrection that fuelled Hansonism. And while opinion polls showed a dip in support for One Nation after the initial media fever wore off, there was never a lag in Queensland.

Queensland is different. It is more decentralised and more rural than the other states, and more Anglo. According to Murray Goot of Macquarie University, more than half of Queensland's federal electorates have populations where at least forty percent of the population left school aged fifteen or under. Queensland has a large Aboriginal population. It has a tradition of mistrust of urban politics. And it has a chippy attitude to Sydney and Canberra. Attacks on any Queensland politician by southern politicians don't go down well.

'We polled every day in the Queensland election,' says Kelly, 'and when John Howard made his comment about Pauline Hanson being "deranged", the poll rating on One Nation jumped five points. When Peter Costello tried to link her to the League of Rights a few days later, her polling went up another three percent. And those ratings held. That was the turning point. Until that week, it had been manageable.'

One Nation also ran a very skilful advertising campaign that played off the aura of martyrdom and suppression. 'It was very simple,' Kelly says. 'The ad ran for a full minute, twice as long as a usual ad. It was just Pauline talking about motherhood issues and it ended with that great Australian phrase as she looked into the camera and said: "Give us a go".'

* * *

2 September 1998.

We are in the land where time stood still. The venue is a beautifully restored timber mansion in Ipswich, the sort of distinctly Queensland architecture that is no longer built. On this night there is a meeting of the Ipswich Rotary Club and the room has forty-one Rotarians (no women), one Deputy Prime Minister and six wombats, as Tim Fischer refers to the journalists who follow his election trail, and now the federal election is officially three days old, though it has been on for months.

Tim Fischer is under intense pressure. Three months before, the headline which summed up the Queensland election—HOWARD'S NIGHTMARE—could just as easily have been FISCHER'S NIGHTMARE. One Nation had cost the Coalition government in Queensland. In its first outing it won 22.7 percent of the primary vote, more than the Nationals (15.2 percent) or the Liberals (16.1 percent). The Nats had been pushed down to fourth position in the primary vote in the state they used to run. They lost five seats to One Nation and another four were saved only by Labor's preferences.

The Queensland election had reawakened support for One Nation around the regional and urban margins of Australia to the realisation that they can get the full attention of the major parties by voting against them all. In the three weeks after the election, the Morgan polls tracked a surge in One Nation's national support from six percent to 13.5 percent. In Tim Fischer's own electorate, support plummeted from the sixty-six percent he won in the 1996 election to thirty-three percent, according to a poll by *The Border Mail* of Albury. One Nation was polling twenty-four percent, one of the highest results in the country.

Dinner at the Ipswich Club is meat and three veg. The evening is supposed to be non-political, but during the introductions one of the office-holders asks: 'All those in favour of a GST stand up.'

Less than half the room stands. There is an embarrassed moment. Tim Fischer then gives a speech about trains. He loves trains. ('A steel wheel on a rail has only one-seventh of the friction of a rubber tyre on bitumen.')

The speech ends to polite applause, then questions, then the raffle draw, then song books are distributed. A man takes his seat at the piano. It is noted that this day is the fifty-ninth anniversary of Neville Chamberlain's declaration of war against Germany in 1939. A song is chosen to reflect the occasion, and the singalong begins:

> *Land of Hope and Glory,*
> *mother of the free*
> *how can we extol thee,*
> *who art born of thee?*

After Fischer and the wombats depart, the night gets more interesting. A group of men gather around the bar and dissect the visit. They are managers, small-business operators and a solicitor.

'We are not represented by either party,' says one man.

'The gun laws are an insult to rural people,' says another.

'They will regret the day they brought the gun laws in,' says a third.

Tim Fischer has not won any votes tonight. But neither has Kim Beazley. Labor held power here during the long years when Ipswich lost its wool stores, coal mines and railway workshops, and ceased to be a blue-collar town. These men believe Labor's policies on capital gains, guns and Aboriginal rights have marginalised Labor in regional Australia.

Pauline Hanson still burns bright here, despite everything. Some of these men voted for her and say they would vote for her again if most of Ipswich had not been stripped from the electorate where Hanson is now running. The reason is simple: they do not believe she is smart, but they have not finished kicking the Establishment.

These men believe that the major parties have become captive to special interests, to big business, big Labor, and tax-funded racial lobbies. Half of them are old Ipswich, which means Old Labor. Men like this, and all supporters of One Nation, along with National Party dissidents like De-Anne Kelly, are described in the cities and in the press as rednecks, even though many of them are middle class. One tart columnist for the *Australian Financial Review* described them as 'dinosaurs', especially De-Anne Kelly. What people forget is how just recent the Jurassic era was in Australia and how far the nation has travelled in so short a time.

In 1972, the same year Gough Whitlam led Labor out of the political wilderness, Arthur Calwell, the old Labor warhorse and Whitlam's predecessor as Labor leader, published his defining memoir, *Be Just and Fear Not*. Read today, it seems Jurassic, but it was written just one generation ago and still sounds like many of the voices at the bar of the Ipswich Club:

> *Australia, like every other country, has the right to determine the composition of its population, the rate of its development, and the measures to be taken to guard its security. These are matters for determination by the Australian Parliament alone. They are not to be decided by newspapermen, multi-racialists, academics, humanists and a handful of assertive, garrulous State politicians and over-zealous do-gooders ... A little idealism must be mixed with large doses of pragmatism ...*
>
> *... The Labor Party's policy on immigration permits of no ambiguity or misrepresentation. Those who think it means that a Labor Government would be authorised to open the flood gates to Indians, Pakistanis, Ceylonese, Indonesians or Caribbean negroes are hopelessly wrong. Such a policy would cause a grievous split and jeopardise Labor's election prospects ...*
>
> *For political and diplomatic reasons, the 1965 Federal ALP conference removed the words 'White Australia' from the Labor Party platform. We certainly did not try to water down the policy nor take the ideal of a White Australia from the hearts and minds of the Australian people ...*
>
> *I maintain that a big influx of coloured migrants*

> would be a menace to social standards and to the trade
> union movement. The coloured people would tend to con-
> gregate in ghettos ... I predicted long ago that
> immigration would become not only a highly emotional
> issue during the 1972 election campaign and all subse-
> quent campaigns, but also an explosive issue.

The notion of Australia as a white island in an Asian sea has no place in the modern world, but the fear of Asian inundation has been a core element of Australian nation-formation for most of our history. The process of shedding this fear is ongoing, and it has been handled both well and badly. But the most lucid warning about the magnitude of the task, contained in the FitzGerald Report tabled in federal Parliament on 3 June 1988, was largely ignored:

> For most Australians, immigration is not about econom-
> ics or demography or the points system. It is about
> change. Change to their own society and often their own
> personal worlds. Continuing change.
>
> This is not easy for a society to accept without contin-
> uing national justification and education and nationally
> attentive management. Immigration is therefore also
> potentially highly volatile ...
>
> There is already a commonly held view that immigra-
> tion has been taken off the main agenda for political
> debate and it is dealt with separately and less openly,
> that the public is not consulted, and that neither direc-
> tion nor rationale is being given. Immigration has many
> supporters. But many Australians feel they are not being

given the facts on immigration and have drawn their own, often erroneous conclusions ...

There is disquiet about the way immigration is thought to be changing Australia. Immigration policy is held by many to be a grab bag of favours. Many Australian-born see governments as protecting all interests but theirs. Multiculturalism, which is associated in the public mind with immigration, is seen by many as social engineering which actually invites injustice, inequality and divisiveness ...

The extraordinary capacity of Australia to take in large numbers of people from different cultural and ethnic backgrounds is not given sufficient credit. On this issue it really ought to be cause for self-congratulation, not self-doubt ...

Almost exactly ten years later, on 20 June 1998, the human thunderbolt, Alan Ramsey, the most senior political columnist in Australia, wrote in *The Sydney Morning Herald* in the wake of the fears (and the hysteria) let loose by the Queensland election result:

Nobody has ever said as much good sense about Australia's immigration program of the past half century as did the three-volume FitzGerald Report. The travesty remains that so much good sense was ignored by the Hawke Government of the day, traduced by its political and ethnic critics, and so little of it ever explained to the Australian people ...

Ten years later and, what? Nothing. The report may never have been written ...

It was the debate we never had. it was a debate set loose by a government report that candidly questioned the structure of Australia's immigration program. It was a debate throttled by a Labor government embarrassed by its own report and hostage to a powerful ethnic lobby fearful of what it would do to the policy of family reunion. It was a debate that died when the Liberals changed leaders. It is a debate that still remains hidden.

15
THE REVENGE OF THE DESPISED

START WITH A GIANT CANE TOAD. Add a pink bridge. Together, they would put Ayr on the map. 'The whole idea is to cause controversy,' said Queensland state MP Jeff Knuth. 'The idea is not to make it look silly or pretty, it's to get tourists stopping here to push money back into town. A lot of people know that there is method in my madness and see a lot of merit in it ...'

Why the cane toad?

'The cane toad is a symbol of the Burdekin. It was introduced here to eradicate the cane beetle and it caused a lot of devastation ... The Burdekin is the first area where the cane toad was introduced. So if we can get that going here it's going to bring money into the centre of town.'

Proposing Giant Things is the oldest trick in the boosterism book and the idea was so bizarre it might have worked. But Knuth could not have anticipated the even more bizarre front-page story his idea generated in the *Ayr Advocate*:

> *Hordes of scantily clad homosexuals parading down the main street of Ayr may next year change the face of our annual mardi gras ...*

AMONG THE BARBARIANS

> *'We'll have all the gays from Sydney up here if you do that,' was one man's outcry at Mr Knuth's pink proposal.*

The story prompted a flurry of comment, radio talk, letters and follow-up stories in the regional media. It ran in the Townsville and Mackay papers. The logic that Ayr could become a gay Mecca was widely discussed. The Burdekin Bridge would be *pink*. The gay community is famous for its love of large bizarre displays. The climate is subtropical, which lends itself to hedonism. And the main pub in Ayr is the *Queen's* Hotel. Say no more.

The matter even reached the Queensland Parliament. On 18 September 1998, the Minister for Transport, Steve Bredhauer, told the House:

> *It could cause the gay community, and not just in Australia, but internationally, a real dilemma. If you were faced with the prospect of going to Sydney for a mardi gras or going to Ayr for a mardi gras, where would you go?*

The *Townsville Bulletin* pointed out, on its front page, that the cane toad was first introduced to Australia in 1935 near Cairns, not Ayr, and therefore Knuth was wrong. The toad was not released to other centres along the Queensland sugar coast until the following year. The paper also complained that Knuth's plan 'would glorify one of our worst introduced pests'.

Queensland is different.

Three months earlier, Jeff Knuth had come out of nowhere during the Queensland state election campaign. On 13 June

THE REVENGE OF THE DESPISED

1998, the day Pauline Hanson's One Nation Party won twenty-three percent of the vote and put eleven candidates into the Queensland Parliament, Jeff Knuth was one of them. Prior to running for Parliament Knuth was a commercial painter, which explains his interest in painting the Burdekin Bridge.

'We lost the seat of Burdekin to a complete unknown,' said De-Anne Kelly, the politician living on the fault-line of the 1998 Queensland election earthquake. All four state seats within her federal electorate almost fell to One Nation, and two of them did fall. 'Jeff Knuth didn't live in the electorate. He didn't advertise. Nobody knew him. Our candidate was well known and well liked. And Knuth won.

'The voters had been waiting for this for years. Now they had an outlet. At the voting booths we saw about a quarter of the voters ignore everyone's how-to-vote cards and say 'no, no, no' and march into the booth. They had a satisfied look when they came out. Now we know how they voted.'

Now we also know how they voted sixteen weeks later, at the federal election of 3 October 1998. Pauline Hanson lost her seat in Parliament. Her chief strategist, David Oldfield, lost his bid for the Senate from New South Wales. One Nation won only a single Senate seat from Queensland. Within De-Anne Kelly's electorate, One Nation's vote plunged from 30.2 percent in the June state election—the highest of any party—to 15.9 percent in the October federal election.

'The bush came back to us in floods,' Kelly said. 'A lot of the farmers had made their statement at the state election.

Once One Nation had MPs in Parliament it was a considerable challenge for them because they had to start to deliver, and they had trouble.'

The foreign media coverage of the federal election was dominated by the fall of Pauline Hanson. As always, it fed off the tenor of the Australian media. One Australian journalist referred to One Nation's 'electoral slaughter'. Another referred to its 'humiliation', and so it went. Yet One Nation had received 930,000 votes, making it the third-largest party in terms of electoral support. It won more votes than the National Party, more than the Democrats or the Greens, and about six times more votes than the Unity Party, which was set up to fight One Nation. It emerged with the same strength in Parliament, one seat, this time in the Senate.

One Nation had achieved this despite a completely incoherent campaign, despite being placed last on the ballots of most major party candidates, and despite incessant public attacks. Almost one million Australians had felt so alienated enough from the political system to vote for One Nation despite everything.

Still, the defeat of Pauline Hanson was a good story to tell abroad after the amount of publicity One Nation had received.

So intimate was the link between the rise of Hansonism and Pauline Hanson's enormous media profile that this protest movement and the media became inextricably bound as a single cultural compound—the Hanson Phenomenon. This compound has made many journalists uneasy, including some of those who form the centre of gravity of political

THE REVENGE OF THE DESPISED

reporting in Australia. Paul Kelly, former editor-in-chief of the *Australian* and historian of the Hawke-Keating years, expressed his concerns in *Two Nations*, an anthology published just before the 1998 federal election:

> *At some future point, the media must assess its own role and motivation and the consequences flowing from its coverage of Pauline Hanson from the time of her maiden speech to the launch of the Queensland campaign. It is the media which made Hanson a national figure and kept her a national figure. The upshot is that Hanson had, by 1998, become the best known and most reported Australian figure in the international media from Europe through Asia. This was a distortion of her importance and news value. In the process, Australia became typecast abroad by Hanson. It is inconceivable that any other nation would have responded with such obsession about an extreme right-wing populist occupying just one seat in the national parliament. Yet the foreign coverage merely reflected the tenor of the local coverage.*

After millions of words were written about Hansonism, it was the shambolic poet laureate of the Labor Party, Bob Ellis, who distilled the essence of the phenomenon in one spectacular passage written for the *Sydney Morning Herald* at the high-water mark of Hansonism:

> *It was a pretty scary night, in the quietest Tally Room I can remember with everyone moving up and down before the big board in restless unbelief, till Pauline Hanson*

*arrived very early and stayed late, in a pale gold spot-
light with a jostling swarm of paparazzi, like Kim Novak
at a Hollywood premiere, to gloat and preen and prattle
and raise her strange yellow devil-cat eyes while everyone looked at her with a kind of erotic, stirred revulsion:
how could this dread improbability be happening?*

A few things should be said.

*One is the obvious, that seven of the One Nation
[Queensland] seats were won with National and Liberal
preferences, and these preferences will never so slavishly
go to One Nation again.*

You have my word on that.

*The next thing that needs to be said is the result
that night had very little to do with racism. A poll ten
days before showed Aboriginal-bludging and Asian-
swamping questions important to only one in ten of
One Nation voters, who like everyone else listed
unemployment, health, the breakdown of rural services,
the ending of rural communities and the break-up of
families as the top concerns. One in ten of One Nation
voters is 2.5 per cent of Queensland, the usual number
of racist obsessives. The usual suspects. The number
hasn't changed.*

Other polls had shown that Aboriginal issues were significant with One Nation voters, but Bob Ellis was basically right. It was the usual suspects. The number hadn't changed.

What has changed is the Australian media. Look back, for a moment, to the time when Australia faced much greater instability from a spontaneous, right-wing populist movement. It was called the New Guard. It sprang up in 1931 from the grassroots of the Depression. Most New Guard members were ex-servicemen, virulently anti-Communist and many of them owned guns. The number of pistol licences taken out in New South Wales rose rapidly that year. By the end of 1931 the New Guard had about 50 000 members.

It was a fertile time for populism. Communism and fascism were on the rise in Europe. New South Wales was roiled by political instability under Premier Jack Lang. In Victoria, a similar movement, known as the White Army, also grew quickly. In South Australia, a Citizens League, run by a former bus operator proclaiming 'We hate all parties' soon had 30 000 members. These three groups had an estimated 100 000 members by the end of the year. They shared a commitment to national unity, a return to Anglo-Saxon values of thrift and self-reliance, and the destruction of the dominance of machine politics.

Sound familiar? But there is one significant difference to the equation now. Imagine what would have happened today if a militaristic right-wing movement with 50 000 members, many of them armed, emerged outside the political party system.

Pandemonium.

The media would be in hyperdrive. The punditocracy would be in a state of apoplexy. Journalists from around the world would be flying in, drawn by the enormous electronic din in Australia.

In 1931, however, there was no pandemonium, no

electronic din. When the New Guard emerged as a news story in April 1931, Sydney had three major daily newspapers, no television, no news channels, no Internet and only six radio stations (now it has twenty-three, plus community stations). *The Sydney Morning Herald* published forty-seven stories about the New Guard in 1931, four of them on page one.

In 1932, an election year, the *Herald* published 107 stories, but only three on page one. Reading through the stories, one is struck by how devoid they are of overt opinion or hyperbole. In the absence of television and the paucity of radio news, this was how most people learned about the rise of the New Guard. The defeat of Jack Lang's government in 1932 took much of the sting out of the movement. The expression of popular will at the ballot box defused the tension (as it would again and again). The New Guard and the White Army fed on their own momentum for another year, but by 1934 had begun to fade quickly. Given that the nation was still in a state of economic depression it is remarkable how serenely Australian society absorbed the upswell, and how calmly the media reported the story.

Move forward to 10 September 1996.

On that day, the maiden speech of an independent member of Parliament triggered an unprecedented campaign against one person, a barrage of attention that could not have been technically possible in earlier times. It ranged from dogged investigation, to insightful analysis, to straight news, to front-page editorials, opinion polls, unflattering photographs, brutal headlines, manipulated quotes, gossip items, hostile columns, prurient speculation, TV confrontations, doorstop

THE REVENGE OF THE DESPISED

ambushes, handwriting analysis, parody, satire, unashamed snobbery, double standards and complete beat-ups. In short, every technique, every weapon, all the destructive power and all the thunderous moral outrage that the modern media could bring to bear.

At the end of eighteen months of massive scrutiny and moral thunder, this one individual had become the most reviled figure in politics. She was also the most famous politician in Australia, had the largest personal following, and led an inexperienced rag-tag party to the greatest first-up election performance in Australian political history.

So much for the moral authority of the Australian news media.

She was also a great story. There was no 'correct' way to handle Hanson, either by the media or the political establishment. The reaction to Hansonism produced a broad range of responses, most of them rational. Hansonism was an intersection of factors that had never quite aligned before. She was neither a media creation nor John Howard's illegitimate progeny. Politics feeds the media's natural biases: it is personality dominated, poll-driven, adversarial and easily accessible. For reporters, politics is a never-ending day at the races.

There is also no question that the lascivious extravagance of the media's coverage of Pauline Hanson was the most powerful ingredient the Hanson phenomenon. To her supporters, her policies didn't matter nearly as much as her 'courage' in the face of a torrent of abuse.

What defeated Pauline Hanson was her own ignorance.

When it came to the big game, a federal election, 'courage' was not enough. The electorate wanted commonsense. And Queensland is not Australia.

What also defeated her was the decision by the major parties to marginalise Hanson, deny preferences, and debate issues which would impact the hip pockets of most Australians. They rarely pointed the spotlight of attention on her, let alone ridicule. They starved One Nation of political oxygen. In doing so, the major parties studiously avoided the issue on which they had expended so much rhetoric for so long—Aboriginal land rights.

The major parties also avoided immigration, which only reared its head when One Nation unveiled a policy of zero net immigration. Yet not even One Nation raised the idea of halting Asian immigration. (It proposed zero net immigration, which still meant 30 000 migrants a year, selected on the basis of skill, not race.) Curbing Asian immigration, which not long ago had been part of the bedrock of Australian nationalism and had been for a hundred years, was simply no longer acceptable in the language of public debate. It would be an insult to the changed face of Australia. This healthy development was largely ignored by the media which instead fixated on Hansonism as proof that Australia was still riddled with racism.

This negative mindset prompted one of the more cerebral members of the federal Government, Dr Michael Wooldridge, the federal Minister for Health, in an essay for *Two Nations*, to write:

THE REVENGE OF THE DESPISED

The larger significance of the mass media at this particular junction of our history is not that it has mishandled the Hanson phenomena. It is that the media reflects and reinforces the pessimistic view of society and our future. There is virtually no area of public policy that is not described at least once a month as being in a state of 'crisis', although most sober assessments would suggest that levels of performance and achievement are better than they have been in decades and constantly improving.

The mass media is the transmission belt of ideas, values and information in society—and if the mass media becomes a dysfunctional institution which focuses only on the negative, with little attempt at perspective, then our nation will be the poorer.

What's more, movements like One Nation will draw ever greater nourishment from the daily diet of gloom served by a media which no longer has genuine interest in reinforcing strong civic values.

This is not an argument for boosterism but an appeal for introspection, about whether media has created a world in which the sky is always falling. The economics editor of *The Sydney Morning Herald*, Ross Gittins, left no doubt he believed negativity was out of control when he blew his top, in print, several times during 1998:

Media coverage of the Asian crisis has gone well beyond the biased reporting of official statistical facts to extensive speculation about the future. Once this barrier is crossed, the scope for imaginative pessimism is almost endless.

The public is entitled to feel hoaxed by business economists and the media. For the whole of this year, it has been consistently misled about the state of the economy.

The boys who cried wolf did so by exaggerating all the bad news and publicising all the most pessimistic predictions ...

While the business economists were making fools of themselves with their forecast of contraction, the less scrupulous elements of the media were having a field day, feigning innocence as they broadcast this foolishness to the nation ...

When we saw the national accounts, this mountain of bulldust came crashing down.

The Australian media does not have the protective ozone layer provided by great publications like *The New Yorker*, *The Atlantic Monthly* or *The New York Review Of Books*, which temper the herd mentality and often snuff out myths with superb reporting. Australia simply does not have the economy of scale to support such products. But now a gaping hole has opened up in the American media's ozone layer. The competition from new technologies is intensifying the pressures for sensation and soap opera. Harold Evans, the former editor of *The Times* and *The Sunday Times* now based in the United States, and one of the finest editors of his era, is one of many who does not like the direction technology is taking the profession:

THE REVENGE OF THE DESPISED

It is now a confusion of news, entertainment, fact and fiction, aggravated by round-the-clock television news programs that add little that is new but whip up emotions and base whole programs on tendentious hypotheticals.

These are concerns about the fundamental structure of the journalism and about the essence of news itself. They go well beyond what usually passes for media criticism in this country.

They reflect the fact that the mild disdain with which journalists have traditionally and honourably been treated by the public appears to be hardening into something more hostile. Cynicism has bred cynicism.

Journalists should be aware of a recent study published in the *Journal of Personality and Social Psychology* in which four experimental psychologists found a startlingly high level of what they called 'spontaneous trait transference'. Example: participants in a study were shown a videotape of a narrator talking about an acquaintance who was cruel to animals. In follow-up surveys, the study group was found to believe that the *narrator* was cruel to animals. We have always known that people tend to shoot the messenger, but these studies found the process of trait transference much more pronounced than previously believed. Given the amount of criticism, bad news and gossip that now flows from the media, and given the exaggerated lens that television places over society, negative trait transference must be at an all-time high.

The conventional media is increasingly trapped in a

narrative box. The standard news story, a three-act play with dramatic opening scene, set-up, and conflict—preferably between good and evil—is now increasingly exposed as an artifact. Most journalism is existential tourism. We journalists create order out of information chaos, but in the process, most of the time, we skate over complexity, nuance, moral ambiguity, and irresolution.

Now people don't have to buy the packaged tour. The Internet, cable television, satellite transmission, news radio, databases, and search engines on the Web offer a river of information, good and bad, available at great speed, enormous quantity, mostly low price, and with or without the filtering of journalists and editors. It is highway around the established order. It allows the younger to bypass the older. The next generation will want to live in a world than is more wired, more green, more republican and more colourblind than the one we have today. It will be a world more like that of Eric Liu, a young middle-class Californian, the son of Chinese immigrants, who writes that, 'the end product of American life is neither monocultural nor multicultural, it is omniculturalism'.

Yet, even in the United States, the wellspring of omniculturalism, multinational corporatism and the WorldWide Web, there is a strong pulse of economic nationalism. Fear of free trade with Mexico split the conservative vote in the 1992 presidential election and delivered victory to Bill Clinton. Fortress America is personified by the Republican presidential pretender Pat Buchanan, who in 1998 published a book entitled *The Great Betrayal: How American Sovereignty and*

THE REVENGE OF THE DESPISED

Social Justice are being Sacrificed to the Gods of the Global Economy. A more scholarly book published at the same time by Harvard economist Dani Rodrik asked a similar question: *Has Globalization Gone Too Far?*

If an articulate ideologue like Pat Buchanan can argue that America is dividing into an elite of prosperous professionals with a majority suffering 'middle-class anxiety, downsized hopes, and vanished dreams', it was inevitable something similar would emerge in Australia, where the academic left is already bristling with protectionist nostalgia.

Which brings us back to Jeff Knuth, a cut-price Pat Buchanan, whose maiden speech to the Queensland Parliament on 30 July 1998, after his improbable launch into politics on the coat-tails of Pauline Hanson, said much about the bottom-up view of the modern global economy:

> *The* [major] *parties ... fawned on foreign policy, globalisation, multinationals, Asia and the United Nations. They were more concerned about the world outside Australia than the Australia that we knew.*
>
> *They gave open slather to the multinationals and provided extended opportunities to the international big boys such as Kmart, Woolworths and Target. They did not want to know small business, especially Australian-owned small business ...*
>
> *... My electorate, like so many other electorates, is facing crippling unemployment ... The situation is the direct result of economic rationalism, globalisation, the non-existent level playing field, the politics of 'get big or*

> *get out' and the Federal and State Governments' sell-out of Australian and Queensland interests to the cartels, robber barons, monopolies and absentee landlords.*

He did not spend his maiden speech talking about Aborigines or immigrants. He talked about guns:

> *The great double-cross of them all was Prime Minister Howard's knee-jerk reaction to the firearm laws, allegedly because of Port Arthur.*
>
> *We now know that Port Arthur had nothing to do with it. That was only the excuse to slug Australians with extremist laws long hidden away in the files, laws hidden away in the dark bogholes of Canberra, awaiting the day when Australian law makers could be scared into passing laws hatched in a far away foreign capital to better fit Australians into their glorified international mould. Howard and his mates condemned hundreds of thousands of Australians as potential murderers ...*
>
> *They really do not want Australia sufficiently armed to defend itself because their loyalties lie elsewhere, outside Australia.*

The Australian people have always exhibited sufficient gravitas at federal elections to snuff out such paranoia. The 1998 federal election was a classic example, an act of collective, intuitive, partly accidental brilliance by the electorate.

On the night of 3 October 1998, when the results began to flow in from around the country, it was astounding how many well-aimed missiles had been fired at all parties. All over the country there were surgical strikes, knocking out target after target, without destroying the Government and the politics of reform.

John Howard's government was returned, but with such damage and with so many hostile minor-party Senators elected that it was clear the people had opted for solidity but would not brook a new tax on food as part of the proposed reforms.

The tax on food was dead on arrival before the voting had concluded on Saturday night.

The Labor Party was given succour, but the electorate declined to give government to a party with no new ideas and the whiff of past arrogance still fresh.

In Perth, however, the ebullient Kim Beazley, who had a great campaign, was given a resounding vote of confidence.

In rural New South Wales, the leader of the Nationals, Tim Fischer was easily re-elected with fifty-two percent of the primary vote despite a swing of 13.4 percent against him, all of which went to One Nation, but much lower than the twenty-four percent One Nation had been polling. Labor made no impact.

In Queensland, Pauline Hanson lost her place in Parliament.

(One Nation's sudden decline in its stronghold, from 22.7 percent to fifteen percent, resonated with the fate of the last great schism in Queensland, when the Democratic Labor Party, after its split from Labor, won twenty-three percent of the primary vote and eleven seats in state Parliament at the 1957 elections, a result mirrored by One Nation forty-one years later. Within three years, the DLP had been cut back to five seats in Queensland and the party never recovered.)

In New South Wales, One Nation's David Oldfield lost his Senate race but received 9.7 per cent of the vote.

In every state but Queensland, One Nation failed to win a seat. The Queensland Senate victory for One Nation's Heather Hill displaced the National's Bill O'Chee, who had helped the counterattack against the High Court's land rights judgements.

In New South Wales, the Democrat's Aden Ridgeway became only the second Aboriginal to win a seat in federal Parliament, defeating One Nation for the final seat.

In the Northern Territory, the vote on whether the territory should become the seventh state was defeated because the region's Aboriginal peoples did not trust the territory's government to be handed power over land rights.

In Brisbane, Cheryl Kernot's media-driven reputation as a people's star was filleted by the voters. The Liberal candidate, Rod Henshaw, almost ran her to ground with a campaign slogan of 'He's a decent *local bloke* for Dickson'. 'She wasn't perceived as a local but as somebody who lacked loyalty because of her defection—we heard about that time and time again.'

In Sydney, another high-profile flag-of-convenience candidate, David Hill, the former head of the ABC, lost a marginal seat Labor needed to win.

In Western Australia, Graeme Campbell, the head of Australia First, the precursor to One Nation, lost his sprawling seat of Kalgoorlie, largely because One Nation ran a candidate and split his vote. 'The decision by One Nation to run a candidate against Graeme Campbell was stupidity bordering on treachery,' said Australia First's Denis McCormack.

Even with the demise of Hanson and Campbell, the number of third party and independent members of the Australian state and federal parliaments was about eighty, the equivalent of an entire state Parliament.

It was, in short, a season in politics which saw the grip of the old two-party system made tenuous. It was the highest vote for third party candidates since the modern two-party system was formed after World War II. The Howard government won re-election, but Labor won more of the primary vote. Even the Democrats, with their control in the Senate, finished well behind One Nation primary vote in One Nation's first federal election.

It was the election everyone lost.

There had been a contained revolt. The political landscape had become more complex, more unforgiving, more unpredictable, and those who felt forgotten or despised had exacted their revenge.

PART FOUR

It is lack of confidence, more than anything else, that kills a civilisation. We can destroy ourselves by cynicism and disillusion just as effectively as by bombs.

Sir Kenneth Clark

16
WHITE DREAMING

I'm not a nice guy. I don't even want to be a nice guy. I have to overcorrect for the mealy-mouthed quality in contemporary Australian life. I try to draw attention to it by behaving in a different way. I just say what I think and it blows up in my face more often than not. But without honesty there can be no literature.

David Foster may or may not be a nice guy, but he won Australia's highest literary honour, the Miles Franklin Award, in 1997. It gave him a little room to move. He says some things I would not dare to say, or even dare to believe, but his courage, his willingness to defend the maligned bushies, the breadth of his knowledge, and the sheer scope of his family, which stretches across the country, up to the Top End and into an Aboriginal clan, make him a remarkable Australian. In some ways his story is Australia's story:

The eucalyptus are in heat at present, determined to seize the window of opportunity which has opened to them; dry storms over dry forests.

Until he won the Miles Franklin and became a best-selling author he was the country's finest unfamous author. It only took him ten novels to make it. 'David Foster is one of a very small handful of Australian writers writing today who will still be read in fifty or a hundred years from now,' wrote the literary critic Andrew Riemer. When his novel, *The Glade Within the Grove,* won the award, it went to a writer who lives so far from the cappuccino ghettos of Sydney and Melbourne that he has worked on prawning trawlers in the Gulf of Carpentaria and knows how to kick his way out of trouble in a fight.

His strongest literary influence is the first-century Roman writer Juvenal, whom he reads in the original Latin. 'Juvenal showed what could and should be done by an artist working in a decadent, or if you prefer, postmodern age such as ours.' Twenty years ago Patrick White described Foster as the most individual and most interesting writer in Australia. Geoffrey Dutton called him the country's most original and daring novelist. Rodney Hall wrote in 1996: 'I am yet again astounded that Foster is not more celebrated. Too much adulation is squandered on light-weight novels masquerading as literary works.'

David Foster grew up in rural New South Wales and graduated with honours from Sydney University. He went on to earn a doctorate in inorganic chemistry and do postgraduate work, left university to work as a postman in a country town, Bundanoon, and take a succession of literary grants. 'No PhD likes to put a postman's uniform on. You swallow your ego. But I was trying to write, and I had to earn an income.'

As recently as the month before he won the Miles Franklin he was working as crew on his son-in-law's prawning trawler in the Gulf of Carpentaria. 'Professional fishing is not much fun. Though green deckies are probably Australia's most highly paid teenagers. It's dirty, dangerous and unremitting work, with stonefish and catfish in the prawn. Deckhands lose fingers. The boats wallow in the big swells.' He goes north so he can visit his scattered family, including those in the Top End, the family one of his sons married into, the Aboriginal branch of the family. Aboriginal with a big dash of Chinese.

The High Court's Wik decision came to mind as I sat in the galley of our trawler, at anchor off the red bauxite beach at Weipa, Gulf of Carpentaria, not far from the Archer River Mission. Wik territory. We were preparing to hunt banana prawn. It's one of Australia's most lucrative fisheries, the northern prawn fishery. A licence for an eighty-footer like ours will cost you $2.4 million.

'This is not fishing the way the Wik fish. I'm not sure the Wik ever fished bananas. But the Croker Islanders want their cut of my percentage. We fishermen understand the Wik. What could be more pathetic than a warrior defeated in war, a hunter deprived of his hunting ground? The prawn farm is the future, but prawn fishermen despise prawn farms. They won't work on prawn farms for the same reason the Wik don't want to work at all: when you have known the real thing, a surrogate becomes unacceptable.

Until he won $27 000 and best-seller status from the Miles Franklin, the rainshowers of high critical praise for Foster had produced little in the way of widespread recognition. He remains a niche novelist, a dense stand of old-growth rainforest amid a sea of prevailing eucalypt.

He writes about Australia with a lucid affinity, and is a gifted naturalist.

> *I felt humiliated that I knew so little of the bush I grew up in and liked to spend so much time in. I'd done a couple of years of botany, and I more or less had to start a field herbarium. I really liked botany. It's one of the less egotistical fields.*

Foster is a wiry, weathered piratical figure who once bemused an academic conference by delivering a large part of his address in Latin. He can be a mesmerising performer. When giving a reading he usually wears the bush working uniform of boots, moleskins and blue singlet, and while he recites he rolls a cigarette with one hand. At the 1996 Adelaide Festival he recited from memory an unbroken passage from his *The Ballad of Erinungarah* for forty minutes. He's memorised the entire two hundred stanzas.

> *While red and black cicadas*
> *Add their stridulating song*
> *To the ceaseless play of rapid spray*
> *Could human voices sing so strong?*
> *Can human voices sing as long?*
> *Why should the glade within the grove*
> *Yield to a city paved with gold?*

His vantage point on the world is an old stone cottage in Bundanoon with views of the escarpments and gorges of the Blue

Mountains. It is the area where Foster was born, where he has lived for more than twenty years, and where he worked as a postie. He writes in a little studio behind his home. Two certificates on his wall say he holds advanced black belts in martial arts. 'Tae kwon do, hard style,' he says. 'Don't worry about that. To a certain extent I don't like to be presented as a martial artist. I did it because it went against the grain.'

Outside his studio window is an enormous eucalypt. 'That's a big ribbon gum. It's one of the reasons we like the place. It's a big fella. We white people have always been uncomfortable with the eucalypt. They are an extraordinary species, and the more you learn about them the more they take your breath away. Especially as they are evolving enormously while most other species are disappearing.'

> *I prefer to be alone and I believe a white man can be more alone in the Blue Mountains than almost any place, because we European settlers don't as yet have eucalypt dreaming. I have oak dreaming. A spell of walking in Ireland left me in no doubt of it.*

'Most of us have no idea what we are looking at when we go out into the bush. It's a tremendously varied landscape here. We never had an ice-age to wipe out botanical species as they did in Europe. And there is a tremendous number of species in Australia, even given the rates of extinction. It doesn't reveal itself in a walk-through once a month.

'My first wife's an anthropologist. My son went through early phases of initiation into an Aboriginal people, one of the few full-blood whites ever to have done so. It was because he was very gifted with the language, and a good dancer, and a good kind of boy. It's a great place for young boys, an Aboriginal camp. Not so good for grown men.'

Much of Foster's life—his experiences visiting his Aboriginal family in the Top End, his spiritual life as a martial artist, and his work in the prawning industry—coalesces in one of his finest novels, *Mates of Mars*, in which Foster, typically, never lapses into sentimentality or cheap second-hand moral superiority:

> *Cyril and the boys had a country once, but that country is dead and all the best wishes of well-intentioned folk from Glebe to Carlton will not revive it. And let these folk live and work with Cyril and the boys for a while, and see how red their necks get.*

'A lot of sentimentality obscures the issues. It's an intractable problem. The issue of colonised peoples. It won't go away. There's a conviction in our society that every problem has a solution, but certain problems don't have solutions. Problems that arise between colonisers and colonised, problems that arise between men and women. There are certain intractables. A proper intelligence recognises that and uses those tensions in their art or in their thinking. The notion that all problems can be removed is not even intellectual.'

> *All eyes are on Cyril that evening when a young lubra collapses, drunk, next to the bowsers at the service station opposite the pub.*
>
> *Cyril doesn't look as though he cares as much as his*

white colleagues, and why should he? He has nothing to do with these Arunta. He inhabits the richest part of the continent; they inhabit one of the poorest. He doesn't speak the same language as the men, doesn't sing the same songs, doesn't dance the same dances. Only a white man would put them on the same committee.

'When you actually look, as distinct from fantasise, you realise that the health problems that so concern us among the blacks are really not of overwhelming concern to them. They are very tough hunter people. Injuries and wounds are something they don't take a great deal of notice of. With all the consequences. They die younger, they get sick, they get injuries, they live in a state of chronic ill-ease. But being healthy and living for a long time is not their goal in life. In that they distinguish themselves from whites ... They are very different to us. Plus we're talking about a culture that has been assaulted and brutalised and really hardly exists any more, except in people's memories. We idealise it.'

Opposite, a young woman, kicking and screaming, is being dragged by her hair from one camp to another. The young men pulling her are swigging at a 2-litre moselle bottle, which is hot stuff and banned.

'I can only apologise,' says Jade to Cyril, 'for what we have done to your people. I think it's absolutely scandalous that they have been introduced to alcohol.'

  'Ah,' Cyril replies, 'reckon dey gotta make up dere own minds dere. Same as de rest of us.'

'I find it difficult to feel an overwhelming sense of guilt or an overwhelming sense of violation about the Aboriginal issue. Many of them went into the stations—they weren't rounded up with stockwhips—because they liked flour and sugar and wanted to avail themselves of some of the advantages of white civilisation. And that's where the problems began. It wasn't only a matter of forcing our civilisation upon them. They changed. There is not one of them who wants to hand in his semi-automatic, I imagine. Things like guns and beer are non-negotiable attributes of modern civilisation which they are not prepared to now do without.

'The big problem for me as a scientist is the word "Aboriginal". What does it mean? Most of the people who call themselves Aboriginal have not been initiated. They don't speak for the cultural elders. People assume they understand Aboriginal issues, but once they get among real experiences, this quickly cures them of their misconceptions ... Genital mutilation is basically the system of Aboriginal initiation. They first circumcise the penis. Some tribes also then subincise the penis. They open the penis up to the urethra ...

'I don't know why they are as they are. Those tribes are very different to us. But if someone is not circumcised in a traditional ceremony, are they an Aboriginal? Nobody has a definition. Is it culture? Is it blood? Are my black grandsons Aboriginals? What does that make me? What is my son, an initiated man? I've got white grandsons and black grandsons.'

If we define an Aboriginal Australian as a person of unmixed Aboriginal descent, no longer living the traditional nomadic lifestyle but residing in a settlement of some sort, retaining traditional language and culture, then such Australians, most to the north of the continent, are held in widespread awe today. There exists towards them, from white country and city both, an unstinting affection ...

But towards the mixed blood Aboriginal there is not much goodwill. Their proclivity for white vice, in the boredom of their chronic unemployment, has also worn the patience of their black kinsmen, many of whom disown them utterly as non-initiated yellow trade-offs. Their seemingly intractable behaviour evokes the wringing of distant white hands, while whites obliged to contend with them daily have a battle on their hands, quite literally ...

In an opinion piece published soon after he won the Miles Franklin Award, Foster suggested that the classification of race in Australia, with people claiming to be Aboriginal with just the barest mix of indigenous blood—hence the explosion of 'Aboriginal' numbers in Australia in recent decades—was exactly the wrong way to go.

A first step toward reconciliation would be to show some of that generosity our indigenous peoples have traditionally shown towards peoples of mixed blood by accepting such mixed blood people as our own. Let us throw this whole business out of reverse gear. Let us regard any person born in Australia as Australian, pure and simple, excepting only those who are initiated and retain a tribal culture.

By this definition my full-blood white elder son, an initiated man, is Aboriginal, and my three coffee-coloured mixed-blood grandsons, who go to school in Darwin, Australians, nothing more. Just Australians, albeit Top Enders with a skin better suited to the climate than most of us. In fairness, I ought to add my son sees himself as white and his boys as Aboriginal. I think he's wrong.

For his frankness Foster was given a head-kicking by the Thought Police in Sydney. But he had raised a fundamental issue. The number of indigenous Australians is exploding. The 1996 census shows that 352 970 people (1.9 percent of the population) described themselves as indigenous, an increase of 87 599, or thirty-three percent, since 1991. The key factor in this surge in numbers, which itself is surely a clear sign of surging indigenous pride and strength, was intermarriage with whites. In contrast with the United States, where the intermarriage rate between blacks and whites is between ten and twelve percent, the intermarriage rate between indigenous Australians and whites is forty-seven percent. Because one Aboriginal parent is enough for someone to claim Aboriginal identity, this accelerates the growth in numbers. The reality of race in Australia, and it is a healthy reality, is that a majority of the 352 970 indigenous population are actually mixed-race Australians.

Forty percent of indigenous Australians now live in the big cities, and the growing stream of mixed-race Australians claming indigenous status—and indigenous rights—is causing problems described bluntly by the black activist and author Roberta Sykes.

> *The black community does have a problem ... just thinking about coping with a flood of white-looking and totally deculturated people poised to demand Aboriginal rights for themselves.*

No-one personifies the growing complexity of racial identity in Australia more than Roberta Sykes. In the wake of publication of the first two volumes of her autobiographical trilogy (*Snake Cradle* that won *The Age* Book of the Year in 1997, and *Snake Dancing* followed in 1998), elders of the Birigubba Juru-Bindal clan, centered around Townsville, commissioned a blistering report about Dr Sykes, written in 1998 by Associate Professor Gracelyn Smallwood, director of Aboriginal Studies at the University of Southern Queensland:

> *She has constructed an identity closely aligned to the snake as a totem in a desperate search for Aboriginality. There is no evidence to show she understands the seriousness of such an action ...*
>
> *Many of our Aboriginal and Torres Strait Islander Townsville community take offence ... Dr Sykes is denigrating our culture and exploiting the Jura/Bindal Birrigubba Nation by using the snake as a literary device*

> in her writing as opposed to having any spiritual connection as a Birrigubba person ...
>
> A large percentage of the Townsville Aboriginal and Torres Strait Islander community including myself remember Roberta Sykes as never associating with us. Roberta was always seen with the white community and at no time do we ever recall her as identifying as an Aboriginal.

Dr Smallwood said that, based on Dr Sykes's own comments and writings, her mother was white and her father was almost certainly a black American. It is an old story. It has always been well known that Roberta Sykes was not regarded as indigenous by Aboriginal people. As long ago as 1980, when asked in a TV interview if she was an Aboriginal, she snapped, 'None of your damn business.'

David Foster, whose life is touched by these complex currents, is as unflinching about the strengths of Aboriginal civilisation as he is about the weaknesses. He regards the spiritual links that many Aboriginal peoples have with their country as the single greatest absence in Australia's dominant white civilisation. 'They have a spiritual connection with the landscape and their totem animals, so death is no big deal to them. That gives them their strength.

'We whites are settled pastoralists and we need a different dreaming. To me, the Irish landscape is a white dreaming landscape because there are myths around every pass, every valley, every rock. There was still an immense amount of wilderness in Ireland in St Patrick's day. The whole island was a wood of cecile oak with hardly a town or village ... White Australians haven't really bothered to know their own landscape sufficiently. I feel we walk in landscapes that have no resonance for us. We know nothing about them scientifically and they have no mythic meaning to us ...

'How long will we be the dominant force on this continent? Our record here is undistinguished and may be short-lived. I see Australia as a potential tragedy because it's a civilisation that has gone into premature decline.'

With his family spread to the Top End, to the Gulf, to Perth and to Sydney, Foster has travelled through the back country of Australia and found the most dangerous erosion of all, the widening divide between city and country.

I found country people are outraged at how they are portrayed and treated in the city. It all began with the gun laws after the Port Arthur massacre, when country people perceived they were all portrayed as rednecks with rifles. It has just gotten worse since then. City people forget that country people are very hard up. And it's easy to mouth platitudes when you are not hard up against it in places like Bourke and Moree. The people in the bush now know they've got no back-up in the city.

It is unfair to expect rural whites to bear the full burden of reconciliation. In the edicts of affirmative action and restitutions from the High Court, rural white Australia, prostrated by drought, abandoned by bankers, commodity prices falling, sees only sanctimony from white lawyers who've never had to face the problems they address. Coming fast on the heels of a gun law that tells us we cannot be trusted with our firearms, this, for many, is the last straw.

The gun law quickly became a struggle between country versus cities. It is so deeply offensive to country people. And frankly, if you're going to disarm all the warriors, humiliate them, you're going to disenfranchise that warrior spirit that is required in times of trouble ...

All our current problems stem from overpopulation, and no-one knows how to cope with it. Too much. Too many. Of everything. We have exceeded the limits of a viable society ... Early in this century Australia was one of the most promising of all civilisations—very democratic, very egalitarian, but also with a fierce racism that became unacceptable. We had a very strong intellectual tradition. Australia and New Zealand were among the first centres of Western civilisation in the modern era. Geoffrey Blainey called Sydney and Melbourne the first high-leisure Western cities. I think a lot of that early advantage has been lost.

Australia needs a stronger sense of its own identity. A stronger faith in its own judgement. A willingness to mix it with the neighbours. A spiritual dimension is crucial. Spiritual hunger is a feature of the modern world and it's usually resolved in escapist activities.

WHITE DREAMING

Drugs, more than anything else. Drugs are taking sacraments for gods you don't know the names of.

Australians are becoming soft. Soft-minded. Soft people are usually knocked over by hard people. And they never thought it could come.

17
A GRAND AND POWERFUL COUNTRY

IN 1911, ONE OF AUSTRALIA'S most highly regarded geographers, Griffith Taylor of Sydney University, predicted that by the year 2000 Australia might support a population of nineteen million people. The prediction ruined his career.

It was viewed as preposterous, even insulting, in a country that most people believed would become a second America. The harsh environment proved Griffith Taylor right, but his remarkable prescience—in the year 2000 Australia's population will be nineteen million—remained largely forgotten until the arrival of Tim Flannery, another environmental pessimist. Unlike Taylor, Flannery's pessimism was greeted by tremendous commercial and critical success when he published *The Future Eaters*, eighty-three years later in 1994.

Flannery quotes the great Charles Darwin who, after a visit to Australia in 1836, predicted with characteristic acuity that Australia's fragile environment would ultimately constrain the nation:

> *I formerly imagined that Australia would rise to be as grand and powerful a country as North America, but*

now it appears to me that such future grandeur is rather problematical.

One hundred and fifty years later, Flannery said the same thing for exactly the same reasons: Australia must give up its century-long delusion of becoming a large population country.

> 'We don't know what the real sustainable carrying capacity of this country is. When I wrote that it may only be twelve million people, it was an intellectually honest attempt to estimate the country's real capacity. Even with all of the benefits of irrigation and technology, our agriculture is at the mercy of the cycle that drives Australia's strange climate, the El Nino Southern Oscillation (ENSO), which brings cycles of drought, fire and flood. The critical difference between an Australian winter and a European winter is predictability. European farmers know almost exactly how long winter will last.'

Flannery's estimate of twelve million people as Australia's sustainable carrying capacity seems absurdly low. Neither the CSIRO or the Australian Conservation Foundation come even close to agreeing with him. They both put a figure of around twenty-three million, by which time Australia may no longer have a surplus of grain production, as the benchmark for imposing population limits.

Flannery, like Griffith Taylor, is a serious scholar not a green fanatic (well, maybe a bit fanatical). Even if he is wrong about the carrying capacity of Australia, he serves as a highly useful counterpoint to the ideology of unlimited growth. Griffith Taylor never backed away from his prediction, despite the ridicule heaped upon him, nor does Flannery. 'There is so much new science since then which supports the arguments in the book, and more is coming out all the time.'

Flannery has Taylor's capacity for stirring up trouble in the most gentlemanly way. At school, he was suspended twice, both times over a moral principle with the abortion debate then raging in Melbourne. 'I had a very unhappy education at St Bede's College, Melbourne. It was such an intellectually closed environment.' He qualified for every university, despite the convulsions at St Bede's, and he noticed an item in the *Catholic Advocate* which referred to Chisholm College at La Trobe University in Melbourne as a 'hellhole of sinners'. That was just the place for young Tim Flannery. 'I thought it sounded great.'

More than twenty years later, as principal research scientist at the Australian Museum in Sydney, he has warned in *The Future Eaters* that Australia is already overpopulated and eating its own future through sheer ignorance. Yet despite this urgent environmental pessimism, Flannery finds plenty to be hopeful about:

> *I find it fascinating to see the growing awareness about Australia's environment and its history. People are opening their eyes. They are going back to original documents that have been ignored. Watkin Tench is an example of someone who provides us with a superb original source.*

AMONG THE BARBARIANS

Captain Watkin Tench was an English officer who arrived in Australia with the First Fleet in 1788 and wrote two superb but largely forgotten eyewitness accounts of the first settlement, particularly the first interactions between the Europeans and the Aborigines. 'Watkin Tench challenges the negative myths that have grown up about Australia, especially about the relationship between the early white settlers and the Aborigines.'

Tench was the key witness of that crucial moment in Australian history when the two civilisations met as equals, with neither dependent on the other. 'It's a first-hand account of the origins of modern Australia. And it's a well-written account.' Tench writes at the outset of his first book, which generated tremendous interest in England when it was published in 1789: 'I have been careful to repress that spirit of exaggeration which is almost ever the effect of novelty on ignorance.' Flannery writes in the introduction of *1788*, the highly successful reissue of Tench's works:

> *Tench's evolving view of the Aborigines is of enduring interest. It is typical of the way humans react to new and different cultures. At first fearful, perhaps even contemptuous of these 'fickle, jealous, wavering' people, Tench gradually came to know them. When he left Sydney in 1791, he also left friends behind ...*
>
> *[Tench] places in sharp focus just how distasteful the Aborigines found the English class system, a structure in which even fully initiated Aboriginal men were systematically relegated to the bottom of the social ladder. They*

> would simply not tolerate being treated so. Instead, they
> laughed at and mocked the Europeans for their clumsi-
> ness and stupidity in the bush. When the exhausted
> Europeans (who in any case were carrying the supplies of
> the Aborigines) showed ill-humour at this, the Aborigines
> promptly called them gonin-patta—shit-eaters.

Flannery revels in what he calls 'unfashionable' history. He has little regard for postmodernism. He does not think much of the multicultural industry either. 'I hate tribalism in any form.' He does not believe in the new academic vogue that Australia is a postgenocidal society that must forever apologise for its existence. 'I think genocide is the wrong word. Disease and social dislocation were more decisive than deliberate extermination.' While not trivialising the privations visited upon the Aboriginal peoples, a subject about which he feels deeply, he believes much contemporary Australian history is fixated on the cruelty directed toward Aborigines while minimising the attempts to form bonds with them and improve their conditions, however misguided, by the European settlers. The observations of Watkin Tench capture the ultimate decency of the first settlers in regard to Aborigines before the two civilisations were in a state of virtual war. Two centuries later, some of the observations Watkin Tench made in that first year of contact remain startlingly relevant:

> With the natives we are hand in glove. They throng the
> camp every day, and sometimes by their clamour and
> importunity for bread and meat (of which they now eat

greedily) are become very troublesome. God knows, we have little enough for ourselves!

During the intervals of duty our greatest source of entertainment now lay in cultivating the acquaintance of our new friends, the natives ... [but] inexplicable contradictions arose to bewilder our researches which no ingenuity could unravel.

They walked stoutly, appeared but little fatigued, and maintained their spirits admirably, laughing to excess when any of us either tripped or stumbled. At a very short distance from Rose Hill, we found that they were in a country unknown to them, so that the farther they went the more dependent on us they became, being absolute strangers inland.

During this trial of their patience and courtesy ... they had manifested no ungenerous sign of taking advantage of the helplessness and dependence of our situation; no rude curiosity to pry into the packages with which they were entrusted ... let him whose travels have lain among polished nations produce me a brighter example of disinterested urbanity than was shown by these denizens of a barbarous clime.

I do not hesitate to declare that the natives of New South Wales possess a considerable portion of that acumen, that sharpness of intellect, which bespeaks genius.

But indeed the women are in all respects treated with

savage barbarity. Condemned not only to carry the children but all other burdens, they meet in return for submission only with blows, kicks, and every other mark of brutality. When an Indian is provoked by a woman, he either spears her or knocks her down on the spot ...

It must nevertheless be confessed that the women often artfully study to irritate and inflame the passions of the men, although sensible that the consequences will alight on themselves.

With a degree in English, a master's degree in geology, a doctorate in zoology, and a high level of computer literacy, Flannery has an exceptionally broad scholarly perch from which he continues to stir the cultural pot. He continues to write books. He is on the advisory panel to the Minister for Immigration—Flannery thinks Australia's high immigration intakes are crazy—and in 1998 he became visiting Professor of Australian Studies at Harvard University. When the *New York Times* reviewed *The Future Eaters*, Professor Paul Rabinow wrote: 'Mr Flannery tells an epic story with a sure-handed, personally implicated perspective ... He tells a wondrous story of extinction, dwarfing, fire ...' *The Future Eaters* may be a wondrous story, but it is, above all, a warning, and Tim Flannery has declined to modify his warning in a time of material abundance.

The deception experienced by each wave of human immigrants into the 'new' lands is one of the great constants of the human experience in the region. To the earliest Aborigines, it must have seemed as if the herds of diprotodons stretched on forever. To the Maori, the moa must have appeared a limitless resource. European agriculturalists saw what they imagined were endless expanses of agricultural land. Early Chinese immigrants to Australia saw san gum shaan *(new gold mountain), and now each new immigrant sees an opportunity to prosper in the land of plenty. In short, they have all seen cornucopia where there is very little ...*

Yet these unoccupied spaces and apparent opportunities in fact represent something very different, for they are necessary accommodations in a hard land. For the Aborigines, it meant forgoing agriculture and hence leaving a very different mark on the land. For the Australians of European origin, it has meant leaving the centre and north largely empty and the creation of vast national parks on what appears to be useable land. It has meant the imposition of what are—by European standards— extraordinarily low stocking rates on rangelands.

These necessary accommodations have created a sense of paranoia in living Australians. Perhaps because of their own recent use of the concept of terra nullius, *many fear that people from Asia will perceive in Australia, if not an empty land, then an under-utilised one.*

Since the publication of *The Future Eaters*, the accumulation of evidence by many other scientists confirms the need for alarm and urgency. Among the most conspicuous of these scientists is Doug Cocks, Senior Principal Research Scientist with the CSIRO's Division of Wildlife and Ecology, who has delivered sardonic assessments of Australia's ongoing degradation in two books, *Use With Care* (1992) and *People Policy* (1996). Using extensive satellite mapping and an abundance of geographic data, Cocks describes a continent with a thin skin of soil, the most basic of all natural resources, which is getting thinner all the time. He tells a story of erosion, salinisation and acidification. Less than ten percent of the continent has rich productive soil. Even areas of deep soils and good rainfall have poor tree growth because of nutrient deficiencies. Pressures which drive artesian water to the surface are declining in large areas. In the Great Artesian Basin, water has to be pumped up another half metre each year. Imported weeds—thorny mesquite, rubber vine, bitou bush, lantana, blackberries, bracken—have collectively wiped out enormous amounts of native biota. The march of the cane toad is wiping out still more. Among Cocks's many diagnoses, warnings and recommendations, there is one subject that gets him agitated:

> *Australia must adopt a 'no immigration' policy. It is the one topic in this book on which I am prepared to take an unequivocal stand ... the economic argument for substantial immigration is in tatters.*

His agitation on this subject had not subsided by 1996 and the publication of *People Policy*:

> *It would not be difficult to assemble a long list of failures and embarrassments in the formulation and administration of Australian immigration policy going*

> *back to 1925 ... More recently, there have been significant failures ... the failure of the 'skills' program to deliver appropriately skilled people, the 'rorting' of the business migration scheme, increasing numbers of overstayers ...*

He lists the large number of constituencies which have self-interest in high immigration policies, which, collectively, explain the powerful forces behind large-scale immigration in Australia.

> 1. *Migrant organisations.*
> 2. *Migrant-dependent bureaucrats.*
> 3. *Migrant-dependent entrepreneurs.*
> 4. *Minority-group expansionists.*
> 5. *Growth-oriented state governments.*
> 6. *Growth-oriented federal politicians.*
> 7. *Economic libertarians.*
> 8. *Open-door humanitarians.*
> 9. *The building industry.*
> 10. *Minority-dependent academics.*

Aligned against this battery of interests, writes Cocks, are several groups that want a reduction in immigration:

> 1. *Environmentalists.*
> 2. *The unemployed.*
> 3. *Aborigines.*
> 4. *Cultural protectionists.*
> 5. *Racists.*

6. *Off-shore humanitarians. (More foreign aid, not more refugees.)*

Obviously the high-immigration groups have more economic firepower than the low-immigration groups. The environmentalists provide the bulk of the counterbalance to the continued supremacy of high immigration.

Doug Cocks, Tim Flannery and most of the environmentalists who have appeared in this book believe Australia should stabilise its population immediately. Cocks advocates annual net migration of between zero and 50 000 people, which he says would produce a stable population of between twenty and twenty-three million by 2045. Growth of per capita national wealth and productivity would continue with minimal population increases. The practical reforms by the Howard government in 1997–98—an intake at 80 000 immigrants a year, a higher proportion of skilled entrants, a clampdown on rorts, a tightening of welfare eligibility—struck a political balance and took immigration off the boil.

Nevertheless, Doug Cocks describes most agricultural practices as the 'slow mining' of the soil, and recent studies have shown that the 'slow mining' of Australia's soil resources is ongoing. Australian farmers are still clearing nearly 500 000 hectares of land every year. Professor Wayne Meyer of Charles Sturt University and the CSIRO warns: 'The day is fast approaching when we cannot afford to irrigate pastures to produce meat and wool because water will have become too expensive.' About seventy-five percent of Australia's water is consumed by agriculture and the rising cost of water is a hidden cost in food. He cites as an example the need for 730 litres of water to produce one kilogram of dry wheat.

When I asked Tim Flannery whether all these problems (most of which are still below the horizon of public concern) would preclude Australia from becoming an eco-superpower, he replied:

> *No, providing we stop the policy of growth for the sake of growth. The high unemployment numbers show we already have a large surplus of workers.*

Flannery does not regard himself as a doomsayer, or a defeatist:

> *Australians have been shaped in a profound way, and in a positive way, by their environment. We are so fortunate that the Australian environment, through its poverty, has forced upon us an ethos of social obligation, of mateship. Australian mateship is a realisation that we either stand together in this environment or fall alone.*

18
GREEN THUNDER

HIGH UNEMPLOYMENT IS KILLING young people. Research by people like Stephen Murrell at Sydney University shows a deep and abiding link between the rate of unemployment among young Australians and the rate of suicide.

Our high rate of youth suicide should be a national emergency. It is one of the durable, structural problems facing Australia, which include high unemployment, drug abuse, Aboriginal wellbeing, environmental degradation, and declining economic sovereignty. (Australia's annual deficit in dividends and interest payments to foreign companies is bigger than the current account deficit; in many ways, it *is* the current account deficit.)

As Australians cast around for ways of tackling these problems there is a scheme which, at least potentially, could strike a blow at all of them. In January 1997 the Australian government allocated 41.6 million dollars to the Australian Trust for Conservation Volunteers to employ 440 young people aged between seventeen and twenty to help in the preservation and regeneration of the Australian environment. The program was to expand to employ 1700 people in the second year.

AMONG THE BARBARIANS

The idea is so unambiguously attractive that its only flaw was its size. It isn't big enough. The Green Corps could be exponentially more ambitious. Obviously it would be exponentially more costly, but the cost of expanding the scheme would be an investment, not an expenditure. There are also ways the Green Corps can help pay for itself in the national accounts, especially as a form of foreign aid.

The Green Corps is not just another unemployment scheme. It is an overdue attempt to link two huge problems—the erosion of the physical environment, and the erosion of employment opportunities for young Australians. The old job-creating tools don't work as well any more. Technocrats and politicians would adjust the macroeconomic dials, cut interest rates, target waste, cut debt. But this has lost some of its job-creating impact. Advanced economies have seen a historic decoupling of economic growth and job-growth. Companies are expanding while shedding workers. Reinventing, reengineering, downsizing, outsourcing—all these buzzwords mean more efficiency, but they also mean that governments have to work harder to create work.

The Green Corps seeks to tap into the deep reservoir of commitment felt by the majority of young Australians to the cause of environmentalism. The urgent national issue of soil erosion and conservation, outlined by the CSIRO's Doug Cocks in the previous chapter, is one that the Green Corps could target. It could also help Australia project green power into its hemisphere. It could give Australians experience of the lives and cultures of our neighbours in the south-west

Pacific and South-East Asia, the two areas where Australia must concentrate all of its foreign aid. Commitment to the environment would be a critical element in the selection process for applicants to the corps. Green Corps graduates would be expected to leave the program with training in skills ranging from bush regeneration techniques to habitat protection and environmental management. There is also the immeasurable benefit of the work done—thousands of small projects—and the work experience.

In its first year of operation, the Green Corps members worked on conserving vegetation along transport corridors, especially around conspicuous assets such as Sydney Harbour; on restoring habitats; creating sanctuaries, especially for endangered species; rehabilitating coastlands, wetlands, mangrove stands and coastal lakes. Green Corps members began work preparing Sydney for the 2000 Olympics. They were clearing and planting along the harbour foreshore, and along major transport corridors. A lot of Green Corps work is grinding, dirty, monotonous manual labour. It is not highly paid. In the first year, corps members were paid a training allowance of between $149 and $246 a week, depending on levels of schooling and time since leaving school.

But the work has a higher purpose and it is no more monotonous than many jobs. And if a tour of duty on the Green Corps is successful, its participants will graduate with a deeper knowledge of Australia and its soul, a sense of teamwork and camaraderie beyond the school environment. Those who are good enough and interested enough would then be ready for the next stage: duty on foreign aid. At the time of writing, Australia was spending 1.4 billion dollars a year on foreign aid, or just 0.29 percent of gross domestic product. The developed world average is 0.41 percent.

This is not the behaviour of a potential eco-superpower. If Australia wanted to project its values, create jobs, help its poorer neighbours, build a multitude of personal links with South-East Asia and the South Pacific, and attack pollution and erosion problems that ignore national boundaries, we could not possibly make a better investment than expanding the Green Corps to regional aid. A commitment to a Green Corps employing and training thousands of young Australians on projects throughout Australia and its region would cost more than the 1.4 billion dollars in foreign aid budget but it would have a major impact on youth unemployment.

The Green Corps does need a budget blow-out.

(1) The Government has already set aside a one-billion-dollar environment fund from the partial sale of Telstra, which could be directed to the Green Corps.

(2) Part of the Green Corps' wage and training costs would be recycled as income taxes.

(3) Funding could come from within the existing foreign aid budget, substituting a portion of foreign aid with work and skills provided by Green Corps members, most of them trained professionals who would work on specific projects.

(4) Some of the ATSIC budget and work-for-the-dole funding for young Aborigines could be transferred to the Green Corps, which offers many possibilities for the indigenous population. Given the deep historic link

between the indigenous peoples and the land, this would appear to be an obvious priority, though no doubt difficult to execute.

(5) Part of the Green Corps's work would be recycled as economic value as it slowed the process of soil and water degradation.

Australia could be delivering specific aid for specific programs under a variety of non-monolithic schemes, both government and non-government. They could replicate the projects of the domestic Green Corps; providing family planning and health services (a nurse can do almost as much good as a doctor where hygiene is poor); upgrading and training in horticulture and agriculture; contributing to fisheries protection; training local administrators. This would provide jobs for Australians and protect, step by step, the regional environment.

Birth control and the education of women are two causes Australia should do more to champion. 'Australia cannot consider population issues and foreign aid issues which fail to consider the global status of women,' says Jim Downey, executive director of the Australian Conservation Foundation. 'Ninety percent of the world's projected population growth over the next thirty-five years will take place in the developing world where the status of women and their access to education and birth control is of grave concern.'

Green Corps members who could manage small-scale projects on conservation, agriculture, education, birth control. Australia should also concentrate solely on its area of influence in the South Pacific and South-East Asia, an area which covers a quarter of the globe.

Why do so many countries in this region have such poor environmental records? ask international law experts, Daniel Esty and Andre Dua. Because of 'the pervasiveness of market failures—the ability of producers and consumers to spill harm onto others, and not have to pay for it'. They write:

> *The trends in China, Indonesia and Thailand remain unmitigatedly negative. China, for instance, is now home to three of the seven most polluted cities in the world. Indonesia suffered a loss of forest cover of almost 110 million hectares between 1981 and 1990. In Thailand, the percentage of the population with access to fresh drinking water has actually fallen as the country's rivers have become fouled with a ten-fold increase in industrial waste.*

The news is also bad in Papua New Guinea, Malaysia, Burma and the island states of the Pacific. The ability of the world to deal with the mess is itself a mess. As Esty and Dua explain:

> *The global environmental regime, comprising the United Nations Environment Program, the Commission on Sustainable Development, numerous treaties and their secretariats, and the environmental work of many other international organisations, is deeply flawed. Authority is fragmented. Coordination across organisations is poor.*

> *Political and financial backing for serious initiatives is limited.*

Instead of attempting to be a second-rank power at the United Nations and multilateral forums—a pocket Britain or America—Australia should concentrate its diplomatic and foreign aid resources on becoming a first-rank nation in environmental diplomacy, research and foreign aid. In other words, an eco-superpower.

Daniel Esty has a brilliant idea:

> *The proper response to this chaos in international environmental management would be the creation of a Global Environmental Organisation (GEO) to bring coherence and structure to the set of environmental activities undertaken at the worldwide scale.*

Why not? The World Trade Organisation (WTO) has grown out of the General Agreement of Tariffs and Trade (GATT), which itself grew out of the multilateralism of the United Nations, and reflects the force of economic globalisation and integration. But the environmental problems facing the world are just as irrepressible, and they, too, need the authority and clarity that come from a forceful and mature world umpire like the WTO. Daniel Esty and Andre Dua have no illusions about the difficulty of setting up anything like a GEO:

> *Creation of a GEO does not presently seem politically feasible ... [In Asia] Korea has gotten no satisfaction from China in response to its entreaties for reduced [acid rain]; regional fisheries continue to fall precipitously;*

> *disputes among China, Taiwan and Vietnam have prevented the successful conclusion of the Regional Seas Agreement for the South China Sea ...*
>
> *The difficulty of achieving successful collective action in response to worldwide environmental harms does not diminish their significance ...*

Australia should push for a GEO. The United Nations is based in the United States. The World Trade Organisation is based in Europe. A third arm of international diplomacy should be based in the Asia-Pacific, the region where so much economic growth, and so much environmental damage, is taking place. The headquarters could be Sydney, with its direct flights to the world, its superb infrastructure, and Australia's environmental leadership in the region. There are two reasons for hope. Daniel Esty and Andre Dua explain one of them:

> *One of the major results of economic integration is that policies previously considered to be within the sovereign authority of domestic officials, especially environmental standards, have come under increasing scrutiny ...*

GEO needs a champion, and it would need a headquarters, supported by the local government. In the wired global marketplace, Australia is entirely suitable. Esty and Dua, both realists, both pessimists, believe GEO has enormous potential:

> *In contrast to trade, spectacular results are, without a doubt, achievable in the environmental sphere.*

19
NOMADS

THE BATTLEGROUNDS OF Mabo and Wik were shrewdly chosen. Of all the hundreds of sites on which to fight for native title, these two places were perfect. Eddie Mabo's land was on a remote island, a distinct physical entity, where indigenous people had been living and fishing for generations. The idea that this island was *terra nullius*, land belonging to no-one, was indefensible.

Wik, too, was a careful choice. The leaseholdings in dispute had largely fallen into disuse for many years. There were no boundary fences, no buildings. The only cattle on one leasehold were feral cattle. Few leaseholdings in Australia could be more tenuous, a fact emphatically pointed out by the High Court's most indefatigable expansionist, Justice Michael Kirby:

> The picture painted of the two leasehold properties ... is somewhat bleak. Each of them, in remote parts of Northern Queensland, offered to the lessee rudimentary and apparently unpromising conditions ... So unpromising was the first Mitchelton lease that it endured for only three years and was forfeited for non-payment of rent. The second lease lasted an even shorter period before it

> was surrendered ... Members of the Thayorre continued living on the land in their traditional way. They would have no reason even to be aware of the grant of any pastoral lease over the land ... it would require very strong legal doctrine to deprive them of their native title.
>
> The position of the Holroyd River Holding is not so extreme a case ... In such a large remote terrain, for most of the year, the Wik could go about their lives with virtually no contact with the lessee or the tiny number of stockmen, wood gatherers and occasional inspectors who entered their domain ...
>
> To the contesting respondents, these facts are irrelevant ... The issue to be resolved was one of legal theory.

True. Australia at the end of the twentieth century is divided more by principles and theories than by anything else. The debate over these principles and theories has become so furious, so tilted with unchecked racial rhetoric, that it is taking the nation to the brink of genuine division and therefore to the brink of genuine cultural decline.

The Wik judgement, in so far as it applies to the specific circumstances before the court, was a victory for commonsense and natural justice. The success of the Wik and Thayorre people hurt no-one. The dispute gave rights to real people—Chocolate Thomas, Sheba Dignari, Button Jones, Dodger Carlton, Paddy Carlton, Ben Ward and many others—in favour of absentee leaseholders with nothing at stake. The judgement protected access to land used by local indigenous people for many generations, at virtually no cost to anyone else.

Of course, the Wik judgement also opened the gates to a flood of litigation elsewhere. The most extreme result was in Western Australia, where Russell Lockyear's Mindara Station was facing fourteen separate native title claims.

In Queensland, a frisson of agitation ran through the huge pastoral leaseholders that soon found potent political expression in One Nation.

> *We are living in a state of mental anarchy,* Queensland grazier Lindsay MacDonald told me. *We've earned less than the cost of production for the last seven years. We've had shocking leaders ... Our faith in the churches has been shaken. The Uniting Church tells us we cannot escape the fact we are living on stolen land ... Our concerns have nothing to do with race. It's all to do with tenure. If we are left with defective title the banks will have to reconsider their position.*

Disillusioned by the urban media's coverage of the debate—'I have lost faith in the media's willingness to deal with the issues fairly'—Mrs MacDonald wrote a paper in early 1998, circulated through the Internet, expressing the impact of the Wik judgement on her family's life. This, in part, is what she said:

> *We had nothing but goodwill towards Aboriginal people and we have clung to that throughout all the trauma we*

have gone through since we first heard of the native title claim on our properties.

My husband's father bought our Blackall property in 1921. He did not steal it, nor was it given to him. There were no Aboriginal people in the area with any connection to this lease for some time previously, and there have been none since. Over time, my husband and I bought my father-in-law out at the prevailing market value, which was the same as freehold value.

We borrowed to buy our Charleville property, which is our son's home, in 1985 to assist in drought management. No people of Aboriginal descent had any connection with this lease and there was no connection to this lease by Aboriginal people for many years previously ... No-one had ever raised the possibility that we had other than exclusive possession ... or indicated that we were to regard the dwellings we built as the limits of what we regarded as home.

Our family took land from no one. All we own, we have paid for, or are paying for. No-one assisted us to establish our water supply ... How then, can our tenures be regarded as merely licences to run sheep and cattle, and not true leases, as Gareth Evans claimed on ABC Lateline on April 1, 1998?

Our son's home is in the area claimed by the Gunggari tribe, affecting a total of 3000 leases in South-West Queensland. It is also the subject of a second claim by the Bidjara tribe, which also includes the Blackall property ...

The Gunggari have claimed 'to be entitled as against the whole world to possession, occupation, use and enjoyment of the claimed land' ... To our horror, we discovered that the legitimacy of a claim was not a prerequisite for acceptance by the Native Title Tribunal ...

Dissension between Aboriginal tribes over claims exists, as in the case of the Gunggari and Bidjara relating to the Gunggari claim. ... I raise it here to highlight the difficulties we are having in trying to sort out who we are expected to deal with ...

This has been a heartbreakingly divisive issue for this country. Great chasms have opened up between city and the bush, between Aboriginal groups and individuals, between indigenous and non-indigenous Australians.

I'm sure the cities are totally sick of hearing about Wik, but I can assure you nowhere near as sick as we are of living with it. We must have some parameters by which we can decide if we can survive, or whether we should go and join those on safe tenures in the cities.

At the other extreme, the fate of many Aborigines disconnected from their land and their family in modern Australia is recorded in the Human Rights and Equal Opportunity Commissions Report, *Bringing Them Home,* a national inquiry into the separation of Aboriginal and Torres Strait children from their families and communities. At this point I would have liked to have quoted some of the harrowing stories from the report to show the other side of the story but reproducing parts of the report is contentious. These stories retell the pain of removal from families, physical and sexual abuse and outline the effects on following generations.

It is easy to forget amid the rhetoric and complexity surrounding land rights that the Australian people have the wealth and the means and the collective desire to restore the land, wherever possible, of indigenous people who have been deprived of their traditional land and the remnants of their traditional way of life. The area now held by traditional communities is larger than the combined size of the United Kingdom, France, Italy and Greece. It is mostly arid land, but it is priceless to those who live on it. The federal Government's Indigenous Land Fund is being built up to 1.3 billion dollars to allow for the spending of up to 45 million dollars a year, in perpetuity, to purchase and manage land for indigenous communities. The process of completing this repatriation will take time and patience and bruise many participants but the resources and the goodwill are there despite the overheated rhetoric.

No clearer symbol of the broad goodwill most Australians have toward reconciliation is the changing attitude toward the ultimate national symbol, the flag. On Australia Day 1997, a nationwide McNair opinion poll asked Australians if they would support using elements of the Aboriginal flag as part of the design for a new Australian flag. The result was a surprise. Fully sixty-six percent said they would consider such a move, 'if a suitable design for a new Australian flag were found' (this phrase had not been used in polling before and made a big difference). The level of recognition of the Aboriginal flag was universal: ninety-nine percent.

This open-mindedness about the flag and what it should symbolise became even more apparent on Australia Day 1998, when Ausflag, the private group which had long been trying to generate momentum for a new national flag, unveiled the hundred finalists in a national competition held among professional designers for a new flag. More than 2 500 entries were received and the overall quality was much higher than in two previous national competitions open to the public. This time *The Sydney Morning Herald* decided to reproduce all one-hundred new finalists, together with the Aboriginal and Australian flags and invited readers to vote for their preference through a phone poll. The paper also published the Internet address of Ausflag so people could examine the new designs.

Frankly, none of the new flag designs were strong enough to win majority support at a national referendum on the flag. The national blue ensign remains safe. However, the *Herald* was not prepared for the response to the phone poll. Some 22 200 calls were registered in forty-eight hours, by far the biggest response to any opinion poll the newspaper had ever conducted. More than a hundred letters also arrived. In the week after publication of the Ausflag Internet address, more than 100 000 people visited the site. The phone poll was repeated by other newspapers and the results were similar.

What stood out was the public's open-mindedness about the national flag. Forty percent of the new Ausflag designs contained elements of indigenous culture. A clear majority voted for flags with an element of indigenous culture. 'We've never had a response even remotely like this before,' the executive director of Ausflag, Harold Scruby, told me.

Almost simultaneously, the Constitutional Convention in Canberra was taking place in an atmosphere of reasoned argument, logical debate, bipartisanship and an overall tone of good humour. Intelligent Australians of widely differing views conducted a dialogue about the soul of the nation and its democratic traditions. The Convention, which had seemed a recipe for inertia when it was announced by Prime Minister Howard, turned out to be a good idea. It clarified the difficulties of change but made clear the desire for change in the symbolism of the nation had become part of the political landscape.

This was the cultural backdrop of the Wik debate. The goodwill was there. But there were enduring problems that mocked the sweet rhetoric of reconciliation. For a start, there was the Native Title Act itself, a bill whose many problems were set out by the former Chief Justice of the High Court, Sir Harry Gibbs, in a speech on Australia Day 1998:

> *No-one of goodwill doubts that it is necessary to act justly to the Aboriginal people, as to all Australians, but ... in many instances, demands are not based on merit but simply on race.*
>
> *The 'right to negotiate', upon which the supporters of the Aboriginal cause place so much value is, of course, not a traditional right ...*
>
> *Aboriginal claimants need not prove the existence of any*

interest before requiring negotiation, and need not have had any physical connection with the land in question ...

It is argued that the pastoralist has no problem, since the High Court has said his or her rights prevail if there is a conflict with native title. The problem is no-one knows what the rights of the pastoral lessee are until the Court has declared them.

It is also said that the Aboriginal people want nothing more than the right to go on their traditional lands for the purposes of hunting, gathering and visiting sacred sights. In fact, some want money, and a lot of it.

It is a defect in the law that the question who is an Aboriginal is undefined.

In summary, Sir Harry asked:

It may be too much to hope that the public in general, and the media in particular, will accept that Aboriginals, who undoubtedly have special needs, should have those needs met simply because they are Australians. The two sections of society cannot be reconciled ... when one of those sections demands a special place and special privileges unrelated to need.

Every problem that Sir Harry Gibbs foresaw has come to pass. A mountain of overlapping, competing and dubious native title claims, as well as simple and legitimate claims, confront the holders of rural leaseholds across Australia.

A confidential report prepared for ATSIC in 1998 conceded that a 'massive build-up' of native title claims was disrupting the mining industry and many of these claims were ill-advised. The *State of the Nation Report on Native Title Outcomes* warned:

> Many claims ... are ambit, covering massive areas, and are poorly researched beforehand ...
> New South Wales is of particular concern because of intra-indigenous disputes and the refusal of different parties to accept mediation in order for the NSW Government to agree to determinations ...

The rate of objections by native title parties is starting to increase significantly, which will mean further delays ... This must be a potent message for the [West Australian] electorate, which perceives its well-being to be based on the mining industry.

Mabo and Wik stand out like beacons of simplicity compared with many of these claims. 'There are now more than seven hundred native title claims on pastoral leases in Australia and many of them are ambit claims, or overlapping claims,' Wendy Craik, Executive Director of the National Farmers Federation, told me in 1998. A lot of pastoralists are despondent. 'Our members have been aghast when confronted with the paperwork.'

It was always going to be a painful process. Australia is now sifting through the history of dispossession and dislocation. The process is made more complex by the ambiguous circumstances in which so many indigenous people left the land. Many indigenous groups have revived land claims despite a long absence from the land, and many of these absences occurred when clans left to follow an easier life around the pastoralists. The arrival of the European pastoralists created not merely a 'line of blood' in Australian history. Among innumerable examples that challenge the rhetoric of cultural annihilation and dispossession, the anthropologist, T.G.H. Strehlow, a man fluent in the Aranda language and passionate in the indigenous cause, saw lands denuded of indigenous peoples for reasons that had nothing to do with dispossession:

> ... the Pitjantjatjara communities of the Petermann
> Ranges, whose lands I found almost completely
> deserted on my two visits of 1936 and 1939, despite
> the fact that their homeland had not been invaded by
> white settlers nor ravaged by police parties. They had
> merely 'drifted out' into areas of adjacent tribes,
> where white people had set up stations or settlements ...
> None of these drifters ever returned to their old
> homelands.

For all the political discussion of recent years about indigenous rights, the standards of health care and life expectancy among the indigenous peoples went nowhere during Labor's thirteen years in federal power even though Labor's heart was in the right place. Rates of imprisonment among Aborigines actually increased. In New South Wales, the Aboriginal proportion of the prison population rose from 5.8 percent in 1982 (the year before Labor came to power in Canberra), to 12.4 percent in 1996 (the year Labor lost power in Canberra). This increase partly reflected the growing lawlessness in New South Wales towns and the heroin trade in Sydney's Aboriginal communities. One in three indigenous males aged thirteen and over had been arrested at least once in the previous five years, according to a 1994 census by the Australian Bureau of Statistics.

The distinguished American scholar, James Q. Wilson, has noted that the advent in Western society of genuine distaste for racism has not been matched by a significant improvement in community trust between blacks and whites:

> *If racist thinking has declined, why are relations between the races so bad? Why do so many whites who cannot be called racists in any fair meaning of the word so often treat blacks warily?*
>
> *Fear. Whites are afraid of young black males. It is not racism that keeps whites from exploring black neighborhoods, it is fear. It is not racism that makes whites uneasy about blacks moving into their neighborhoods, it is fear. It is not racism that leads white parents to pull their children out of schools with many black students, it is fear. Fear of crime, drugs, of gangs, of violence ... Fear can produce behaviour that is indistinguishable from racism.*

Substitute the word 'Aboriginal' for 'black' and you have exactly the same problem in Australia. The state of life in country towns such as Moree, Bourke, Walgett, Brewarrina and Wilcannia is a state of permanent bubbling tension marked by stone-throwing, pub brawls, break-ins, bag snatching, rapes, assaults, racist insults and intermittent riots.

NOMADS

On Australia Day 1998 the Premier of New South Wales, Bob Carr, announced he would visit the western town of Walgett in the wake of a riot in which shops were smashed and looted, the TAB robbed, and police showered with bottles and rocks by a crowd of Aborigines, many of them drunk. That same day, in Sydney's Redfern, a crowd of more than two hundred Aborigines pelted police with rocks and bottles in Eveleigh Street after six police had sought to make an arrest. The previous week, in the New South Wales town of Moree, a general meeting was held after people were stabbed in two separate armed hold-ups. A month before that, an Aboriginal pub mob rioted in another western town, Bourke. And so it goes, a problem getting worse not better.

The simmering problems at the grassroots are fanned from the top. Indigenous leaders maintain a drumbeat of comments about 'racists' and 'rednecks'. Aboriginal leader Noel Pearson described the Howard government as 'racist scum' because it did not agree with him on Wik.

The Aboriginal legal activist Paul Coe was disbarred from legal practice on 3 July 1997 after the New South Wales Legal Services Tribunal found him to be 'not a fit and proper person to remain on the roll of legal practitioners'. The finding was the latest and most fateful episode in twenty years of accusations and controversy. A few minutes after the judgement was handed down, Coe spoke to reporters on the steps of the court: 'It confirms my view that it is still a white man's world.' Asked what skin colour had to do with this case he simply repeated, 'It's a white man's world.'

Charles Perkins told Olympian Cathy Freeman she had

'symbolically turned her back on Aborigines' when she did not carry an Aboriginal flag during a lap of honour at the Atlanta Olympics even though such actions are expressly banned at the Olympics. He has called repeatedly for boycotts of the 2000 Olympics.

Mick Dodson used the Human Rights and Equal Opportunity Commission as a blunt political instrument and a platform for his high-octane blame throwing. His influence is evident in the Commission's 1997 Report, *Bringing Them Home—Report of the National Inquiry into the Separation of Aboriginal and Torres Strait Islander Children from Their Families.*

Bringing Them Home is an important document. Australia must confront the mistakes of its past, not bury them. The heartache caused to thousands of Aboriginal families by the removal of children into foster homes is something Australians should acknowledge, not deny. That this was widely understood in the community was reflected in *Bringing Them Home* becoming a best-seller.

However, under the influence of Mick Dodson, the Report was also used to make the claim, the very grave accusation, that the treatment of Aboriginal children constituted 'genocide'.

Dodson received plenty of support from the news media, which did not blink at the use of the term 'genocide'. In the hands of the media, the Report mutated into the 'stolen' children. And even though the Australian *Year Book* showed that only ten percent of Aborigines had been taken away from their families, the media was uniformly enthusiastic in promoting the impression that entire generations of children were forcibly taken away.

It was left to Dr Ron Brunton, an anthropologist, business consultant and former academic, to go where no journalist would go. In February 1998, the Institute of Public Affairs in Melbourne published Brunton's 16 000-word response to *Bringing Them Home*, entitled *Betraying The Victims*:

> • *Only nineteen of the individual witness accounts or their accompanying commentary provide any hint of the reason that was offered for their separation from their families ... [Yet] it is fair to state that the report attempts to give the impression that the bases for removal were nearly always unjustified.*
>
> • *Many non-Aboriginal children who became wards of the state also had appalling experiences. From the late nineteenth century until the mid-1960s thousands of British children were sent to Australia and Canada ... and many of these children had families who had not consented to their migration.*
>
> • *The most egregious aspect of the Inquiry is its 'finding' that the forcible removal policy constituted 'genocide' and 'a crime against humanity'.*
>
> • *Assimilation policies directed at indigenous or tribal people were strongly promoted by international bodies at least until the 1960s.*

Ron Brunton also makes two points about the then Chairman of the Human Rights Commission, former High Court judge

Sir Ronald Wilson. First, even though the churches were prime agents in the removal of children, they receive only light criticism in the report. Second, when Sir Ronald was a Moderator of Assembly in the Presbyterian Church in Western Australia, he sat on the board of Sister Kate's home for Aboriginal children and thereby played a role in the removal of children from their families and communities. The submission of Millicent D. would have been a searing experience for Sir Ronald:

> *During the course of the Inquiry,* [Sir Ronald] *apologised ... He has also been quoted as stating 'I had no knowledge of the wrongness of the practice', a remarkable admission given that he now claims that the practice constituted 'genocide', which is generally seen as the ultimate crime against humanity.*

Finally, Brunton makes the point that the unchallenged accusation of genocide has quickly metastasised into the academic mainstream.

> *Already it has become part of the conventional wisdom of many academics who are blithely speaking of 'the cultural and biological genocidal policies of the stolen generation years' ... These assessments will quickly find their way into the texts which are used to give young Australians their understanding of the past and they are also likely to be thrown back in Australia's face when complaints are made about human rights abuses in other countries.*

As for apologies, they are easy to demand but not as easy to give when the entity in question is a government. When the Canadian government made a formal apology to Canada's indigenous peoples in 1997 it was thrown back in the government's face. Sir Harry Gibbs, the former Chief Justice, expresses an opinion about apologies that is sharply at odds with his former brother judge Sir Ronald Wilson.

'It seems to be the fashion to demand apologies for iniquities long past,' Sir Harry said in 1998. 'It is almost beyond belief that the question whether the Prime Minister should apologise for policies which neither his government nor its predecessors instituted or had constitutional power to prevent, should be a serious political issue ... surely the discussion of this matter shows a lack of proportion.'

Lack of proportion? Sir Harry should know that the politicians who helped drive the Labor government's race-based agenda—Nick Bolkus, Laurie Brereton, Gareth Evans, Simon Crean, Daryl Melham (with his references to 'white sheets' and 'burning crosses')—were, together with some indigenous leaders like Mick Dodson and Noel Pearson and their allies in the news media, at the centre of the push for a so-called 'race election' based on the Wik decision. Gareth Evans pronounced at the front door of Parliament House in Canberra on 2 April 1998: 'This bloke [Prime Minister Howard] seems to be never so happy as when he's bashing blackfellas.'

The determination with which these men were prepared to put this nation on the rack of a race election, depict any reform as discriminatory, and raise the stakes to a destructive pitch, were exposed by Father Frank Brennan, Jesuit priest, son of Justice Brennan of the High Court (himself the author of the key opinion in the Mabo judgement), passionate and influential advocate of the indigenous peoples, and critic of the Howard government. But Father Frank Brennan drew the line at Labor's Wik race strategy. In a letter written on 5 March 1998 to a Melbourne QC, he wrote:

> *As a Catholic priest involved in this issue, I have always tried to be attentive to the conflicting claims of miners, pastoralists and Aborigines, and to enunciate a decent moral bottom line within the prevailing political context. I have always regarded working relations with the Government of the day, whatever its political hue, as essential in the political process ... For the ALP, which coined the phrase 'unrepresentative swill', to craft 350 amendments to a bill and later inform its national conference that, in government, it would call all parties to the table (not having done so before presenting 350 amendments) is to strain the credibility of anyone committed to real legislative outcomes ...*

Father Brennan then reiterated his belief that the determination of Labor to make any Wik legislation subservient to the Racial Discrimination Act was a prescription for chaos.

Labor's willingness to throw the race card does not sit well with Bill Hayden, the former Governor-General and leader of the Labor Party (and former holder of the seat of Oxley won by Pauline Hanson in 1996). Hayden now spends his time asking the big questions that his own party prefers to avoid:

> *Why was Pauline Hanson so strong? Why did her issues take off? Because people are sick and tired of being screeched at by certain groups. Robert Tickner* [a former federal Minister for Aboriginal Affairs who lost his seat in the 1996 election] *was a classic case. He would say 'Racist, racist,' screaming it all over the ABC. So people were not saying anything publicly but they were saying a lot privately. And the tragedy of all this is that Aboriginal policy can be set back enormously because of the way it has been run for so long.*
>
> *In Aboriginal welfare, there is a very serious alcohol problem, but if you raise it, there are well-meaning, fashionable, small-l liberals and lefties who will say, 'This is all exaggerated.' It is not. I have been in so many Aboriginal communities on what they call 'pay day', when the social security money comes in, and it's pretty awful. You don't want to hang around there for long. People say, 'There has been all this expenditure on health. Why hasn't it improved?' A lot if it* [is self-inflicted] ... *We need to be able to discuss these things without being accused of being racist. But a lot of the Aboriginal leaders, like Mick Dodson, I suspect, feel that once they allow that*

discussion to take place they will lose control of the direction of policy.

Many of the problems in Aboriginal Australia are the direct result of past mistakes by the dominant white culture. But many of the ongoing problems, notably the stark disparities in life expectancy and general health, also reflect a chasm in value systems, a primal disparity between a hunter-gatherer civilisation and a mercantile-pastoral-industrial culture. The story told in the opening chapter of this book about Stephen Barnes Jungarrayi, the man who went back to his community to endure brutal traditional 'payback' tribal punishment, expressed the unease with which these differing universes coexist.

The complexity of this uneasy coexistence and the need for indigenous solutions to indigenous problems is largely ignored by those who portray all these problems as the result of white subjugation. In the words of Professor Kenneth Maddock, quoted earlier, we are witnessing 'the politics of embarrassment. The aim is to soften up your opponents by making them feel bad about themselves or their ancestors.' The 2000 Olympics in Sydney will be treated as the perfect platform for internationalising the politics of embarrassment.

All the strains caused by the strident politics of race and identity, the wear and tear of high and inefficient immigration, the toll of environmental stress, the hard-eyed efficiencies of economic rationalism and free trade, have exacted a toll on this prosperous nation. A 1996–97 survey by the CSIRO found that the average Australian was five times wealthier at the end of the twentieth century than at the beginning of the century, but noted that material wealth was no longer enough to measure the progress and mental well-being of a nation:

Material progress now presents developed nations with diminishing benefits and escalating costs. It appears to be becoming increasingly irrelevant, even hostile, to wellbeing and quality of life through the impacts on both the natural environment ... and social structures.

The nation that arduously won the 2000 Olympics must now endure those who will use this world event to pursue their domestic political agendas, including accusations of racism and genocide, ignoring the reality of Australia's fundamental tolerance. If those who are agitating are true to their word, when the world's news media descend on Sydney in 2000 to dispense instant analysis of contemporary Australia, the media will be fed an image of a racist nation. Australians will have to work hard not to allow this to happen. A successful Olympics would be the best way. We have already seen that Australia can be an eco-superpower; and Australia will likely play the role of sporting superpower in 2000. It is amazing what a nation can achieve when the people commit their hearts and minds to a national effort.

Sport is not a trivial subject. It is an arena which almost all the world takes seriously. It is the most important single form of cultural expression in the global marketplace. It matters more to more people than any other form of culture. Billions of dollars are spent in the cause of national pride on the sporting fields. It is the global surrogate for war and personal combat. And it is certainly not a trivial subject to many of Australia's Aborigines.

Anyone who doubts the potency of sport and sporting symbolism in the life of a nation need only remember the sight of Cathy Freeman, carrying the Australian flag in her moment of international glory at the 1996 Olympics and the Aboriginal and Australian flags after her victory in the 1997 World Championships, and the catharsis and joy these sights gave the nation. Freeman's reaction to those who called on her to boycott the 2000 Olympics and 'to stand and mourn with us' is instructive. She said she had not devoted her life to achieving international success so she could become a tool for moral blackmail.

Sport proved a potent weapon in breaking down racial exclusion in the United States.

The 1996 Olympics in Atlanta proved, once again, that Australians' passion for sport has given their country a sporting record that most nations would like to achieve and few have attained. More than a hundred nations sent teams to the 1996 Olympics, and seventy-nine of them won medals. Thirteen nations reached the plateau of twenty medals. Only five reached the plateau of forty medals. One of them was Australia.

When the relative size of nations is taken into account, Australia becomes the singular performer of the 1996

Olympics. Not only did Australian men and women win forty-one medals but they won across a remarkable range of sports—fourteen—a breadth exceeded only by the United States. Above the plateau that defines a major Olympic nation—thirty medals would seem a reasonable benchmark—Australia's performance, in per capita terms, was outstanding. Measured in medals (weighted for gold, silver and bronze performances) per million population, this is how the top nations performed:

1 **Australia 3.78**
2 Germany 1.46
3 France 1.27
4 Italy 1.22
5 Russia 0.92
6 United States 0.82
7 China 0.09

It was the perfect springboard for the 2000 Olympics where Australia would have the largest team, the home ground advantage and home waters. These advantages are tempered by the dangers of unrealistic expectations, excessive jingoism and political propaganda stunts.

If we are truly fortunate, Sydney 2000 will replicate the 1998 World Cup in France, when a polyglot, stylish French national team whose families came not merely from France, but from Algeria, New Caledonia, Martinique, Guadeloupe, French Guiana and Spain, created a defining moment of national cohesion.

However, if we are less fortunate, some of the people who

will be working to undermine Australia's reputation will win a place in the global Olympic spotlight.

The most spectacular difference between the staging of these Games and the 1956 Olympics in Melbourne will be the role of Australia's indigenous culture. Anyone perusing the newspaper clippings of 1956 would be struck by the invisibility of Aborigines, even in any token role in the Olympics. The opening ceremony was dominated by the presence of His Royal Highness the Duke of Edinburgh, who opened the Games, and by the Russian team, which caused a stir during the ceremonial march into the Melbourne Cricket Ground when it failed to salute the royal box. REDS REFUSE SALUTE said one headline.

Less than fifty years later, a white Australian Olympics is unthinkable. Indigenous cultural symbolism has become central to Australian cultural symbolism. The nation has made a collective journey.

This time, the Olympic torch that lights the way to the Sydney Olympics begins its hundred-day journey in the red centre, Uluru, the geographic and mythical centre of Australia. And the first runner in the torch relay is an indigenous Australian and Olympic gold medallist, Nova Peris-Kneebone. Speaking through an interpreter, Tony Tjamiwa, chair of the Mutitjulu Community, Uluru's traditional owners, said his community was 'overjoyed at having the Olympic torch come to Ayers Rock first and then on to Sydney'.

The world will come to a land of nomads, a rich mixture of characters, bush people who lived off the land, wanderers who travelled across the world, sojourners, immigrants, adventurers, a nation open to the world, a curious amalgam, a success. It is a country where, when the Olympics first came in 1956, the athletes were encouraged to break from their national teams and mingle during the Closing Ceremony, a show of mass egalitarianism and informality that has endured ever since.

AFTERWORD
A DANCE WITH THE THOUGHT POLICE

A POLITICAL BUREAUCRACY CAN work in subtle ways. In 1996, the Human Rights and Equal Opportunity Commission received a complaint about me from the editor of the *Chinese Post*, a small Chinese-language newspaper in Sydney. The editor of the newspaper, an immigrant from China, did not inform me he had complained to the Commission. I found out by accident when a Commission staffer let it slip during conversation.

The editor's complaint said that a front-page story I had written would cause 'severe and possibly irreversible damages to the group-image of the whole Chinese Communities'. He wanted a front-page retraction by the newspaper and legal action by the Commission.

The story had been published in the *Sydney Morning Herald* on 1 July 1996 under the headline: FEDERAL LAWS BLAMED FOR SYDNEY'S WELFARE GHETTOS. Prior to publication, it had been read back to the source at Monash University. The Monash academics blanched at the use of the word 'ghetto', preferring the euphemism 'enclave', but journalism is antagonistic toward academic euphemisms.

In lodging a complaint of racial discrimination, what the

editor may or may not have told the Human Rights and Equal Opportunity Commission is that he had a vested economic interest in the matters broached by the story. The *Chinese Post* is a newspaper whose primary market is the so-called Bob Hawke special immigrants from the People's Republic of China. Front-page stories published in the *Post* at the time the complaint was being lodged included, *'The Howard government has been in office six months and new immigrants face fierce attacks'* and, *'Ruddock guarantees that students whose 816 applications were refused will no longer be sought by the immigration department'*.

Nothing was ever heard from the Commission, but not long after the complaint from the *Chinese Post,* the 'ghetto' story was included in a media handbook compiled by the Commission.

Without ever checking with the *Herald* about the accuracy of the story, or informing the *Herald* that it had received a complaint, the Commission determined that the piece was inaccurate and, by clear implication, racist. It was included prominently in a handbook on the Racial Hatred Act to be distributed to news media and journalism faculties throughout Australia as an example of how *not* to write a news story. The chapter began:

> *Partly due to their necessarily reductionist nature, news stories created from reports on complex research findings, surveys and polls are often inaccurate and misleading. In many cases misinterpretations may be the inadvertent result of carelessness or deadline pressures,*

but there are clearly instances where journalists have deliberately misinterpreted and manipulated reports to reflect their own opinion and agenda.

Exhibit number one was the *Herald*'s front-page 'ghetto' story. Even though the factual accuracy of the *Herald* story had never been challenged, it was used as an example of a story that was 'reductionist', 'inaccurate', 'misleading', 'careless', 'manipulated' and 'irresponsible'.

This is how the Thought Police work.

The Human Rights and Equal Opportunity Commission, together with its allies in the state ethnic affairs commissions, state ethnic community councils and state anti-discrimination tribunals, are now armed with the broad and amorphous weapons of the Racial Hatred Act and various anti-discrimination statutes. These laws give power to control or sanction what people say by legal action, legal threat or professional rebuke.

Although the vast majority of cases are mediated or dropped, and only a small percentage are litigated, every year hundreds of Australians receive letters from government bureaucracies or corporations informing them they have been accused of discrimination or, worse, racism and need to explain themselves. This is a powerful ideological weapon. Given the wide definition of discrimination used by some of the people quoted in this book, the possibility for misuse of this power is overwhelmingly obvious.

Most of the doctrinal head-kicking in Australian society goes on in the universities. But the most overt enforcers are in the news media, where re-education and rebuke can be meted out in public. What the media and academia have in common is a propensity to play the man, not the ball. It is not enough to disagree with the argument, you must discredit the person who made it. After this book became a best-seller it was inevitable I would be re-educated and rebuked.

The process by which I went from being anti-Hanson in my book to a Hansonite in the media is instructive:

In a chapter, 'Love At First Sight', I argued there was a strong undercurrent of class snobbery in the media's response to Hanson:

> *For the media, the story was simple. It was black and white, good versus evil, middle-class enlightenment against redneck prejudice. There was more than a touch of class war—focaccia and cappuccino versus fish and chips.*

I then quoted Zita Antonios, the Race Discrimination Commissioner who made a similar point.

The class angle was picked up by the *Sunday* program which interviewed me for a story about the media and Hanson. The passage in the book became a TV interview, which became a soundbite:

> *The news media gave her an enormous amount of publicity. They gave her the oxygen and then they sneered and jeered and ridiculed her and ordinary people were saying, wait a minute, wait a minute, she's raising issues that we would like raised and she's getting bucketed. And they*

> *felt that by being bucketed that they themselves were being bucketed by this cappuccino ghetto, these little cappuccino-quaffing journalists who were sneering at the working class Australians.*

The soundbite then became part of a column by a pundit:

> *So it's all the media's fault. More or less. Paul Sheehan, a journalist with the* Herald, *explained One Nation's support to* Sunday *as a 'working class' backlash against 'this cappucchino gateau', 'these little cappuccino-quaffing journalists who were sneering' at Ms Hanson and her supporters.*

The column contained sardonic references to coffee and cake, which made no sense to the editor who received the story, who then did what journalists do, but which the pundit did not do, and checked the obviously strange reference to gateau, and found out I'd actually said ghetto.

Thus corrected, the column was published and it begat another column in another newspaper:

> *According to a rising tide of critics, the media act as an 'elite', with little or no interest in the wishes and aspirations of ordinary working people. The recent reference by Paul Sheehan, analysed by* [the gateau pundit] *to 'cappuccino-quaffing journalists' was sneered at the working class was a shining example of the genre.*

These defensive columns begat a third, outraged, column by a pundit who got his material from the gateau pundit who had massaged a soundbite, which was a paraphrase of a passage, which was in a book, which none of them had read:

> *Damn right I am biased against Pauline Hanson and all that she imagines she stands for, and I am happy to admit it ...*
>
> *To be biased against her is therefore, not merely the rational approach of a thoughtful mind but a patriotic duty, however her gaggle of apologists in the media might wriggle to present it, in the words of Paul Sheehan, as the 'sneering of these little cappuccino-quaffing journalists'.*

In the space of a week, through a process of Chinese whispers, misquotes and escalating outrage, I had metamorphosed from a Hanson opponent into a wriggling apologist for Hansonism.

That's how the Thought Police work.

The third columnist—the brave and thoughtful one—had not long before been on the phone to the editor of a major newspaper imploring him not to run a story about his personal life because it would damage his family. The story was not run, and should not have run, but the incident was a metaphor for the columnist's art: he was a man as careless with the reputations of others as he was careful with his own.

Let me repeat: thrashing Hanson as a racist and a fool is no substitute for actually doing some work. Moral outrage failed to explain what caused the groundswell that propelled Hanson to Canberra.

Craig McGregor, the award-winning author of *Class in*

A DANCE WITH THE THOUGHT POLICE

Australia, wrote a feature published in *The Sydney Morning Herald* on 13 October 1997 entitled 'The new ghettos of Sydney' about the growing divides in Australian society:

> *Ghettos? In Sydney? Aren't they a phenomenon of American cities? Answer: Sydney, which is now well on the way to becoming a global city, is also developing one of the most brutal characteristics of the planet's First World metropolises. It is developing ghettos.*
>
> *Not just racial ghettos, either. Ghettos of poverty, unemployment, violence, social distress and desolation which are only too familiar in Los Angeles and in Brasilia, but which the Australian Dream always thought it could avoid. And, worst of all, there is now a permanent underclass which is being concreted into these ghettos from generation to generation.*
>
> *If you redefine the term 'ghetto' a little, Sydney also has developed—ahead of all other Australian cities—ghettos of wealth and privilege which are visibly transforming themselves into American-style redoubts ...*
>
> *This is brave new Australia, in the era of globalisation and post-modern capitalism. While some surf the new technowealth, others end up in social compounds where a culture of poverty, joblessness and low expectation means people are trapped there for generations. If this isn't a ghetto, what is?*

A high level of denial permeates the immigration issue in Australia, for ideological reasons. Bob Birrell and Byung-Soo Seol described one response to the evolving immigrant urban underclass in Sydney:

> *One response common among scholars is to simply deny the situation. Alternatively, some romanticise the diversity and bustle of it all. The reality is that Sydney is focussing the social and economic problems associated with low income NESB migrant communities in one suburban region. The stress of such accumulating disadvantage threatens the capacity of the government authorities to deal with the resulting problems.*

The immigration scholar John Atchison is one of the many people who see the most insidious problem coming not from the xenophobes and racists in society, who have a voice but little real power, but from those censorious forces who seek to control the debate and have considerable power. Atchison wrote in 1997:

> *One of the most disturbing features of the so-called and inaccurately described Blainey debate was the associated latent fascism in the labeling of opponents as racists.*

The problem of ideological orthodoxies imposed through the agencies of bureaucracies, lobbyists, and the legal system was foreshadowed with remarkable clarity more than a 150 years ago, in Alexis de Tocqueville's *Democracy in America,* one of history's most enduring works of social insight. He believed that once a democratic society had been built, the greatest threat to individual freedom was the insidious dominance of the state:

> *Government extends its embrace to include the whole of society. It covers the whole of social life with a network of petty, complicated rules that are both minute and uniform, through which even men [and women] of the greatest originality and the most vigorous temperament cannot force their heads above the crowd. It does not break men's will, but softens, bends, and guides it; it seldom enjoins, but often inhibits action; it does not destroy anything, but prevents much being born; it is not at all tyrannical, but it hinders, restrains, enervates, stifles, and stultifies ...*

Given the tremendous achievements of Australia, it should be a time of national confidence, but it is not. Thirty years of poisoning of the nation's history has taken its toll. Many histories now parrot a hatred of Australia. The politically motivated accusations of racism, made hollow by overuse, have been pumped up to include 'genocide' and 'holocaust'.

The mud has stuck. The nation's sense of certainty at the end of the century has been eroded by the politics of stealth and division. Australians are caught in a moment of collective hesitation, still exuberant, hedonistic, open-minded, successful, yet their everyday freedoms are being eroded behind the rhetoric of equity.

AMONG THE BARBARIANS

The real methods of political control have become subtle, evasive, sweetly ruthless, a billion-dollar lie, an inability to see that Australians have built a prototype for a new way in the twenty-first century, an eco-superpower, a society that is both a haven for the world's most ancient human ecology and a culture that transcends tribalism.

SOURCES

THIS IS A BOOK OF reportage. It is a depiction of Australia at a moment in time. The primary sources were telephone and face-to-face interviews. These were supplemented by *Hansard*, court records, annual reports, scholarly papers, government reports, and newspaper articles.

Most direct quotations are from interviews with the author. Most sources are noted at the time they are quoted.

I am indebted to colleagues at John Fairfax, publishers of the *Sydney Morning Herald*, notably defamation lawyer Mark Polden, and librarians Helen Bayliss and Franca Bopf. Thanks to the *Herald*'s former Editor-in-Chief John Alexander, for the time and space to write stories which later expanded into the chapters 'An Empire Of The Soul', 'White Dreaming', 'The Man Who Wasn't There', 'Strip Mining', 'The Vote Eaters' and 'A Grand and Powerful Country'.

Particular thanks go to Susan Wyndham.

Four scholars—Richard Basham, Tim Flannery, David Foster and Bob Birrell—contributed significantly to this book. Another scholar, Stephen J. Pyne, is quoted through his book, *The Burning Bush*.

Sang Ye, journalist and oral historian, has made an important contribution to the understanding of Chinese immigrants to Australia and to this book.

David Reid, formerly of the Department of Social Security, stuck his neck out by agreeing to be interviewed. Given his new career as a school teacher and the ad hominem treatment meted out to critics of immigration rorts, I changed his second name.

William Whitworth, Editor of *The Atlantic Monthly*, and, in my opinion, the finest editor of his era, has provided many years of unobtrusive excellence, some of which has guided this book.

The following court judgements were used extensively:

Equal Opportunity Tribunal of New South Wales, *The Hellenic Council of NSW v The Macedonian Youth Association* (10/1995), Sydney, 1997.

High Court of Australia, *Mabo and others v State of Queensland* (FC 92/014), Canberra, 1992.

High Court of Australia, *The Wik Peoples and Thayorre People v the State of Queensland and others* (FC 96/044), Canberra, 1996.

Industrial Relations Court of Australia, *Battese and Election for Communication Workers Union (Postal and Telecom branch)* (169/96), Sydney, 1996.

Industrial Relations Court of Australia, *Cook v Australian Postal Corporation* (NI4428/1995), Sydney, 1997.

The following books all provided material for *Among the Barbarians*:

Atkinson, Alan, *The Europeans in Australia*, Volume One, Oxford University Press (Melbourne), 1997.

SOURCES

Barmé, Geremie, *In the Red: Chinese Contemporary Culture*, Columbia University Press (New York), 1998.

Bernstein, Richard and Munro, Ross, *The Coming Conflict with China*, Knopf (New York), 1997.

Betts, Katherine, *Ideology and Immigration* (Australia 1976 to 1987), Melbourne University Press, (Melbourne), 1988.

Bird, Carmel (ed) *The Stolen Children: Their Stories*, Random House (Sydney), 1998.

Birrell, Robert, *A Nation of Our Own*, Longman (Sydney), 1995.

Bookman (anthology) *Two Nations: The Causes and Effects of the Rise of the One Nation Party in Australia*, Bookman Press (Melbourne), 1998.

Browne, Janet, *Charles Darwin—Voyaging*, Random House (London), 1995; Pimlico, 1996.

Calwell, Arthur, *Be Just And Fear Not*, Wilke and Co (Melbourne), 1972.

Carew, Edna, *Paul Keating: Prime Minister*, Allen & Unwin (Sydney), 1992.

Caruana, Wally, *Aboriginal Art*, Thames and Hudson (London), 1993.

Castles, Stephen; Foster, William; Iredale, Robyn; Withers, Glenn; *Immigration and Australia: Myths and Realities*, Allen & Unwin (Sydney), 1998.

Cocks, Doug, *People Policy: Australia's Population Choices*, NSW Press (Sydney), 1996.

Cocks, Doug, *Use with Care*, University of NSW Press (Sydney), 1992.

Daws, Gavan, *Prisoners of the Japanese*, William Morrow (New York), 1994.

Dodd, Helen, *Pauline: The Hanson Phenomenon*, Boolarong Press (Brisbane), 1997.

FitzGerald, Stephen, *Is Australia an Asian Nation?*, Allen & Unwin (Sydney), 1997.

Fitzgerald, Tom, *Between Life and Economics*, [The 1990 ABC Boyer Lectures], ABC Books (Sydney), 1990.

Flannery, Tim, *The Future Eaters*, Reed Books (Melbourne), 1994; George Braziller (New York), 1995.

Foster and others, David, *Crossing The Blue Mountains*, Duffy & Snellgrove (Sydney), 1997.

Foster, David, *Mates of Mars*, Penguin, 1991; Vintage (Sydney), 1996.

Foster, David, *The Ballad of Erinungarah*, Vintage (Sydney), 1997.

Foster, David, *The Glade within the Grove*, Random House (Sydney), 1996.

Frost, Alan, *Botany Bay Mirages: Illusions of Australia's Convict Beginnings*, Melbourne University Press (Melbourne), 1994.

Gammage, Bill, *The Broken Years,* ANU Press (Canberra), 1974; Penguin Books (Australia), 1975.

Gill, Alan, *Orphans of the Empire*, Millennium Books (Melbourne), 1997.

Grant Blight (editor), *Pauline Hanson—One Nation and Australian Politics*, University of New England Press (Armidale, NSW), 1997.

Grover, John, *The Struggle For Power*, E.J. Dwyer (Sydney), 1980.

Hanson, Pauline, *The Truth*, Pauline Hanson's One Nation (Adelaide), 1997.

Hayden, Bill, *Hayden*, Angus & Robertson/HaperCollins (Sydney), 1996.

SOURCES

Horne, Donald, *The Lucky Country*, Penguin Books (Melbourne), 1964.

Howitt, A.W., *The Native Tribes of South-East Australia*, [first published 1904], Aboriginal Studies Press (Canberra), 1996.

Hughes, Robert, *The Culture of Complaint*, Oxford University Press (New York), 1993.

Hughes, Robert, *The Fatal Shore*, Knopf (New York), 1986.

Irving, Helen, *To Constitute a Nation*, Cambridge University Press (Melbourne), 1997.

Jacobs, Bruce and Yu, Ouyang (editors and translators), *Bitter Peaches and Plums: Two Chinese Novellas (My Fortune in Australia*, by Liu Guande, and *Australia—Beautiful Lies*, by Huangfu Jun), Monash Asia Institute (Melbourne), 1995.

Kelly, Paul, *The End of Certainty*, Allen & Unwin (Sydney), 1994.

Latham, Mark, *Civilising Global Capital*, Allen & Unwin (Sydney), 1998.

Lingle, Christopher, *The Rise and Decline of the Asian Century*, Asia 2000 (Hong Kong), 1997.

Lines, William, *Taming the Great South Land: A History of the Conquest of Nature in Australia*, Allen & Unwin (Sydney), 1991.

Little, Reg and Reed, Warren, *The Tyranny Of Fortune*, Business & Professional Publishing (Sydney), 1997.

Murray, Les, *Subhuman Redneck Poems*, Duffy & Snellgrove, 1997.

Pasquarelli, John, *The Pauline Hanson Story*, New Holland (Sydney), 1998.

Pyne, Stephen J., *The Burning Bush: A Fire History of Australia*, Henry Holt (New York) 1991; Allen & Unwin (Sydney), 1992.

Reynolds, Henry, *Aboriginal Sovereignty*, Allen & Unwin (Sydney), 1996.

Reynolds, Henry, *Fate of a Free People*, Penguin (Melbourne), 1995.

Samuelson, Robert, *The Good Life and Its Discontents* (The American Dream in the Age of Entitlement, 1945-1995), Times Books (New York), 1996.

Sang, Ye, *The Year The Dragon Came*, University of Queensland Press (Brisbane), 1996.

Schama, Simon, *Landscape And Memory*, Knopf (New York), 1995.

Seagrave, Sterling, *Lords of the Rim*, Bantam (London), 1995; Corgi (London), 1996.

Shelton, Judy, *Money Meltdown: Restoring Order to the Global Currency System*, The Free Press (New York), 1994.

Sleeper, Jim, *Liberal Racism*, Viking (New York), 1997.

Spillman, Lyn, *Nation and Commemoration (Creating National Identities in the United States and Australia)*, Cambridge University Press (Cambridge), 1997.

Tench, Watkin, *1788*, [first published 1789, 1793], edited and introduced by Tim Flannery], Text Publishing (Melbourne), 1996.

de Tocqueville, Alexis, *Democracy in America*, [first published in this edition, 1848], Doubleday/Anchor (New York), 1983.

Vasta, Ellie and Castles, Stephen (editors), *The Teeth are Smiling (The Persistence of Racism in Multicultural Australia)*, Allen & Unwin, 1996.

Viviani, Nancy, *The Indochinese in Australia, 1975-1995*, Oxford University Press (Melbourne), 1996.

Walsh, Peter, *Confessions of a Failed Finance Minister*, Random House (Sydney), 1995.

SOURCES

White, Mary E., *Listen ... Our Land is Crying*, Kangaroo Press (Sydney), 1997.

Wilson, Dulcie, *The Cost of Crossing Bridges*, Small Poppies (Melbourne), 1998.

Wright, Alexis, *Grog War*, Magabala Books (Broome, WA), 1997.

The following reports, scholarly papers and journal articles were also used:

Aboriginal and Torres Strait Islander Commission, *State of the Nation Report on Native Title Outcomes*, (Canberra), 1998.

Amnesty International, *Australia—Silence on Human Rights: Government responds to 'Stolen Children' inquiry*, Amnesty International Secretariat (London), 1998.

Atchison, John, 'The Sad State of the Immigration Debate,' in *Pauline Hanson—One Nation and Australian Politics*, University of New England Press (Armidale, NSW), 1997.

Bureau of Statistics, Australian, *National Aboriginal and Torres Strait Islander Survey, Social Atlas,* Report 4155.0 (Canberra), 1994.

Bureau of Statistics, Australian, *Law and Justice issue, Indigenous Australians*, Report 4189.0 (Canberra), 1994.

Bureau of Statistics, Australian, *Agriculture and the Environment*, Report 4606.0 (Canberra), 1996.

Bureau of Statistics, Australian, *Australian Social Trends, 1997*, Report 4102.0 (Canberra), 1997.

Bureau of Statistics, Australian, *Labour Force—and The Youth Labour Market*, Catalogue no. 6203.0 (Canberra), November 1997.

National Audit Office, Australian, *Follow-up Audit, Department of*

Immigration and Multicultural Affairs, 1997-98, Canberra (1997).

Basham, Richard, *Australia and Asia: Race, Ethnicity and the Golden Triangle*, Graduation address, Bond University, June 1997.

Birrell, Bob, Spouse Migration to Australia, *People and Place* (Monash/Swinburne), vol. 3, no. 1, 1995.

Birrell, Bob, Policy Implications of Recent Migration Patterns, *People and Place* (Monash/Swinburne), vol. 3, no. 4, 1995.

Birrell, Bob, Our Nation: The Vision and Practice of Multiculturalism Under Labor, *People and Place* (Monash/Swinburne), vol. 4, no. 1, 1996.

Birrell, Bob, and Seol, Byung-Soo, 'Sydney's Ethnic Underclass', *People and Place*, vol. 6, no. 3, September 1998.

Brunton, Ron, *Betraying the Victims: The 'Stolen Generations' Report*, Institute for Public Affairs, February, 1998.

Downey, Jim, *Population Policy and Ecological Sustainability*, AESP national conference paper (Sydney), 1997.

Dua, Andre, and Esty, Daniel, *APEC and Sustainable Development*, Yale Center for Environmental Law and Policy (New Haven, CT), 1996.

Eckersley, Richard, *Perspectives on Progress: Is life getting better?*, CSIRO Resources Futures Program (Canberra), 1997.

Ethnic Affairs Commission of NSW, *Annual Report 1993-94*, (Sydney), 1994.

Ethnic Affairs Commission of NSW, *Annual Report 1994-95*, (Sydney), 1995.

Federal Bureau of Investigation, *Overview—Asian Criminal*

SOURCES

Enterprises in the United States, Department of Justice (Washington DC), 1993.

FitzGerald Report, The, *Immigration, A Commitment to Australia*, Dr Stephen FitzGerald (Chairman), Australian Government Publishing Service (Canberra), 1988.

Gibbs, Harry, Sir, *Australia Day Message 1998*, The Samuel Griffith Society, January, 1998.

Gruen, Fred, 'The Quality of Life and Economic Performance', in *Dialogues on Australia's Future*, Centre for Strategic Economic Studies (Melbourne), 1996.

Healy, Ernest, Ethnic ALP Branches—The Balkanisation of Labor Revisited, People and Place (Monash/Swinburne), vol. 3, no. 3, 1995.

Healy, Ernest, 'Unemployment Dependency Rates Amongst Recently Arrived Migrants: An Update', *People and Place*, vol. 2, no. 3, 1994.

Healy, Ernest, 'Welfare Benefits and Residential Concentrations Amongst Recently-Arrived Migrant Communities', *People and Place* (Monash/Swinburne), vol 4, no 2, 1996.

House of Representatives Standing Committee for Long Term Strategies, *Australia's Population Carrying Capacity: One Nation—Two Ecologies*, Australian Government Publishing Service (Canberra), 1994.

Human Rights and Equal Opportunity Commission, *Bringing Them Home, Report of the National Inquiry into the Separation of Aboriginal and Torres Strait Islander Children from Their Families* (Canberra), 1997.

Human Rights and Equal Opportunity Commission, *The Racial*

Hatred Act: A Guide for People Working in the Australian Media (Sydney), 1996.

Human Rights and Equal Opportunity Commission, *Annual Report 1995-96* (Canberra), 1996.

Human Rights and Equal Opportunity Commission, *Annual Report 1994-95* (Canberra), 1995.

Hunter, J.C. and Altman, B., Welfare Assistance and the Indigenous Labour Force: An Analysis, *People and Place* (Monash/Swinburne), vol. 4, no. 2, 1996.

Institute for Aboriginal Development, *Current Distribution of Central Australian Languages*, IAD (Alice Springs), 1990

Joint Standing Committee on Electoral Matters, Report on the inquiry into the role of the Australian Electoral Commission in conducting industrial elections, Parliament of Australia (Canberra), October 1997.

Jones, Barry, *Political Challenges of Population Planning*, AESP National Conference Paper (Sydney), 1997.

Jones, Barry, *Australia's Population 'Carrying Capacity': One Nation—Two Ecologies*, Australian Government Publishing Service (Canberra), 1994.

Kaufman, Henry, *Structural Changes in the Financial Markets: Economic and Policy Significance*, Henry Kaufman & Co. (New York), 1994.

Joske, Stephen, *The Economics of Immigration: Who Pays?* and *The Economics of Immigration: A Postscript*, Parliament of Australia Legislative Research Service (Canberra), 1990.

Malouf, David, Foreword to the Third Edition of the *Macquarie Dictionary*, Macquarie University Press (Sydney), 1997.

SOURCES

Moore, Des, *How Labor Targeted Votes And Opinion*, Institute of Private Enterprise (Melbourne), 1996.

Morrisey, Patrick, 'Undermining Rural Sustainability', *Policy*, Winter 1997.

Nagle, QC, John, *Report of the Special Commission Of Inquiry Into The Police Investigation of the Death of Donald Bruce Mackay*, (NSW Government Printer), 1986.

Department of Corrective Services, NSW, *NSW Inmate Census 1996*, Statistical Publication, October 1996.

Government Green Paper, NSW, *Building on our Cultural Diversity*, Draft Report, NSW Government, May 1996.

Price, Charles, *Immigration and Ethnicity*, Department of Immigration (Canberra) 1996.

Price, Charles, Net Immigration and Population Growth, *People and Place*, (Monash/Swinburne), vol. 1, no. 2, 1993.

Russell, Bill, and de Roos, Nicholas, *Towards an Understanding of Australia's Co-movement with Foreign Business Cycles*, Reserve Bank of Australia (Sydney), 1997.

Ye, Sang, *Unfair Competition*, Heat 6 (Sydney), 1997

Stilwell, Frank, *Economic Policy and Population Policy: Is Stability Uneconomic?*, AESP national conference paper (Sydney), 1997.

Sullivan, Lucy, and Maley, Barry, and Warby, Michael, *State of the Nation*, Centre for Independent Studies (Sydney), 1997.

Sullivan, Lucy, *Rising Crime in Australia*, Centre for Independent Studies (Sydney), 1997.

World Bank, The, *Expanding the Measure of Wealth*, (Washington D.C.), 1997.

World Bank, The, *Monitoring Environmental Progress: A Report on Work in Progress* (Washington D.C.), 1995.

Year Book Australia, *1997*, Australian Government Publishing Service (Canberra), 1997.

Zubrzycki, Jerzy, *The Evolution of the Policy of Multiculturalism in Australia, 1968-1995*, Global Cultural Diversity Conference, April, 1995.

A number of rigorously researched magazine articles are also quoted in the text:

Binyan, Liu, and Link, Perry, 'A Great Leap Backwards?' *The New York Review of Books*, 8 October 1998.

Calvin, William, 'The Great Climate Flip-Flop', *The Atlantic Monthly*, January, 1998.

Cassidy, John, 'The Melting-Pot Myth', the *New Yorker*, 14 July 1997.

Hertsgaard, Mark, 'Our Real China Problem', *The Atlantic Monthly*, November 1997.

Kaplan, Robert D., 'Was Democracy Just A Moment?', *The Atlantic Monthly*, December 1997.

Schwarz, Benjamin, 'The Diversity Myth: America's Leading Export,' *The Atlantic Monthly*, May 1995.

Soros, George, 'Toward a Global Open Society', *The Atlantic Monthly*, January 1998.

Thurow, Lester, 'Asia: The Collapse and the Cure', *The New York Review of Books*, 5 February 1998.

INDEX

A
abalone 85, 86, 190
Aboriginal flag 322
Aboriginal people
  alcohol and 8–15
  apology 332–3
  arrival of Europeans and 19–20, 30, 298–301
  customary law 7–15
  definitions of 13, 283–90
  drugs and 194, 327
  environment and 3, 298, 310–11
  Hanson and 224, 228, 236
  initiation 11, 15, 286–8
  land rights 266, 321–2
  Liberal government and 104
  native title 4, 230, 240, 315–19, 324–27, 333
  prison statistics and 130, 193–4, 327
  reconciliation xi, 96, 235–6
  sport and 329, 337–40
  Stolen Children report 319–21, 329–33
acid rain 50
aging population 148
Albanese, Anthony 126
Alcorso, Caroline xii
American Civil War 24
Amnesty International 11, 14
Antarctic Treaty 78, 83–5
Anti-Discrimination Act (NSW) 146–64
Antonios, Zita 121, 233, 344
aquaculture 84
Arena, Franca 186

Asia, Australia's image in 232–3
Asia-Pacific conservation 309–14
Asian crime 182–200
Asian crisis 42–9, 267–8
  Australia and 53–6
Asian Organised Crime Group 184, 192
Asian values 72–6, 190–1
Asian-Australians 128–30
  student success 201–3
assimilation 33, 118
Atchison, John 125, 128, 348
Atkinson, Alan 18–19
Atlantic Monthly 160, 268
Ausflag 322–3
Australia
  art 25
  China, relationship with 69–71
  Chinese immigrants and 60–8
  cuisine 5
  culture 5, 25, 31, 35–6, 38
  democracy 7, 25, 37–8, 76, 107, 240
  East Asia and 72–6
  eco-super power 78–86, 310–14
  economy, Asian crisis and 53–6
  egalitarianism 25, 37–8, 76
  environmental degradation 80–1, 149, 295–303
  environmental history 1–5, 21–2, 77–8
  history, contrasting views 23–5, 34
  industry development 25
  intellectuals and 31–3, 232–3, 345
  nation building 33–4

nativism 25, 31
  rural resentment in 152–4, 243–9, 272, 291–2
Australia—Beautiful Lies 62, 63
Australia First Party 225, 275
Australia Post 166–78
Australian 231
Australian Against Further Immigration 225
Australian Book Review 71
Australian Bureau of Statistics 80
Australian Conservation Foundation 296, 311
Australian Financial Review 117, 252
Australian Labor Party (ALP)
  Aboriginal issues 333–4
  branch stacking 94, 102, 103, 174–8
  CEPU election and 167–78
  ethnic vote and 96, 98–102, 110–16, 120, 122, 132, 133–4
  grant allocations and 96, 98–102
  immigration policy 109–16, 122, 132, 253–6
  multicultural/ethnic lobby and 95–6, 98, 256
  NSW Right 94, 106, 172–5
  1996 election defeat 93–4, 96, 153
  political patronage 119–20
  Victorian branches 158, 162, 175
  white collar activists 119
Australian National Audit Office 131
Australian national character 293
  environment and 77–8, 81, 306
  post war boom and 31
  soldiers and 26–31
Australian Nature Conservation Authority 84
Australian Rules football 25
Australian Taiwan Friendship Society 134
Australian Trust for Conservation Volunteers 307

Australian Workers Union (AWU) 106
Australian's Review of Books 62
Australians for an Ecologically Sustainable Population (AESP) 109, 147–8
Ayr 257–8
Ayr Advocate 257

B

Babb, Jeff 227, 229
Baldwin, Peter 97
Ballad of Erinungarah, The (Foster) 282
Barme, Geremie 57, 60–1, 65–6
Barry, Graham xii
Basham, Charoen 188
Basham, Dr Richard
  crime 63, 181–2, 187–92, 194–5, 197–200
  social security fraud 204, 212, 219
Battese, Noel 169, 170
Be Just and Fear Not (Calwell) 119, 253–4
Beazley, Kim 132, 134, 177, 252, 273
Beijing 50, 56, 57
Beijing Man in New York (TV program) 60–1
Bidjara people 318–19
Bieddulph, Michael 158
Birrell, Robert
  Australian nationhood 22, 23, 24, 33
  immigration 63, 113, 124, 132, 216–17, 348
Birrigubba Juru-Bindal people 289–90
birth control 311
Bitter Peaches and Plums (Jacobs and Ouyang) 62–3, 218
Blainey, Geoffrey 126, 127, 231, 240, 292, 348
blue revolution 84

INDEX

Bolkus, Nick 97, 104, 125, 127, 161, 162, 333
boosterism 257
Border Mail 251
Borjas, George 123, 234
Botany Bay Mirages (Frost) 20
Bredhauer, Steve 258
Brennan, Father Frank 333–4
Brennan, Justice Gerard 333
Brereton, Laurie 94, 126, 333
Bridgewater, Dr Peter 84
Bringing Them Home 319–21, 329–33
Broken Years, The (Gammage) 26, 27
Brown, Gordon 48
Brunton, Ron 330–2
Buchanan, Pat 270–1
Bureau of Immigration and Multicultural Population Research (BIMPR) 122
Burning Bush (Pyne) 1–3
bush xv, 1–6, 21, 279, 282–3
business migration program 192
Byung-Soo Seol 113, 124, 348

C

Cabramatta, NSW 165–6, 181, 182–4, 209, 213–15
Calwell, Arthur 119, 252–4
Campbell, Graeme 226, 275
Canada 83, 139, 332
cane toads 257, 258, 303
Carr, Bob 102, 134, 147, 177, 328
Cassidy, John 234–5
Castles, Stephen 33–4, 145–6, 162
Cavalier, Rod 177
Centre for Population and Urban Research 161
Ceresa, Maria 9
Chan, Angela 116, 117, 145, 186
China 48–53, 55–6, 151, 312
 nationalism 59–60
China's Pitfall (He) 52
Chinese athletes 58–9

Chinese immigrants 60–8, 133–4, 215–16
Chinese lobby groups 72, 133–4, 342
Chinese Post 341, 342
Chinese students 61, 62–3, 74, 133, 212, 342
Chow, Carmel 192–3
Christofedes, Sheila 115
Citizens League 263
Civilising Global Capitalism (Latham) 112–13, 120
Clark, Sir Kenneth 277
Clark, Manning 22–3
Class in Australia (McGregor) 347
coastal piracy 190
Cocks, Doug 302–5, 308
Coe, Paul 329
Collins, David 21
Collins, Peter 102
Communication Electrical Plumbing Union (CEPU) 100, 167–78
community group grants 98–102, 111
Confessions of a Failed Finance Minister (Walsh) 122
Confucian values 74
Conroy, Stephen 169, 170, 176
Constitution 22–5
Constitutional Convention 323–4
Cook, Peter 79
Cook, Quentin 168
Cope, Bill 34
corruption 189
 China 49–53
Costello, Peter 249
Craig, Mark 195
Craik, Wendy 326
Crean, Simon 333
crime 181–200
 Asian 187–8
 gangs 184, 190, 194
 immigration and 130–1
 organised 181–6, 213–16
 rural areas 152

Vietnamese immigrants and 183–4, 192–3, 214–16
violent 150, 182, 185
Croker Islanders 281
Crokett, Gary xii
CSIRO 296, 303, 336
Culture of Complaint (Hughes) xiii–xiv

D

Dalai Lama 68
Danforth, Loring 158, 159
Darwin, Charles 17, 35, 295
Darwin, Susan 17
Daws, Gavan 28–9
Deakin, Alfred 24
Della Bosca, John 172–3, 178
democracy 7, 25, 37–8, 76, 107, 240, 349–50
Democracy in America (Tocqueville) 349
Democratic Labor Party (DLP) 273–4
deregulation 245, 247
diversity 100–1, 147
divorce rates 217
Dodd, Helen 223, 229, 232
Dodson, Mick 121–2, 329–30, 333, 335
Dooley, Glen 10
Downey, Jim 311
drought 1–2, 21, 150
drugs 131, 181–200, 214, 292–3
in sport 58–9
Dua, Andre 49, 312–14
Dutton, Geoffrey 280

E

East Asia, Australia and 65, 72–6
East Timor 239
Eastman, D. x
economic rationalism 111
egalitarianism 25, 28, 37–8, 76
electoral fraud, trade union 166–78
elites 146, 232–5, 345

Ellis, Bob 261–2
environment 1–7, 21–2, 78–86, 149, 150, 295–6
China 49–53, 151, 312
Green Corps and 307–11
immigration and 129
Pacific region, aid and 309, 311–14
Equal Opportunity Tribunal 156, 157
Esty, Daniel 49, 312–14
Ethnic Community Councils 100, 116, 186
ethnic vote, ALP and 109–16, 132, 133–4, 253–6
Ettridge, David 227
eucalypts xv, 1–3, 21, 279, 283
Europeans in Australia, The (Atkinson) 18–19
Evans, Gareth 161, 318, 333
Evans, Harold 268

F

family reunion program 110, 112, 132, 192, 256
Fatal Shore, The (Hughes) 19, 30–1, 77
fear 328
Federal Court 133, 212
federal election (1998) 244–52, 259–61
Federation 21, 22–5, 65
Ferguson, Laurie 112, 177
Ferguson, Martin 134
Fields of Wheat, Hills of Blood 159
financial crisis 42–9, 54–5, 267–8
fire 1–3, 21
South East Asia 41–2
Fire Under the Snow 69
firestick farming 3
First Fleet 17–21, 298–301
Fischer, Tim 250–2, 273
fishing 83–5
FitzGerald, Stephen 38, 72–3
Report 254–6
Fitzgerald, Tom 45

INDEX

5T gang 183–4
Flannery, Tim 149, 295–302, 305–6
foreign aid 309–14
Foster, David xv, 279–93
France 83
Fraser, Malcolm 118
Freeman, Cathy 229–30, 329, 337–8
Freeman, Richard 123
Frew, Todd 212
Frey, William 124
Friedman, Thomas 82
Frost, Alan 19–21
Future Eaters, The (Flannery) 295–302

G

Galbally Report 118
Gallipoli 27
Gammage, Bill 26, 27
gangs and crime 184, 190, 194
Geebung, Elsie 224
Ghost Shadows gang 200
Gibbs, Sir Harry 324, 332–3
Gibian, Jane xi
Gittens, Ross 267–8
Glade Within the Grove, The (Foster) xv, 280
Global Environment Organisation (proposed) 313–14
globalisation 245, 271
Gluyas, Rick 224, 229
Good Life and Its Discontents, The (Samuelson) xiii
Goot, Murray 249
Graff, Julius 150
Graham, Gladys 224
Grassby, Al xi, 96, 118, 139–43
Great Betrayal, The (Buchanan) 270–1
Greece 155–64
Green Corps 308–11
greenhouse gases 49–51, 149
Grog War (Wright) 12
Gruen, Fred 36
GST 178, 246, 251, 273

gun laws 149, 246–7, 248, 252, 272, 291
Gunggari people 318–19

H

Hall, Rodney 280
Hanson, Mark 223, 229
Hanson, Pauline xiii, 71, 115–16, 127, 259–60, 273
    Asian crime and 187–8
    Australian of the Year remarks 230
    estrangements 229
    family history 223–4
    Ipswich rally 241–3
    maiden speech 221–2
    news media and rise of 224–9, 232–40, 248–9, 344–5
    resentment of major parties and 221–2, 234–6
Hansonism 111, 115–16, 260, 265, 345–6
Harris, Dr Graham 80
Hasluck, Paul 235
Hawke, Bob 61, 67, 342
Hayden, Bill 334–5
Haymarket Property Owners Association 70–1
Hazelton, Barbara 223, 229
He Qinglian 48, 52
Healy, Ernest 161–2, 207
Heaney, Seamus 154
Heat 59
Hellenic Council of NSW 156–64
Henshaw, Rod 274
heroin 182, 185, 193, 194, 196–8
Herron, John 104
Hertsgaard, Mark 49–50, 51
Higher School Certificate 201–3
Hill, David 274
Hill, Heather 274
HMS *Beagle* 17
Hogan, Warren 118
home invasion 189
Hong Kong 66, 72, 189

Horne, Donald 31–3, 35, 36–7
Howard, John 92, 105, 107, 120, 170, 273
  Aboriginal people and 329,
  Constitutional Convention 323
  gun laws 246, 272
  Hanson and 230, 239, 249, 265
  immigrants and 70, 115, 342
  Tibet 68
Hudson, Graham 176
Hughes, Robert xiii-xiv, 19, 30–1, 77
Human Rights and Equal Opportunity Commission 117, 121–2, 225, 237–8, 329, 341–4

I
I Married a Foreign Woman 62, 218
immigrants
  abuse of the system by 125, 131–3, 204–13, 216–19
  illegal 195–6
  skill levels and 124
  underclass 110, 113–14, 152, 341, 347
immigration
  Chinese 60–8, 302, 341–2
  composition of 127–30
  crime and 130–1, 181–200
  demographic shifts and 124–5, 128–30
  economics of 122–4, 147–8
  environment and 129, 296–303
  Hanson and 222
  Keating maiden speech 95
  marriage racket and 206–7, 216–18
  media and 233–4
  policy 70, 103, 109–16, 122, 132, 203, 253–6, 266
  social cohesion and 147–8, 152, 203–4
Immigration and Ethnicity (Price) 128–9
Immigration Review Tribunal 127, 133

imprisonment rates 130, 193–4, 327
Independent Council for Refugee Advocacy 70
Indonesia 41–3, 151, 238–40
Industrial Relations Court 167
information technology 270–1
Institute of Public Affairs 330
interest groups, ALP and 109–16, 120, 132, 133–4, 253–6
Ipswich, Qld 241–3, 250–2
Ireland 283, 290–1
Irian Jaya 151
Irving, Helen 23, 24–5, 64–5
Is Australia and Asian Nation? (FitzGerald) 38

J
Jacobs, Bruce 62–3, 218
James, Clive 35, 56
James, Neil 62
Japan 83, 151
Japanangka, Martin Johnson 9
Jews, Muslims and 43–4
Johns, Gary 177
Johnson, George 124
Jones, Barry 109–11, 134–7, 147, 148
Jones, Nick x
Jose, Nicholas 71–2
Journal of Personality and Social Psychology 269
journalists 267–70
Jungarrayi, Stephen Barnes 7–15, 335

K
Kalantzis, Mary 34, 162
Kaplan, Robert 160
Katherine Aboriginal Legal Service 10
Katz, Larry 123
Kaufman, Dr Henry 45–6
Keating, Paul 91–6, 98, 104–7, 161, 240
Kelly, De-Anne 244–9, 259

INDEX

Kelly, Paul 261
Kelly, Ros 98
Kennett, Jeff 104
Kerkyasharian, Stepan xi, 145
Kernot, Cheryl 248, 274
Kirby, Michael 315
Knuth, Jeff 257–9, 271–2

L
Lacey, Josie 116
Lajamanu, NT 9, 13
Lamb, Peter 184
Lang, Jack 263
Latham, Mark 112–13, 120, 177
Law of the Sea 78–86
Le Geng Jia 211–12
League of Rights 249
Leaituaalesi, Davina 150
Lebanese immigrants 193, 206–7, 208, 210
Lee Kuan Yew 73–6
Lenders, John 175
Lewis, Michael 47
Liar's Poker (Lewis) 47
Liberal Party 102
    bureaucracy and 120–1
    federal Aboriginal policies and 104
    Hanson pre-selection 224
    immigration and 125–7, 218–19
    multiculturalism and 118
Liberal Racism (Sleeper) 145
Lindsay electorate 174, 178
Lines, William 3–4
Link, Perry 52
Little, Reg 65, 191
Liu Binyan 52
Liu, Eric 270
Lo Po, Faye 207
Locke, Joan 168
Lockyear, Russell 317
Long, Malcolm xii
Long-Term Capital Management (LTCM) 47–8
Lonsdale, Tom 150
Loo, Pamela 134
Lucky Country, The (Horne) 31–3, 35, 36–7

M
McCormack, Denis 225, 275
McCubbin, Fredrick 25
McDonald, Lindsay 317–18, 320
McGregor, Craig 347–8
McGuire, Noel x
Mackay, Donald 139–43
Mackay, Qld 245–7
McKee, Alice 223
Mackie, Jamie 62
McLeay, Leo 170
Ma, Tony 71
Macedonia 104, 155–64
Macedonian Conflict, The (Danforth) 159
Macedonian Youth Association 156–64
Maddock, Kenneth 231, 336
Mahathir, Dr Mohamad 43, 46
Maher, Dr Lisa 194
Maher, Michael 141–3
Malaysia 42, 43
Malouf, David 35
marine environment 4, 83–6
marriage racket 63, 206–7, 216–18
Marsden, Maurie 226, 228, 229
Marsic, Sonja ix
Marxism 23, 33
Massie, Marcella 247
Mates of Mars (Foster) 284–5
mateship 28
Meagher, Reba 103
media 262–70, 333, 337
    Hanson and 224–9, 232–40, 248–9
    NESB 115
Mekong Club 165
Melham, Daryl 104, 333
melting-pot theory 124
Merrit, George 229
Merriwether, John 47

369

Meyer, Wayne 305
Micaleff, Eddie 176
Mighell, Dean 175–6
Milan, Nigel 145
Mildren, Justice Dean 8, 13
Miles Franklin Award 279, 280, 281, 287
military spending 26
Minns, John xi
Mistaken Identity (Castles ... [et al]) 34
Moffitt, Justice Athol 214
money laundering 213–16
Moore, Des 99
Moore, Justice Michael 167, 169, 173
Moree, NSW 329
Morgan Stanley 42
Morrissey, M. 34
Mount Druitt High School 203
multicultural industry 96, 102, 111, 114, 117–18, 123, 132, 299
  cultural federation fantasy 143
  Hansonism and 115–16
  Les Murray and 153–4
  social security fraud allegations and 209
  thought police 341–50
multiculturalism 33–4, 118
  Hanson and 222
  origin of the term 139
Murray, Les 146–7, 153–4
Muslims 43–4
Mutijulu community 340
Murray-Darling River 149–50
My Fortune in Australia 62, 218

N
Nagle, John 139–43
Nation of Our Own, A (Birrell) 22, 24
National Crime Authority 184, 185, 215
national identity 292–3
National Party 244–52

nationalism, overseas Chinese 61–8
native plants xv, 1–5, 21, 279, 283, 303
native title 4, 240, 315–19, 324–7
Natour, Jamal 171, 172, 173
Neal, Belinda 178
negative trait transference 269
Nelson, Camilla ix
NESB immigrants 95, 98
  ALP and 98–102, 110, 120, 122, 174–7, 253–6
NESB news media 115
New Guard 263, 264
New York Review of Books 52, 268
New York Times 82, 234, 301
New Yorker 234–5, 268
New Zealand immigrants 130, 194
Newman, Jocelyn 96–8
Newman, John 165–6, 167, 172
Nichols, George 195
No Aircraft Noise Party 115
non-English Speaking background immigrants *see* NESB immigrants
NSW Anti-Discrimination Board 143–4
NSW Teachers Federation 203
nuclear weapons testing 83

O
O'Chee, Bill 274
O'Connor, Mark 147
O'Donnell, Penny xi
Oldfield, David 227–8, 229, 259, 274
Olympic Games 55–6, 57, 60–1, 82, 329, 336–40
omniculturalism 270
One Nation Party *see* Pauline Hanson's One Nation Party
organised crime 181–6, 213–16
Our Nation 162
outworkers 206–7
Ouyang Yu 62–3, 218
ozone layer 149

INDEX

P
Palmer, Mick 196
Palmer, Vance 36–7
Pasquarelli, John 223, 225, 226–7, 229, 237–8
Patten, Chris 57–8
Pauline—The Hanson Phenomenon (Dodd) 223
Pauline Hanson—the Truth 228
Pauline Hanson Support Movement 227
Pauline Hanson's One Nation Party 103, 104, 124, 126, 227, 235, 236–7, 317, 345
　1998 federal election 247–52, 259–61, 273–5
　Queensland elections 241, 244–5, 249, 257–8
Pearson, Noel 329, 333
People and Place 161, 207, 216–17
People Policy (Cocks) 303
People's Action Party 74
People's Daily 68
Peris-Kneebone, Nova 340
Perkins, Charles 329
Phuong Ngo 103, 165–6, 172–3
Piccone, Vic 227, 229
Pioneer Valley (Qld) 245–6
politics of grievance 119, 232
population debates 109–11, 125, 128–9, 136, 147–8, 295–303, 311
Price, Charles 129
Prince, Greg 6
Prisoners of the Japanese (Daws) 28–9
Pun, Dr Anthony 116
Pyne, Stephen 1–3

Q
quality of life 36, 336
Quang Dao 166
Queensland elections (1998) 124, 241, 244–5, 249, 258–9
Queensland Times, The 224, 225

Queensland, why it is different 249
Quinlan, Michael 207

R
rabbits 21
Rabinow, Paul 301
Racial Hatred Act 116, 342
racial tensions 124
racial vilification legislation 164
racism 116–17, 121, 125, 145, 232, 327–8, 333
Rakuyo Maru (ship) 29–30
Ramsey, Alan 178, 255–6
Ransley, Paul 175, 176
reconciliation xi, 96, 235–6, 287, 291
red cedar trees 4
Redfern, NSW 328
Reed, Warren 191
Refugee Review Tribunal 211
refugees 118, 210–11
Regional Institute of Environmental Technology 51
Reid, David 204–10
Reimer, Andrew 280
Reith, Peter 170–1
Reynolds, Henry 230–1
Richardson, Graham 114, 177
RICO law 199–200
Ridgeway, Aden 274
right wing movements, media and 263–5
Rising Crime in Australia (Sullivan) 185
Roberts, Tom 25
Rodrik, Dani 271
Ruddock, Philip 127, 129–31, 133, 134–5, 342
rural Australia 152–4, 243–9, 272, 291–2
Russia 54
Ryan, Peter 186

S
Salmon, Ian 142
Samios, Jim 145

Samuelson, Robert xiii
Sang Ye 59, 61–2, 66, 215–16, 218
Sartor, Frank 71
SBS ix, xii, 118, 144
Schama, Simon 77–8
Schurmann-Zeggel, Dr Heinz 11, 14
Scott, Les 224, 225
Scruby, Harold 323
Seng, Ted 71
1788 (Tench) 298–301
Sham-Ho, Helen 134, 186
Sharp, Tom 190
Sheehan, Paul 83, 111, 135, 345
sheepdog trials 5–7
Silas, Ellis 26–7
Singapore 73–6
Singh, A.K. x
single parent families 206–8
Sister Kate's Home 320
Sleeper, Jim 145
small pox 19–20
Small, Clive 184
Smallwood, Prof. Gracelyn 289–90
Smith, Robert 83
Snake Cradle and Snake Dancing (Sykes) 289
social conditions 147, 151–2
social justice 25
social security 25
    fraud 96–8, 125, 131, 204–13, 216–19
soil erosion 80, 303, 308
Soros, George 43, 46–7, 48, 55, 89
South Korea 43
Spain 83
Spillman, Lyn 81
Spitzer, Dr Gisether 59
Springvale, Vic. 183
Stehlow, T.G.H. 326–7
Stevenson, Jan 172
Stilwell, Frank 147
Stolen Children report 319–21, 329–33
Stone, Shane 11
Streeton, Arthur 25

Subhuman Redneck Poems (Murray) 153–4
Suharto, President 238–40
Sullivan, Lucy 185
Sunday (TV program) 175–6, 344
Sydney
    Olympics 56, 57, 60–1, 82, 329, 336–40
    traffic problems 152–3
Sydney Morning Herald 134, 135, 152, 261, 264, 267, 322, 341
Sykes, Roberta 289–90

T
Taming the Great South Land (Lines) 3–4
Tan Le 230
tariffs 25
tax avoidance 213, 215–16
Taylor, Griffith 295, 296, 297
Teeth are Smiling, The 145–6, 153
Telstra 246, 247
Tench, Watkin 21, 297–301
terra nullius 315
Thailand 42
Thayorre people 316
Theophanous, Andrew 158, 162
thought police 341–50
Thurow, Lester 48
Tiananmen Square 61, 67, 210, 211
Tibet 68–9
Tickner, Robert 104, 334
Tinker, Ray 184, 197
Tjamiwa, Tony 340
To Constitute a Nation (Irving) 23–5, 64–5
Tocqueville, Alexis de 349
Townsville Bulletin 258
trade unions 25
    elections 166–78
    grants to 101–2
Transport Workers Union (TWU) 169
triads 189, 190, 191, 193
Trigg Point, Perth 85, 86

INDEX

Truth and Immigration article 127
Tsang, Henry 134
Tsung Tsin Association 200
Tuan Van Tran 166
Tuckey, Wilson 91
Turkish immigrants 193, 208, 209–10
Two Nations 261, 266–7
Tyranny of Fortune, The (Little and Reed) 65, 191

U

Uluru 340
underclass 110, 113–14, 152, 341, 347
unemployment
    NESB migrants and 110, 112–14, 203
    young people and 307–11
Uniana (ship) 196
United Nations International Conference on World Population and Development 136
Unsworth, Barrie 142
USA
    China and 69
    immigration research and 123
Use With Care (Cocks) 303

V

Vasilopoulos, E. xi
Vasta, Ellie 146–7
Venton, Noel 246
Vichitthavong, Lilly 235
Vietnam War 33
Vietnamese immigrants
    crime and 183–4, 185, 192–3, 214–16
    postal workers 166–7
    social security fraud and 205–6
violent crime 150, 182, 185

W

Walsh, Max 54, 120
Walsh, Peter 114, 117, 122, 177
Wang, Lucy 165
Warburton, Keith 236
Warlpiri people 9, 13, 14, 15
water conservation 81, 305–6
Watson, Trevor 233
Webster, Frederick Charles 223
weeds 303
Welfare Rights Centre 209
White Army 263, 264
White Australia 65, 254
white dreaming 283, 290–1
white racism 72
White, Patrick 280
Whiteside, Bruce 227, 229
Whitlam Gough 96, 118, 252
Wik people 281
    High Court decision 230, 315–19, 333
Willesee, Geraldine ix, xii–xiii
Wilson, James Q. 327
Wilson, Sir Ronald 238, 331–2
Winton, Tim 79–80, 85, 86
women and the vote 25
Wooldridge, Michael 266–7
World Cup 339
World War I 26–8
World War II 28–30
Wran, Neville 142
Wright, Alexis 12
Wu, Spencer 68

Y

Yangtze River 49–50
Yau-Ming, Chiam 74
Year the Dragon Came, The (Sang) 61–2, 215–16, 218
Young, Jun 134
youth suicide 307

Z

Zagorski, Walter 223, 229
Zhou Ming 58
Zubrzycki, Jerzy 139